Southern Africa: Regional Security Problems and Prospects

ADELPHI LIBRARY 14

Edited by
ROBERT JASTER
IISS

Published for
THE INTERNATIONAL INSTITUTE FOR
STRATEGIC STUDIES
by
Gower

Published by
Gower Publishing Company Limited
Gower House
Croft Road
Aldershot
Hants GU11 3HR
England

British Library Cataloguing in Publication Data

Southern Africa: regional security problems
  and prospects.–(The Adelphi library; 14)
  1. Africa, Southern–National security
  I. Jaster, Robert S.   II. International
  Institute for Strategic Studies   III. Series
  327.0968   UA885.6

ISBN 0 566 00866 1

Printed and bound in Great Britain by
Biddles Ltd, Guildford and King's Lynn

Contents

Contributors

Robert Jaster is now a freelance analyst and part-time lecturer based in the US. He specialises in the international security dimensions of Southern Africa.

Christopher Coker is a lecturer in international relations at the London School of Economics.

Garrick Utley is a news correspondent with NBC based in New York. He was formerly Senior European Correspondent for NBC in London, specialising in the problems of Southern Africa.

Bukar Bukarambe is a Research Fellow at the Nigerian Institute of International Affairs in Lagos.

Introduction

Early in 1984 the log-jam in southern Africa seemed suddenly to break, and regional detente appeared to many to be in the offing. A US-mediated ceasefire in the Angolan War was signed in February of that year. It provided for the withdrawal of South African forces from Angola, and joint monitoring of the Namibian border by the Angolans and South Africans to prevent SWAPO (South-West Africa People's Organization) from infiltrating its guerrillas into the territory. It was hoped this would pave the way for a general Namibian settlement, including the withdrawal of Cuban combat troops from Angola and South Africa forces from Namibia.

In March 1984 South Africa and Mozambique signed the Nkomati Accord, a mutual security pact pledging each country to prevent its territory being used as a base for aggression against the other. Mozambique would no longer allow guerrillas of the ANC (African National Congress) to attack South Africa from Mozambican bases, and South Africa would close down the MNR (Mozambican National Resistance), a South African-sponsored guerrilla group (also known as RENAMO) operating against the Mozambican Government.

Yet, in spite of these remarkable developments, conflict has continued and regional security remains an elusive and perhaps still distant hope. The ANC, though denied bases in neighbouring states, has nevertheless maintained its low-level campaign of bombings and sabotage against targets inside South Africa. In Mozambique the signing of the Nkomati Accord failed to put an end to MNR attacks on Mozambican settlements and transport; indeed, MNR activities were intensified, leading South Africa to mediate an uncertain truce between the MNR and the Machel Government in October. As 1984 drew to a close, South African forces remained inside Angola, and SWAPO infiltration into Namibia continued. UNITA, Angola's most durable national movement, continued to operate in large parts of the Angolan countryside without serious challenge, while its leader, Jonas Savimbi, was demanding a voice for UNITA in the central government. Cuban combat troops remained in the country to defend the dos Santos Government against UNITA and the unpredictable South Africans. After seven years of intensive Western peace efforts, the Namibian conflict was still unsettled.

Why has detente failed to take hold? Why are southern Africa's conflicts so intractable? What are the dangers for the West in continuing warfare between South Africa and its neighbours?

The essays in this volume analyze the sources of conflict in the region, discuss the likely outcomes, and suggest the implications for Western security interests. They explain why these conflicts are not easily or quickly resolved.

South Africa's central role in these conflicts, and its power to block any regional settlement it does not favour, are analyzed in the Coker paper and in the study of South Africa's security options. The analysis traces the growing militarization of the society and the recent emergence of the South African military as a major influence on policy: parallel developments that reflect the Republic's increasing isolation, particularly since the end of Portuguese rule in Africa in 1974, in a world hostile to *apartheid*.

Having failed in their long quest for admission to a Western defence alliance, and more recently in their bid to organize a 'constellation' of regional states friendly to South Africa, its leaders appear to have adopted a belligerent 'go-it-alone' policy. This policy involved South Africa in virtually a continuous state of border warfare against neighbouring states – particularly those offering sanctuary to guerrillas operating against South Africa and Namibia. The leadership has convinced the majority of its white constituents that the opposition to *apartheid* and to South African rule in Namibia is the result of a massive, Communist-orchestrated onslaught against the Republic. Thus Pretoria's belligerent policy toward nearby states was designed in part to shore up white confidence by demonstrating that the government is uncompromising in the face of this alleged 'Total Onslaught'.

While chapter 2 warns of the problems posed for the West by a defiant and isolated South Africa, which is likened to a cornered wildcat – 'small but potentially lethal, unpredictable, dangerous to approach, and difficult to control' – Christopher Coker shows what can happen when the wildcat breaks loose. He analyzes the sharp rise in the scale of South African military operations since 1978, when the new Botha Government's so-called 'destabilization policy' entered full stride. In addition to South Africa's well-publicized ground-and-air strikes against guerrilla targets in Mozambique, Angola and Lesotho, Coker cites armed attacks on Zambia and Zimbabwe as well.

Moreover, in contrast to the South African Defence Force's (SADF) 1975 invasion of Angola, in which the attacking force included fewer than 2,000 South African troops, SADF operations against Angola in the 1980s have sometimes engaged as many as 11,000 or more troops, supported by armour and heavy weapons. As Coker notes, operations on that scale were directed not just at SWAPO guerrillas, but also at the Angolan Army.

This is consistent with the evidence of South Africa's growing preparations for a conventional war. As its neighbours acquire more sophisticated weapons and a greater defence capability, South Africa will find it increasingly costly to conduct military strikes inside their territories. Indeed, the prospect of higher casualties in its border wars has undoubtedly been one of the factors leading the Botha Government to seek detente, though on its own terms.

The roles of other African states in regional conflict management are examined in Bukar Bukarambe's analysis of the OAU and in the paper on the Front-Line States. While giving full credit to the OAU's achievements, Bukarambe at the same time probes its failure to live up to early expectations – particularly its failure to resolve various regional conflicts. He attributes this in part to the early notions of Pan-Africanism which led to false expectations of a continental consensus among the newly independent states. Except on a few issues, like *apartheid*, such a consensus was not to be. Bukarambe notes, too, that the weakness of the African states, has led to the rapid internationalization of conflicts: these states have had the capability to initiate a conflict, but seldom the capability required to carry it through. He also cites structural problems. OAU resolutions are only advisory. The Organisation has no authority to invoke sanctions or other coercive measures, or even to collect membership dues, which have been in chronically serious arrears. Bukarambe offers specific suggestions for making the OAU more effective, but he thinks that sub-regional groups, like ECOWAS (Economic Organisation of West African States), may come to play a more significant role in conflict management, particularly if, together, such regional groups are able to provide a federal framework for the continent as a whole.

One such group, the so-called Front-Line States, has for some time been playing an important role in the management of southern African conflicts. It began in the mid-1970s, when the presidents of four states (Botswana, Mozambique, Tanzania and Zambia), concerned over the escalating Rhodesian conflict and the prospects of outside military intervention, decided to work jointly toward a negotiated settlement. Since the more radical OAU member states opposed such a settlement, the four presidents moved effectively to by-pass the OAU while seeking a peaceful resolution of the conflict in its name.

In analyzing the Front-Line States' *modus operandi*, which has been described as *'ad hoc* summitry', Jaster shows how their leaders have served as a bridge between the Western powers seeking a settlement and the guerrillas. In both the Rhodesian and Namibian conflicts, the Front-Line presidents have supported Western peace initiatives. And in both conflicts they have helped to keep the USSR out of the negotiations and from exercising a veto over Western-led initiatives. Front-Line leaders have forced intransigent guerrilla chiefs to come to the bargaining table and, once there, to negotiate seriously. By building the guerrillas' confidence in the negotiating process, Front-Line officials have been able to persuade them to abandon extreme positions and to make critical concessions.

The Front-Line States also took the lead in initiating a regional economic development programme – the first in southern Africa. Their conflicts with South Africa and its guerrilla proxies, together with the effects of economic mismanagement and several successive years of devastating drought, have diverted attention and resources away from economic development. Jaster argues in favour of Western support for this programme, not least because it can be an important factor in linking *all* the regional states, including Marxist-oriented regimes, with the West and weakening their ties to the Communist countries.

It is significant, however, that Front-Line initiatives, both in regard to regional conflicts and regional economic development, have depended heavily on Western leadership and support. Like the OAU itself, the Front-Line States are not strong enough to carry out such initiatives by themselves.

Examining US policy in southern Africa, Garrick Utley traces the shifts in policy with each change in Administration, and even within a single presidential term. He frames his argument in terms of 'globalists vs. regionalists': those who view the region primarily as an arena in the US-Soviet power struggle, against those who see it as a region dominated by its own internal dynamics. As Utley points out, this split reflects widely differing conceptions of what is actually happening in southern Africa. Indeed, the sorts of policy zig-zags he describes have often been the result of defective intelligence and flawed analysis.

During Angola's independence struggle, to cite a particularly sobering example, the US slid into providing clandestine military aid to the FNLA (National Front for the Liberation of Angola). By any informed standard the FNLA was the most feckless of Angola's three contending national movements, and the one that stood the least chance of coming to power. The Americans were unfamiliar with Jonas Savimbi's UNITA (National Union for the

Total Independence of Angola), the movement of Angola's Ovimbundu people, who make up over 40 per cent of the population. Nor did the US know much about Agostinho Neto and the MPLA (Popular Movement for the Liberation of Angola), which represented Angola's educated urban elite. The head of the CIA's Angola Task Force at the time would later write that 'our knowledge of the MPLA was almost nil' (John Stockwell, *In Search of Enemies*). Neto spouted Marxist rhetoric, and that was enough. (Ironically the Russians, too, were initially hostile to Neto, and only after repeated Cuban urging did they eventually provide the massive infusion of arms which, together with the Cuban combat brigade, enabled the MPLA to consolidate power.)

Utley notes that 'it was not precisely an American policy decision' to back the FNLA. Its leader, Holden Roberto, was the brother-in-law of Zaire's President Mobutu. Through Mobutu the FNLA had established close relations with the CIA, which mistakenly believed the FNLA to be the best fighting force of the three movements. Since no one was in a position to challenge these judgements, the US threw almost all its support behind the FNLA. Meanwhile growing Congressional opposition to US military involvement in Angola meant that the aid had to be both clandestine and on a small scale – too small a scale to have any appreciable effect on the outcome.

Ignorance of the situation in Angola thus did not inhibit the use of clandestine aid, which was extended without any coherent idea of the forces involved or the sort of political settlement that should be sought. The US made no effort to stimulate Portuguese or collective African action to promote reconciliation among the Angolan parties and to avoid South African or Communist intervention. Instead the US launched a confused and misguided operation to pre-empt the Soviet Union, encour-

aged South African military intervention, and helped bring about just the sort of result it least desired.

Utley notes the Soviet readiness to expand its influence in southern Africa, provided it can do so at an acceptable cost and without weakening its capability to deal with problems in regions of higher priority. Its fear of incurring excessive costs has been shown in its restrained and token responses to South Africa's military occupation of Angolan territory and to armed South African attacks inside Mozambique. Utley makes the point that instability and conflict in the region are essentially of local origin, and are not simply a product or symptom of superpower rivalry. Even without South African support, UNITA would continue to pose a threat to the MPLA Government of Angola. Nor do South African blacks need Soviet encouragement to take up arms against *apartheid*. South Africa was prompted to pursue its war against guerrilla sanctuary states precisely because the superpowers had left a power vacuum in the region. Neither the US nor the USSR was prepared to put pressure on South Africa or its neighbours.

Utley argues that the US has no real policy option in the region other than to remain engaged in what he aptly terms 'preventive diplomacy'. He also stresses the importance of joint Western initiatives, as in the Western Five's Contact Group on Namibia. Even though the US was the dominant member, the collapse of the Contact Group, which fell out over the US insistence on linking a Namibian settlement to a Cuban troop withdrawal, has nonetheless weakened the US position as a mediator in the conflict. Without the support of other Western countries for the notion of linkage, the US and South Africa are its only promoters: a fact which has fuelled African suspicions of US-South African collusion in Angola and Namibia.

Thus the major sources of conflict in southern Africa remain what they have been for the past 25 years: the challenge, internal and external, to white minority rule, and the white minority's response to that challenge. In the past few years, however, since South Africa has become the last surviving member of the 'white redoubt' in southern Africa, the conflicts have become more dangerous and perhaps even less tractable. Dangerous because, in Angola, South African forces have fought against Cuban and Angolan troops in a conflict that has shifted increasingly toward conventional warfare with tanks, artillery, and a more sophisticated Angolan air defence capability. Dangerous, too, because the failure of South Africa's counter-insurgency to halt infiltration by ANC and SWAPO guerrillas has led the Botha Government to enlarge its tactical objectives. South Africa has used political, economic or clandestine military means against every one of its neighbours in an effort to force them to sign mutual security pacts; in other words, to win their formal acknowledgement of South Africa as the regional superpower.

Although South Africa has succeeded in clubbing several of its neighbours into submission, this by no means signals an end to the region's conflicts. Indeed, on at least a couple of counts these conflicts have grown less tractable. For one thing, the setbacks which South Africa has dealt to SWAPO in battle have not been matched by political successes inside Namibia. Without any credible political force to oppose SWAPO at the polls, the South African Government is unlikely to risk a settlement that would include free and open elections with SWAPO taking part. South Africa will instead continue to try to arrange a settlement in which SWAPO would play a minor or subsidiary role, or from which SWAPO would be excluded entirely. There is little reason to think SWAPO would accept such terms.

Moreover, as the essays in this volume show, southern Africa's conflicts have become increasingly institutionalized. Over the years almost all the parties to the conflicts have developed vested interests in maintaining a hard line. Particularly as the established political orders in Namibia, Angola and Mozambique have been weakened by prolonged conflict, their challengers — SWAPO, UNITA and the MNR, respectively — have had greater reason to reject concessions and to hold out for their maximal demands. Yet in none of these cases has the established authority been challenged to the point of giving in to such demands. In South Africa, too, the growing confidence of the military, together with its leading role in policy-making under P.W. Botha, suggest that an aggressive, uncompromising stance toward South Africa's opponents will continue.

Finally, successful guerrilla movements — even proxy groups like the MNR, which began not as a legitimate national movement but as a band of mercenaries — tend in time to take on independent life and goals of their own. It remains to be seen whether South Africa can really call off the MNR or Mozambique close down ANC operations as promised, or Angola put an end to SWAPO infiltration.

It may be that South Africa's Nkomati Accord with Mozambique, and its ceasefire with Angola, will not only have dampened down those conflicts, but will prove to have been a historical turning point leading eventually to the settlement of those and other conflicts in the region. Given the underlying sources of conflict which have yet to be resolved, however, and given the growing interdependence and intractability of southern Africa's conflicts, they are not likely to be ended soon. Nor are long-term settlements likely to be brought about without the direct involvement and mediation of the Western powers. Only by acting in concert can the Western powers bring credible pressure and prestige to bear on all the contending parties to move toward a mutually acceptable *modus ivendi* and to lay the groundwork for eventually resolving the region's conflicts.

Robert Jaster

1 Globalism or Regionalism?

United States Policy Towards Southern Africa

GARRICK UTLEY

INTRODUCTION

I have come to Africa with an open mind, and an open heart to demonstrate my country's desire to work with you. . . . My journey is intended to give fresh impetus to our co-operation, and to usher in a new era in American policy.

Dr Henry Kissinger
Lusaka, 27 April 1976

Although Africa forms one-fifth of the world's landmass (as Dr Kissinger recognized in his speech), he had never visited that dominant portion of the continent which lies south of the Sahara. There was no surprise in this. The political instability of many of the new black African nations, the ethnic clashes based on tribal rivalries, the problems of economic development, even the wars of liberation against white rule, had exerted little attraction on a mind more interested in great-power relationships.

During the rush to independence in the early 1960s the United States realized that the new African states would become important, if only in terms of the number of votes they would soon command in international organizations. Beyond that there was considerable optimism over what the winds of change would bring in Africa, particularly in the field of economic development during the first 'development decade' of the 1960s. The emergence of the black African states also accorded with the optimism of the 'new generation' of Americans which was running the Kennedy Administration.

Early on it was decided that each new nation would have a fully staffed United States Embassy with an ambassador, instead of one ambassador to serve a cluster of small neighbouring countries. Aid programmes were established; the United States Information Agency launched major schemes for informing black Africans about American life; black performers such as Louis Armstrong made highly publicized tours of African countries. Because of its sheer size Africa became important in the lower and middle levels of the foreign policy bureaucracy in Washington – but it never commanded sustained attention at the highest decision-making level. The United States, after all, had been little involved in, and had had no deep experience of, African affairs. It was the European countries who had 'scrambled' after Africa's riches in the nineteenth century, who had staked out their claims in Berlin in 1885 and who had overseen (with varying degrees of success) the transition from colonial to black rule. As long as development in Africa did not upset the fundamental balance of power and influence in the world, the European nations could be left to look after it. A most telling illustration of this attitude is the pattern of presidential trips. American Presidents have covered the world on state visits, but it was not until 1978 that a President visited sub-Saharan Africa.

What brought President Carter to Lagos was the same consideration that had prompted Dr Kissinger's visit to Lusaka two years earlier: the possibility that events in Africa, particularly the growing Soviet and Cuban involvement in the affairs of the continent, could aggravate the general instability of the region and could even upset the perceived balance-of-power relationship between the United States and the Soviet Union.

The military revolution in Portugal in April 1974 had set off a chain of events, the result of which was predictable, if not inevitable. The

1

independence of Angola and Mozambique under Marxist leadership provided the basis (and the bases) for increased military pressure on white-ruled societies, as well as (potentially) on moderate, pro-West black nations. Southern Africa had become a prize for competing political interests to fight over.

The prize is worth fighting for. Historically, the strategic importance of southern Africa has focused on the Republic of South Africa because of her role as guarantor of trade routes between the Indian Ocean and the Atlantic – trade routes which today still carry the bulk of oil from the Middle East to Europe and the United States. Nevertheless, today the importance of southern Africa to the West lies largely in the mineral wealth to be found there. It must be emphasized that the loss of southern Africa's minerals to the West is an exceedingly remote possibility. Even if there were to be Marxist rule in southern Africa (including South Africa), the West would probably continue to have access to the region's mineral resources. Marxist governments that have come to power in the region have recognized, sooner or later, that their economic interests (if not their political sympathies) lie with the West. This has been seen in Angola, in Mozambique, and, more recently, in Guinea, to cite three examples. Despite this, it is important to recognize that southern Africa has become a new and important area of competition between the West in general – and the United States in particular – and the Soviet Union. Southern Africa must now be a factor in the geo-political equation facing American policy-makers.

It is one of the premises of this paper that the Soviet Union has a strong but not vital interest in southern Africa. Unlike the West, the Soviet Union does not have historic roots in Africa, nor does she have a serious economic stake in the continent, for she is not dependent on Africa's raw materials. Moreover, in any listing of Soviet foreign policy priorities Africa would rank below a number of other areas and interests. These are Eastern Europe (and Europe in general), the Soviet Union's growing pre-occupation with China, and developments in Central Asia as well as in the Middle East, to which Moscow itself may soon need to turn for oil supplies. All of these concerns are of 'vital' interest to the Soviet Union for reasons of political security or economic necessity. Africa falls into a different category of Soviet policy: the desire to expand Soviet political influence in those areas where such expansion can be accomplished at an acceptable cost and without weakening the Soviet Union's ability to deal with more important foreign policy problems closer to home. Soviet (and Cuban) intervention in Africa is an example of this. It was made possible by the instability in the southern third of the continent (as well as in the Horn) and because the United States, along with other Western nations, was not prepared to offer a military response to Soviet initiatives.

Important as the geo-political implications may be, the instability of southern Africa cannot be viewed solely in terms of the relationship between the two super-powers. The region must be treated on its own terms.

The purpose of this paper is to study the development of American policy in southern Africa during the three-year period from April 1976 to April 1979. Following a brief review of American attitudes and policy towards Africa in general and South Africa in particular, the paper will offer a more detailed account of American efforts in Rhodesia, Namibia (South-west Africa) and Angola. The three are treated separately, not only because each has posed a different problem for American policy-makers, but also because each represents a different policy approach. In Rhodesia the United States (with Britain) has pursued a consistent policy line; in Angola American policy has been anything but consistent; while in Namibia American policy has been marked by close co-operation with four of the United States' principal allies. At the conclusion of the paper an attempt is made to define the shape of future American policy towards South Africa (a subject that will be of prime concern for the rest of this century), and there is a discussion of various policy options which might be open to the United States.

The author is a journalist who has spent some considerable time following developments in southern Africa. What follows is the 'story' of those developments, along with the author's observations and analysis. It is a story of almost unending complexity, involving the traditional East–West conflict as well as the growing North–South disputes. It is a political story but also one of great economic importance. It demands the establishment of priorities; a belief in human rights as opposed to pragmatism; a concern for short-term arrangements (for example, with South Africa) rather than for the long-term implications of such arrangements. For American policy-makers southern Africa raises the issue of regional versus geo-political priorities. Finally, the story is linked inextricably with race.

I. SOUTH AFRICA

A major (and delicate) question for the United States in the formulation of her policy towards southern Africa is her relationship with South Africa. By virtue of its location, its economic strength, its military capability and its internal racial policies, the government in Pretoria must play a central role in southern Africa. It has been a premise of American policy that the United States should maintain a working relationship with South Africa while at the same time supporting aspirations for majority rule among Africa's blacks. The evident contradiction in this is recognized and considered unavoidable, given the black/white conflict.

Within this overall approach to southern Africa, the debate in Washington has been about the degree to which the United States should support black aspirations, and therefore about how much pressure the United States should apply to South Africa.

In April 1969, less than three months after he joined the Nixon Administration, Dr Kissinger asked for an inter-departmental review of American policy towards southern Africa. The report of the National Security Council (NSC) group was ready by mid-August. It suggested a series of options, ranging from closer association with the white regimes in southern Africa to a virtual cutting of ties with Pretoria. One of the options was the continuation of current policy. In the end the Nixon Administration compromised. Although it called for continued support for black aspirations and aid to black governments, the Administration subtly but perceptibly tilted in favour of the ruling white governments. Possible measures included retaining the American Consulate in Salisbury and the easing of sanctions against Rhodesia. (The Consulate was eventually closed at British insistence, but in 1971 the Nixon Administration did not oppose the Byrd Amendment which allowed the importation of Rhodesian chrome into the United States.)

As regards South Africa, the Administration moved to ease economic restrictions. The sale of computers to the South African military was allowed. The Export–Import Bank guaranteed a long-term loan to the South African government for the purchase of railroad equipment. In the political arena the United States adopted a more sympathetic attitude towards Pretoria and a less vocal posture towards South Africa in the United Nations.

Although the new policy was never announced publicly, the Nixon Administration justified it on the grounds that closer ties with South Africa would encourage moderation of her racial policies, and that increased pressure on South Africa would not in any case change the policy there. The rationale for the Nixon policy was found in the premise which accompanied the favoured option:

> The whites are here to stay, and the only way that constructive change can come is through them. There is no hope for the blacks to gain the political rights they seek through violence, which will only lead to chaos and increased opportunities for the Communists.

Within five years events in Angola and Mozambique would prove the premise false and would change dramatically American perceptions of southern Africa.

The policy debate of 1969 brought out two other points. One was the strong opposition mounted by Africanists in the State Department towards the policy favoured by Dr Kissinger and his White House staff. (Almost a decade later the same attitudes are being expressed and the same lines drawn between the Africanists in the State Department and the NSC.) The other conclusion of the 1969 NSC study was that American interests in southern Africa were 'important but not vital'.

When President Carter took office on 20 January 1977 his Administration, like President Nixon's eight years earlier, had to define its relationship with South Africa. The policy bequeathed by Dr Kissinger was that pressure was not to be applied against South Africa. The

3

Kissinger thesis (as will be shown in the following chapter) was that the United States could not try to force South Africa to change her internal policy and at the same time expect South African help in Rhodesia and Namibia which had become the immediate problems of the day. In a word, the Kissinger policy was 'linkage'.

If the Carter Administration represented anything, though, it was change. Mr Carter had been elected largely because he emphasized the importance of moral values which, translated for foreign policy purposes, meant human rights. The appointment of Andrew Young to the post of Ambassador to the United Nations underlined the special attention the President was prepared to give to the Third World in general and Africa in particular. The issue (human rights), the spokesmen (Mr Young and the President) and the target (South Africa) were all in position. Certainly, Pretoria was braced for an onslaught from Washington, but it did not come immediately. Instead, the Administration directed its human rights offensive against the Soviet Union. President Carter openly criticized the treatment of dissidents and wrote a letter to Mr Andrei Sakharov – an action that may not have done much for the Administration's Soviet policy, but it did provide a breathing space for its Africa policy.

For two months (until the end of March 1977) the policy towards South Africa was reviewed and debated. William Schaufele (Assistant Secretary of State for African Affairs), who had stayed on from the previous Administration, advocated the continuation of the Kissinger policy of not putting pressure on South Africa.

The counter-argument, articulated by Andrew Young and supported by Anthony Lake (the new head of the State Department's Policy Planning Staff), was that the Carter Administration, to be true to what it stood for, had to take a firmer line against South Africa and to be seen publicly to do so. African policy should not be dominated by East–West geo-political considerations and the Kissinger concept of linkage should be dropped. The new premise was that it must be in South Africa's own interest to help to resolve the problems of Rhodesia and Namibia, and that therefore there was no need for the United States to seek an accommodation with Pretoria. This was thought to be especially important, since the new goal of the overall Africa policy was to strengthen American standing among the black African nations in order to assure them of American support.

The conclusion of the policy review under the Carter Administration led to the resignation of Mr Schaufele, who was succeeded by Richard Moose. It also led to a clear demonstration of the new policy, when Vice-President Mondale flew to Vienna to meet the South African Prime Minister, John Vorster, in May 1977. Although the new Carter Administration policy envisaged the possibility of applying some direct pressure on South Africa, it was acknowledged from the outset that this pressure would be limited. In order to send Pretoria a 'message', the Administration was prepared to adopt a series of progressively tougher measures (including the withdrawal of military attachés and commercial representatives, and the limitation of Export–Import Bank guarantees), but it was not about to brandish the threat of serious sanctions. Accordingly, the principal thrust of the American effort was to be seen in public pronouncements and gestures, such as Mr Young's travels through black Africa and Vice-President Mondale's Vienna meeting. Those talks ended in what Mr Mondale called a 'fundamental and profound disagreement'. A formal statement by him at the end of the conference set the tone of the Carter Administration's approach to Africa.

There has been a transformation in American society of which we are very proud. It affects not only our domestic life, but our foreign policy as well. We cannot accept, let alone defend, the governments that reject the basic principle of full human rights, economic opportunity and political participation for all its people regardless of race . . . I made it clear that without evident progress that provides full political participation and an end to discrimination, the press of international events would require us to take actions based on our policy and to the detriment of the constructive relations we would prefer with South Africa. . . . We hope that South Africa will review the implications of our policy and the changed circumstances which it creates. We hope that the South Africans will not rely on any illusions that the US will in the end intervene

4

to save South Africa from the policies it is pursuing, for we will not do so.

At the end of the news conference which followed his statement Mr Mondale was asked whether a distinction was to be made between the Administration's demand for 'full political participation' for blacks in South Africa and 'one man, one vote'. The Vice-President said he made no distinction; the two were the same.

Mr Mondale could have offered no other response, despite the fact that he was handing Mr Vorster a valuable political weapon with which to strengthen his own position among South Africa's whites. At the same moment as Mr Mondale was speaking in Vienna, Andrew Young was in Maputo, in Mozambique, at the United Nations Conference on Southern Africa. Mr Young was telling black Africa – especially liberation movement leaders like Robert Mugabe and Sam Njomo – that the United States was on their side and that this time she really meant it. Mr Young's background as a noted civil rights leader gave him privileged access to black leaders, but the policy he brought with him was nevertheless treated with prudent scepticism. Indeed, the

steps taken by the Carter Administration against South Africa have been seen by black Africans to be far short of effective pressure. In October 1977 the United States did support the United Nations resolution banning arms sales to South Africa (a unilateral American arms embargo had been imposed in 1964), but she vetoed economic sanctions. The Administration also banned the sale of non-military supplies to the South African police and armed forces and leading American banks were encouraged to halt loans to the South African government. However, no pressure was put on the more than 300 American corporations doing business in South Africa. Indeed, the Carter Administration's attitude towards business in South Africa did not change from that of the previous Administration: the United States 'neither encourages nor discourages investment in South Africa'. The ambivalence of that statement sums up the contradictions inherent in American policy towards South Africa. The dilemma posed by the South African government is that it is at one and the same time the biggest obstacle to majority rule in its own country and a necessary participant in promoting black rule in Rhodesia and Namibia. It is there that changes must first come.

II. RHODESIA

American diplomatic efforts in connection with Rhodesia have been carried out in full recognition of the fact that legally the future of the country is primarily Britain's responsibility. The two allies have worked closely together in the attempt to bring about a peaceful, stable settlement. Although the United States considered herself, initially at least, the junior partner in that relationship, at times she has unmistakably assumed the leading role.

This was evident in Dr Kissinger's speech in Lusaka in April 1976, in which the Secretary of State called on South Africa to 'promote a rapid negotiated settlement for majority rule in Rhodesia'. What had moved him to take Africa seriously and to invest his personal prestige in the solution of the continent's troubles is what motivates most Western statesmen to action – the fear of instability and its consequences. The American analysis was straightforward: black insurgent movements would eventually win the

war against the white government; the longer the fighting continued, the greater the likelihood of serious Communist involvement and influence in the nationalist camp; it was probable that the future black leadership of Rhodesia would be radical rather than moderate. Thus the American goal was to end the war as quickly as possible, permitting the hand-over of power to the more pro-Western of the black leaders. Dr Kissinger recognized that if he was to achieve this, he needed South Africa's help to put pressure on Ian Smith, the Rhodesian Prime Minister.

Rhodesia declared her unilateral independence in November 1965. For more than a decade the country has survived (and even prospered), despite her political isolation and economic sanctions. The first selective sanctions against Rhodesia were imposed by the United Nations in December 1966. Full sanctions were voted in May 1968. However, it was evident that sanctions could never be effective as long as they were

5

not applied either by or against South Africa, which provided the conduit for Rhodesia's imports as well as her exports. (This was equally true of Mozambique prior to the Portuguese collapse.) Indeed, the disclosure that successive British governments were aware that sanctions on oil deliveries were being violated demonstrates how hollow the sanctions policy was.

The result was that Rhodesia experienced steady economic growth through the late 1960s and early 1970s, as well as an annual net inflow of white immigrants. Sanctions did hurt, certainly, but they also necessitated a restructuring of the economy. Rhodesia became self-sufficient in agricultural crops (wheat, corn, foodstuffs and cattle). Rhodesian industry claimed that by the early 1970s a young couple setting up home could find 90 per cent of what they wanted made in Rhodesia. Clearly, in such a situation the only effective pressure on the white Rhodesian government could come from South Africa, which controlled Rhodesia's life-line to the rest of the world. How Dr Kissinger went about mobilizing that pressure merits careful attention, since it marked the first major and direct American intervention in the Rhodesia problem.

Dr Kissinger's meeting with Prime Minister Vorster in Bavaria in June 1976 was the first time that such a high-level American official had met a South African Prime Minister since the Nationalist Party won power in 1948. Nevertheless, the meeting was held in a third country: an American Secretary of State was not yet prepared to visit Pretoria, nor was Washington yet prepared to receive a South African leader. The South African government recognized the importance of the meeting in Germany, however. Not only was it an acknowledgment by the United States of South Africa's key role in Africa, but it also showed that Dr Kissinger's aim in Rhodesia coincided with South Africa's interests and that it was preferable to have a moderate black government in Rhodesia rather than a radical one.

This was not a sudden shift of attitude on the part of Pretoria. South Africa too had recognized the fundamental change brought about by Portugal's withdrawal from Mozambique. The South African government understood that the level of fighting in Rhodesia would continue to intensify to the point at which South Africa might one day have to decide whether to intervene actively on the side of the white minority government or abandon it. Abandonment would be interpreted by other African nations (as well as by South Africa's white electorate) as a sign of weakness. South Africa's political and economic support for Rhodesia was not the total commitment white Rhodesians would have liked. For example, South Africa has never extended full diplomatic relations to Salisbury, although South Africa maintains a diplomatic mission there. Rhodesia also has a diplomatic representative in South Africa, but there has been no formal exchange of ambassadors. This has caused some resentment among the white population of Rhodesia, particularly since the Portuguese collapse in Mozambique, which rendered Rhodesia completely dependent on South Africa for her survival. It was hardly surprising that when Dr Kissinger and Mr Vorster met in Germany Mr Smith suspected that a deal was being concluded behind his back.

At their meeting Dr Kissinger and Mr Vorster were able to establish some common interests. Mr Vorster could offer to put pressure on Rhodesia and Kissinger could offer the assurance that the United States would exert minimal pressure on South Africa. Both men believed that the time was ripe for a Rhodesian initiative. The insurgent forces were penetrating deeper into the country. Although most of the guerrilla incidents were on a small scale, there was no doubt that the intensity of the war was increasing. What was especially worrying was Rhodesian intelligence reports that the insurgents were planning a major offensive in November, when the seasonal rains would provide heavy vegetation cover and would limit the effectiveness of the Rhodesian army and air force. This military prognosis, taken with Mr Vorster's readiness to apply pressure, made it appear that the time had come to act. By late July, South African Railways reported 'congestion' on their lines, which caused backlogs of export goods to pile up inside Rhodesia. Similarly, the amount of oil shipped through South Africa to Rhodesia was reduced. By mid-September Rhodesia's fuel reserves were down to less than three weeks' supply. The South African government, which had paid half of Rhodesia's defence bill in the first six months of the year, gave no indication that the largesse would continue. Finally, in August 1976, in order to remove any doubts, South Africa withdrew most of the 40 helicopters she had loaned to Rhodesia, along with the South African pilots and technicians who had manned them. All these actions, plus the economic indicators which were pointing downwards under the war's pressures (Rhodesia's GNP fell 3·4 per cent in 1976), were intended to have a softening-up effect on Rhodesia's leadership.

Between 4 and 6 September 1976 Dr Kissinger and Mr Vorster met again, this time in Zurich. At the end of the talks Mr Vorster announced publicly his acceptance of the principle of majority rule in Rhodesia. What promises he received in return have never been revealed, but it seems certain that they included financial assurances (direct or indirect) and the promise of a more sympathetic American attitude towards South Africa in the United Nations. Two months later the United States voted against a UN 'program of action against apartheid'.

Following the Zurich meeting, Dr Kissinger briefed the French, British and West German leaders and then set off to confront Mr Smith face to face. On the way he held talks with President Nyerere in Tanzania and President Kaunda in Zambia, two of the Front Line Presidents (the others were President Machel of Mozambique, President Neto of Angola and President Khama of Botswana) through whom the United States had been dealing with the Patriotic Front.

In Pretoria Dr Kissinger met Mr Vorster for two days of additional talks. At this late date, Ian Smith had still not been definitely told that he would see Dr Kissinger, a meeting the Rhodesian Prime Minister had long sought. However, on 20 September Dr Kissinger and Mr Smith met at the American Embassy. Mr Vorster was not present, for his role in squeezing Smith had already made him vulnerable to attacks from the hardline elements in his own party. However, Mr Vorster had reacted swiftly and forcefully to the black riots which had broken out in Soweto in June and had continued there and in other parts of South Africa through August and this had clearly pleased his supporters. To a considerable degree, therefore, the riots obscured the fact that Rhodesia's fate was becoming a dominant political issue in South Africa, and this gave Mr Vorster considerable freedom of action in his dealings with both Henry Kissinger and with Ian Smith.

At their meeting Dr Kissinger laid out before Mr Smith the agreement he had brought with him. The main terms were: majority rule within two years; a multi-racial interim government; and a trust fund to compensate white Rhodesians should they be forced to leave the future Zimbabwe. Dr Kissinger told Mr Smith that if he rejected the agreement and returned to Salisbury, he (Kissinger) would understand his action. The Secretary of State merely added, 'but next year the terms will be even tougher'. Ian Smith did not give in easily but in the end he accepted. After his return to Salisbury he made his historic broadcast (on 24 September 1976) announcing acceptance of the Kissinger proposal in its entirety. Further changes, he said, were not negotiable.

The apparent success of the Kissinger peace missions was short-lived. It started to unravel over the fundamental question of who would control the army and the police in the interim government. In Pretoria Mr Smith had demanded that whites should retain control and Dr Kissinger had agreed. But after the Pretoria meeting Dr Kissinger had flown to Dar es Salaam to present the agreement to President Nyerere, who balked at the idea of continuing white control over the two instruments of power in Rhodesia. Despite this, Dr Kissinger sent Mr Smith and Mr Vorster a message that the agreement had been accepted by the blacks. It is interesting to speculate whether the American Secretary of State was misled in his contacts with the Front Line Presidents (the people of Rhodesia think he was) or whether he deliberately deceived Ian Smith in order to make sure he would go through with his speech and announce his formal acceptance of majority rule.

Whatever the reason, the result was that all parties were offered the prospect of a conference in Geneva at the end of October 1976, at which to negotiate the details of an interim government and a new constitution. Britain took the chair at the conference. Mr Ivor Richard, Britain's Ambassador to the United Nations, had the unenviable task of trying to keep the Kissinger agreement from falling apart completely. He had little chance of doing so, despite the presence in Geneva of all the key Rhodesian figures, including Mr Smith, Robert Mugabe, Joshua Nkomo, Reverend Ndabaningi Sithole, and Bishop Abel Muzorewa. The question of who would hold effective power in Rhodesia was as unresolved after the Kissinger mission as it had been before. Shortly after the conference opened President Ford was defeated by Mr Carter. Dr Kissinger and his policy were undercut and so, inevitably, was the conference. It struggled on for some weeks before breathing its last in December 1976.

In early January 1977 the British took the initiative again. Ivor Richard began to conduct his own version of shuttle diplomacy around southern Africa.

The new proposal presented by him to Ian Smith bore little resemblance to the Kissinger plan of just four months earlier. It called for a 30-member Council of Ministers of which one-third would be white (and half of those appointed by Britain). In addition, a Commissioner appointed by Britain would preside over a Security Council, which would appoint the chiefs of the police and the military. Mr Smith, not surprisingly, rejected the proposal, demanding that it was either the full Kissinger plan or nothing. However, Britain had introduced a new character into a possible peace settlement – a British Commissioner – who would be given a more prominent role in the Anglo–American proposals to be advanced later in the year. For the moment, though, negotiations could not go forward.

During his final nine months in office Henry Kissinger had raised southern Africa to a position of priority in American policy-making. His performance was like the tightrope walker who tries to perform his act first without a net, then without a pole, and finally without a rope. If Dr Kissinger's goal was to achieve a fully implemented agreement, it can be argued that the American effort was doomed to failure from the start, for the Rhodesian nationalist leaders would never accept a plan which left Mr Smith controlling the security forces. If, however, his goal was more limited, something of importance can be found amid the debris of what he had cobbled together – specifically Mr Smith's acceptance of the principle of majority rule. That alone changed the route of future negotiations. The issue was no longer whether there would be black rule in Rhodesia, but how it would be brought about. That was Dr Kissinger's accomplishment, and it was his legacy to the new Administration.

President Carter's appointment of Andrew Young as Ambassador to the United Nations meant that American policy in Africa would undergo dramatic changes. The continuity of policy which traditionally exists between one Administration and the next would be observed in the Middle East, in Western Europe and in relations with the Soviet Union (aside from the initial human rights issue). In southern Africa, however, the new Administration would change direction, and through its first ten months in office Mr Young and the State Department would lead it in that new direction unchallenged.

A Congressman from Georgia, Mr Young lacked experience in international affairs and in the formulation of foreign policy. What he brought to his new job was a long and committed involvement in the civil rights movement (as an aide to Martin Luther King) and an enduring faith in the ability of blacks and whites to live together. Most important, Mr Young had a close rapport with, and the full backing of, President Carter.

A close examination of Andrew Young's approach to Rhodesia reveals that in one respect there was little difference between his goal and that of Dr Kissinger – a shift of power from white to black hands as peacefully and as swiftly as possible, in order to avoid a larger-scale war which could provide an opening for greater Communist intervention. What distinguished Mr Young from the previous policy-makers was his apparent lack of concern over the political leanings of a new black government. Mr Young's argument was that even a leftist 'liberation' government, despite past attitudes and future rhetoric, would look to the West for its economic ties rather than to a Soviet Union which has no historical links with Africa, little economic interest in the continent and no common ideological ground. He supported the premise that Communism does not root in African soil.

In essence, Andrew Young endorsed a common criticism of American foreign policy – that it frequently supports an eroding *status quo* rather than siding with the emerging force of change. In Rhodesia events had forced Dr Kissinger to abandon a *status quo* approach and to intervene personally, in an effort to transfer power to the black majority. Mr Young and the State Department pursued that policy vigorously and with even greater emphasis on American support for

8

black nationalist movements. The policy was unconventional, as were Mr Young's personal style and public statements. It was also consistent with the Carter Administration's rejection of a geo-political approach to the problems of southern Africa. This was particularly significant because less than two months after the Carter Administration took office, President Podgorny and President Castro both made trips to southern Africa. President Castro visited Tanzania, Mozambique and Angola. The Soviet President, in addition to visiting Tanzania and Mozambique, also visited Zambia. At the time American policy was not to make an issue of Communist involvement in Africa. African leaders were sceptical of the renewed promises of American support (even if made to them by an American black), and they were sensitive about being considered prizes in a traditional East–West struggle. The American attitude was summed up in a speech by the American Secretary of State, Mr Cyrus Vance, in St Louis on 1 July 1977, in which he stated that the most effective African policy was an affirmative one. He said, 'A negative, reactive policy which seeks only to oppose Soviet or Cuban involvement in Africa would be both dangerous and futile.' The statement reflected two important considerations in American policy formulation. First, the Soviet Union possessed an inherent political advantage in bidding for black African support, since she was not constrained by any commercial or economic interest in southern Africa. Second (and of more immediate importance), American policy decisions in southern Africa were conditioned by the fact that the United States was not prepared to 'react' (that is, to use force), either overtly or covertly to counter Soviet/Cuban intervention.

In the end American diplomats seeking a Rhodesian settlement could try to persuade the various parties to reach an agreement, but they did not have the power to compel them to do so. In an important way this diplomatic weakness strengthened Mr Young's position. For although his approach and his comments would be criticized by many, no one had a viable alternative policy to propose.

In March 1977 the United States agreed to co-sponsor, with Britain, a constitutional conference for Rhodesia. Proposed by the British Foreign Secretary, David Owen, the initiative came to nothing, due this time to opposition from the Patriotic Front. The Front's leaders, Joshua Nkomo and Robert Mugabe, were feeling increasingly confident. Following the establishment of their political alliance, they claimed that they were the sole representatives of Zimbabwe nationalism – a claim given formal recognition by the Organization of African Unity (OAU) at its conference in Gabon in the summer of 1977. As the Patriotic Front denounced the Anglo-American peace efforts more stridently, Mr Smith was talking about his plans for an internal settlement with black leaders who had been ignored by the OAU. That Mr Smith had the power to do this was evident, especially after the 31 August elections in Rhodesia, in which his party had once again won all 50 seats in Parliament. The momentum was clearly moving away from negotiations and towards increased confrontation.

On 1 September Britain published a White Paper on Rhodesia. This was another attempt to allay the mistrust of both sides. The goal was an independent Zimbabwe by the end of 1978. The main points were: the surrender of power by the white government; free and impartial elections; a British-appointed transitional administration, with a Resident Commissioner controlling the army and police; the presence of a UN force during the transition period; an independence constitution; and a billion-dollar development fund (not a compensation fund for whites, which the Kissinger plan a year earlier had called for).

Neither side was happy with the plan. The Patriotic Front had been demanding that power should be handed over to it and that it should organize elections. Neither Mr Nkomo nor Mr Mugabe relished the prospect of having to compete in open elections which would be internationally supervised; nor did they like the idea of the introduction of a UN force into Rhodesia. Mr Smith's government, on the other hand, was opposed to the absolute powers to be conferred on the British Resident Commissioner. It was especially opposed to the idea of a new Zimbabwe army, which would include elements of the Patriotic Front forces. Mr Smith, however, did not reject the Anglo-American plan. This was partly because, since the Patriotic Front did not accept it, there was no need to, and partly because South Africa did not want the plan to be rejected. The United States and Britain had both won Pretoria's tacit support for the proposals by warning that they might not oppose UN oil

9

sanctions if South Africa rejected the latest peace initiative. South Africa knew that the question of economic and military embargoes would be debated and voted on in the UN that autumn.

Quite aside from South Africa's position, it was evident to Mr Smith (and to most others) how events were moving. On the one hand the Patriotic Front was not prepared to accept the Anglo–American plan and, on the other, the military and economic pressures against the white Rhodesian government were building up. Conscription was extended to the 38–50 age group, and every able-bodied white male faced the prospect of spending half of every year on active duty. The economy continued to decline, with projections indicating a 7 per cent drop in GNP by the end of 1977. Finally, whites were leaving in greater numbers. There was a net emigration of 10,908 by the end of 1977. Many more would have left had government controls not prevented them from taking their money with them. All of these pressures had the effect of moving Mr Smith inexorably towards an attempt to bring off an 'internal settlement'.

There was little that the United States could do as she watched Ian Smith enter into negotiations in December with Bishop Muzorewa, the Reverend Ndabaningi Sithole and Chief Jeremiah Chirau. Mr Smith's attempts to work with the three black leaders (two of them proven nationalists) were inadvertently aided by the American and British governments when they invited him (but not the internal black leaders) to meet with Robert Mugabe and Joshua Nkomo in Malta early in the new year. Mr Smith was later to call this a 'fatal mistake', for it convinced Bishop Muzorewa, Reverend Sithole and Chief Chirau that the only way they could seek power was through an arrangement with the existing government. A more fundamental reason for Mr Smith's success, however, was the history of tribal and personal rivalries that has debilitated the nationalist movement in Rhodesia.

In Rhodesia today approximately 80 per cent of the African population is Shona-speaking, although one cannot speak of a single Shona tribe. These people live in the northern, eastern and south-eastern part of the country. About 14 per cent of the African population is Ndebele, living in the southern part of Rhodesia. If there were a united Shona leadership, stable black rule would be easier to achieve, since the Shona would have overwhelming numerical power: that, however, is not the case. Moreover, the most experienced of the black leaders, Mr Nkomo, is a Kalanga, a tribe linked to the Ndebele. Consequently, Nkomo's political strength derives from one (rather small) part of the country.

In addition to the tribal differences, there are the personal rivalries, many of them of long-standing. Mr Nkomo emerged in 1957 as the first of the black leaders when he was chosen to head the new African National Council (ANC). This was banned in 1959. In 1960 he became the leader of the National Democratic Party. This was banned in 1961. In 1962 he formed the Zimbabwe African People's Union (ZAPU), which was also banned but continued to operate from outside Rhodesia. ZAPU's chief representative abroad was Reverend Sithole. In 1962 Sithole led a faction (including Robert Mugabe) which broke with Nkomo and formed its own movement, the Zimbabwe African National Union (ZANU). The reason for the split was as much conflicting personalities as conflicting policies. The pattern of internal party strife persisted. In 1970 Mugabe drove Reverend Sithole out of the ZANU leadership, who thereupon claimed that he and his supporters constituted the legitimate ZANU. The ZANU feuding continued until Presidents Kuanda and Nyerere threw their support and recognition behind Mr Mugabe. However, that hardly settled matters. In March 1975 Mr Herbert Chitepo, a leading ZANU official, was assassinated in Zambia. Many ZANU members blamed the murder on supporters of Josiah Tongogara, ZANU's military commander-in-chief. The result was a ZANU blood-letting in which several hundred ZANU members were killed. The inevitable consequence was yet another split in ZANU. Although it was never made official (on paper ZANU remains a monolithic movement), the split has led not only to more feuding but also to periodic clashes among various ZANU factions.

The record of instability in the nationalist movements is due not only to tribal friction and personal rivalries, but also to the history of harsh persecution of the black movements by the white Rhodesian government. Mr Nkomo, Mr Mugabe and Reverend Sithole have all shared the experience of spending years in Rhodesian prisons. Each claims to be Zimbabwe's true nationalist leader. Nevertheless, the continuing level of political strife among the black nationalist movements is difficult to comprehend, given the fact that the movements and their leaders share a common goal.

To a considerable extent, it is this record of rivalry that explains the rise of Bishop Muzorewa as a nationalist leader. A Methodist bishop, Muzorewa rose to prominence in 1971 when he took over the leadership of a reconstituted African National Congress. His popularity was due to the fact that he seemed unlike the other nationalist leaders. He did not appear to be power-hungry. He was not tarnished by the internecine struggles of the other movements. Although a colourless personality, he was a figurehead behind which those Rhodesian blacks who rejected the other leaders could unite. By 1975 it was estimated that Bishop Muzorewa was the single most popular leader among blacks; however, the bishop did not command any military power.

This factionalism among Rhodesia's blacks provided Mr Smith with the opportunity to push ahead with his version of an internal settlement. Nkomo and Mugabe would reject any negotiations because they had their armies and each hoped to seize power for himself. However, Bishop Muzorewa and Reverend Sithole looked more promising to Mr Smith. The former had popular support and the latter possessed considerable shrewdness. Both men saw the personal advantages of an agreement with Mr Smith, provided the terms were acceptable. Chief Chirau also participated in the negotiations. Rhodesia's tribal chiefs supported the government in order to preserve their own power, but Chief Chirau seemed unlikely to be a key figure in an internal settlement.

Following protracted negotiations, agreement on an 'internal settlement' was announced on 3 March 1978. A transitional government was established, led by an Executive Council consisting of the four signatories. Decisions were to be by consensus. A bi-racial Council of Ministers served as the Cabinet, with black and white co-ministers for each portfolio. Elections were to be held by 31 December 1978.

From the beginning, however, it was clear that the 'internal settlement' was a shrewd manoeuvre by Mr Smith to maintain white control in Rhodesia. This was evident in his insistence that whites were to be guaranteed a large enough number of seats in the 100-seat Parliament to block any constitutional changes to the agreement for a period of ten years. The most important of the 'entrenched' white powers was control of the police, the army, and the government administration for the same period.

The announcement of the settlement demanded a response from the United States. The plan had surface appeal, so explaining to American public opinion why it should not be supported was difficult as the country was not familiar with the details of the Rhodesian problem. Although clearly imperfect, the plan did appear to provide exactly what American policy had been working towards – universal suffrage, the orderly transfer of political authority from whites to blacks and provisions which would encourage whites to remain in Rhodesia to provide expertise and stability. Moreover, the agreement appeared to meet the basic criteria established by Britain in the 1960s for formal recognition of Rhodesia's independence. The Foreign Secretary, Dr David Owen, called the agreement a 'good step forward' but not good enough to be blessed with formal British recognition. The American response, however, was adamant; the settlement was deemed 'inadequate'. The analysis was that whatever its attractions, the internal settlement was internal; it did not include all the parties to the dispute, and there was little faith that the transitional government could stop the fighting and organize elections even if it wanted to. Time, it was thought, would demonstrate the inadequacies of the internal settlement and also the extent to which Mr Smith remained in control of it.

An added burden for American policy-makers was that the announcement of the settlement came less than a month before President Carter's visit to Nigeria. The visit was intended to demonstrate American support for black Africa. Any sign of sympathy for the Salisbury agreement, which had been denounced by most African leaders as well as by the Patriotic Front, could have led to the cancellation of the President's visit – a trip which was assuming considerable political importance. Soviet/Cuban involvement in the Ogaden fighting between Somalia and Ethiopia (plus the prospect of similar involvement in Eritrea) was rapidly bringing Africa to the forefront of American strategic thinking. The Carter Administration was painfully aware of its vulnerability in the face of possible Soviet/Cuban

11

intervention in Rhodesia. The only answer the American Administration could find was renewed efforts to get all the parties in the Rhodesian dispute to sit down and talk.

In late March 1978 Mr Young met the Front Line Presidents in Dar es Salaam. When he flew on to Lagos to meet President Carter he thought he had achieved a major breakthrough. He reported that he had been assured by the Front Line Presidents that the Patriotic Front was now prepared to attend an all-party conference and that they had accepted the Anglo–American plan. The news was so encouraging that the President ordered a new mission to southern Africa, headed by his Secretary of State. Although Dr Owen joined the mission, it was clearly the result of an American initiative. In mid-April Mr Vance, Dr Owen and Mr Young met Mr Mugabe and Mr Nkomo in Dar es Salaam. Once again they watched an alleged agreement disappear before their eyes. Mugabe and Nkomo did agree to attend a new conference and to accept key portions of the Anglo–American plan, including those covering elections, the presence of a British Commissioner and UN forces. However, the two men then made the demand that the Patriotic Front should in effect control the Rhodesian security forces. The result was disappointment for Cyrus Vance and a chastening experience for Andrew Young. When Mr Vance flew on to Salisbury (the first visit of so senior an American official to Rhodesia) he and Dr Owen asked Mr Smith and his black colleagues on the Interim Government's Executive Council to attend an all-party conference. A week later (to no one's surprise) the Executive Council turned down the invitation.

Once again the Anglo–American initiative on Rhodesia was suspended. If the Interim Government in Salisbury had not won the recognition it sought, it had at least had the opportunity to demonstrate that it would work. Success would ultimately depend on one thing only – the ability of the government to persuade the soldiers of the Patriotic Front to lay down their arms. Political detainees were therefore released and the government talked of cease-fires and of organizing elections. However, it was soon clear that little real progress was being made in either of these areas. Indeed, Mr Smith began to say that elections might not be possible by the end of the year. Moreover, the fighting increased in intensity,

and within the Executive Council serious friction between Bishop Muzorewa and the other members became evident. Although the terms of the internal settlement were officially considered by its members to be inviolate, everyone was aware that new deals and sudden realignments were possible. This was most conspicuous in Ian Smith's appeal to Mr Nkomo to return to Rhodesia to join the Interim Government. The internal settlement clearly posed an awkward problem for the Carter Administration in terms of American public opinion. It was difficult to explain why the United States should withhold support from an agreement which claimed to lead to majority rule, while maintaining ties with the Patriotic Front, one of whose leaders was proclaiming his goal of one-party Marxist rule. It was not the first time the Carter Administration would be caught between its idealistic pronouncements and its need to pursue a pragmatic policy. And in Rhodesia, despite Mr Young's widely publicized statements, it *was* a very pragmatic policy. The United States had given priority to staying on good terms with the side she felt was going to win (or at least was going to play a major role in a new Zimbabwe), namely the Patriotic Front. It was an effort to pre-empt (or at least minimize) Soviet/Cuban influence over the Front and its armies by American default. As for 'one man, one vote' elections, here too American policy was guided by no illusions. An election leading to majority rule was not expected to be a seed which would put down firm democratic roots in Zimbabwe. The recent history of too many African states crushed any such hope. Rather, elections were considered essential as a device to provide international acceptability and legitimacy for the transfer of power into black hands. It appeared that the only way to carry out that transfer of power in a politically stable environment was to secure the agreement of all the factions involved. That meant convening an all-party conference, the policy doggedly pursued by the United States and Britain.

Frustrating as the political and personal rivalries among the various black leaders might be, the major obstacle to an effective and stable Rhodesian settlement has been the absence of a common interest between the West (including South Africa) and the white population of Rhodesia. The single most important fact concerning Rhodesia is that the ruling party (the Rhodesia Front), which has led the country since its unilateral declaration of independence, is not interested in a genuine multi-racial state. It is interested not in sharing power but in holding on to power. This attitude was seen in Mr Smith's negotiations with Dr Kissinger, as well as in the concessions he was able to win from his black partners in the internal settlement. This refusal to give up power is more than a government policy; it reflects the dominant feeling among Rhodesian whites and it is the fundamental reason why diplomacy has failed. Mr Smith's attitude is that of the white population, which explains why he has survived for so long. He has shown considerable toughness and an ability to fight rearguard actions to preserve white rule. His problem is that one rearguard action leads to another and, eventually, to defeat. The danger for the West has been that the longer this process continues, the greater the instability and the greater the possibility of direct Communist intervention in Rhodesia. If the prospect of that is frightening to the West, it is not necessarily daunting for Mr Smith. He may hope that Cuban intervention will create a traditional East–West confrontation, which will compel the United States at least to choose between supporting Rhodesia's whites and siding with Cuban- or Soviet-backed nationalist forces – a nightmare prospect for American policy-makers.

If the Carter Administration could find any consolation, it was that its analysis of the Rhodesian situation was proved correct by events in the summer of 1978. The level of fighting again increased as the Government lost control over more and more areas of the country. The government also showed little sense of urgency in removing racial discrimination legislation and in organizing elections. The diplomatic effort of the United States and Britain was devoted essentially to continuing to urge the reconvening of an all-party conference. The fact that the Salisbury government refused to join the talks did not come as a surprise to Washington and London, where policy-makers were following Mr Smith's efforts to persuade Joshua Nkomo to return to Rhodesia to participate in the internal settlement.

On 14 August 1978 Ian Smith met Mr Nkomo secretly at the State House in Lusaka. Also present at the meeting were the Zambian President, Kenneth Kaunda and the Nigerian Foreign Minister, Joseph Garba. It has been American policy throughout the Rhodesian effort to work closely with the Front Line Presidents, and particularly with Presidents Nyerere and Kaunda. But during his visit to Lagos in the spring of 1978 President Carter had urged Nigeria to become more active in the effort to negotiate a Rhodesian settlement. Nigeria's size and oil wealth gave her a major political voice in African affairs, and the military government headed by General Olusegan Obasanjo considered southern Africa an area of legitimate concern for Nigeria. Throughout the summer of 1978 Mr Garba played an active role in trying to arrange a meeting between Smith and Nkomo. Although details of what transpired at the meeting are not known, it is believed that a deal was proposed which would have seen Mr Nkomo returning to Rhodesia as the Head of the Executive Council. The obvious difficulty was that Robert Mugabe (who had not been informed of the Lusaka meeting) had to be included in a lesser role in the settlement if Mr Nkomo was not prepared to break completely with his co-leader of the Patriotic Front. The Smith–Nkomo talks ended with the declared intention to hold a second meeting approximately a week later. However, at this point it was necessary to inform Mr Mugabe of what was being proposed. Five days after the Lusaka meeting he was flown by the Nigerian government to Lagos, where General Obasanjo tried to persuade him to accept the settlement. Mr Mugabe did not accept the proposals, and he was supported in this by President Nyerere, who felt he had been deceived by Kaunda, who had acted as host during the Smith–Nkomo talks. A week later, news of the Smith–Nkomo meeting began to leak out. On 1 September Joshua Nkomo announced publicly that the meeting had taken place. Rhodesian politics would never be the same again.

The Lusaka meeting confirmed what almost everyone on both sides had been thinking: first, that the internal settlement was not working and, second, that the Patriotic Front was not a united front. It was, in fact, two separate armies, whose two leaders were united only by a common desire to destroy white rule in Rhodesia. Indeed, any analysis of the events of the summer of 1978 must examine whether it was really in the interests of the United States and Britain to encourage an agreement between Mr Smith and Mr Nkomo at the expense of Mr Mugabe. If British and American policy was to promote stability in Rhodesia, it would have been prudent to encourage closer co-operation between the Nkomo and Mugabe factions rather than to follow a course which could only have led to a definitive split between them and to even greater factionalism and instability. There are two possible answers to this. First, the United States and Britain were not the prime instigators of the Lusaka meeting (although they were informed and were watching it closely). The meeting took place because Mr Smith, President Kaunda and the Nigerian government wanted to try to do a deal with Mr Nkomo. Second, it was already recognized that the Patriotic Front was not a lasting institution and that the chances of civil war in Rhodesia between the Mugabe and Nkomo armies (based as they were on tribal foundations) was likely in any case. Therefore a secret approach to Joshua Nkomo by Mr Smith could scarcely do any harm. What followed was a sequence of events which brought the American and British peace effort in Rhodesia to a halt.

Less than forty-eight hours after Mr Nkomo's public confirmation of his meeting with Ian Smith an Air Rhodesia Viscount was shot down by a ground-to-air missile after taking off from Kariba, near the Zambian border. Ten survivors of the crash were subsequently massacred by insurgents. The outrage among the white population of Rhodesia was compounded when Mr Nkomo claimed that his army had shot down the plane, although he denied that it had murdered the survivors. Mr Smith was vilified by some of his supporters for having held talks with Mr Nkomo.

This sudden turn of events and the prospect of Rhodesian retaliation worried American policymakers, who saw the chance of an all-party conference rapidly receding. On 9 September American and British officials met in London. They publicly reaffirmed their confidence in the Anglo–American plan. There was even an expression of hope that the events of the previous four weeks had broken the political deadlock over Rhodesia and that a new flexibility and certain factional realignments might now be possible. However, American and British officials realized that their settlement plan had to be revised. The new version, known as 'Option B', had been shown to the Front Line Presidents and

the Patriotic Front earlier in the summer. It was a dramatic watering down of the previous Anglo–American proposal. An all-party conference remained the starting point. The conference would agree on a transitional constitution, which would designate a new governing body composed of the four members of the Salisbury Executive Council, the two leaders of the Patriotic Front and two other Patriotic Front representatives. Once this body was formed, sanctions would be lifted. Then, at the earliest possible moment, a referendum would be held on the constitution before formal voter registration. If the referendum was approved (as it certainly would be by Rhodesia's black majority), Her Majesty's Government would formally grant Zimbabwe independence.

The new plan clearly reflected the mood of desperation in Washington and London. Gone was the requirement that elections would have to be held before the new government was recognized; gone also was the requirement that Zimbabwe's leaders would have to be elected. The fundamental issue of who would control the army and police – even who would serve in the two security forces – was evaded.

The abandonment of the key provisions of the original Anglo–American plan indicated not only a general feeling that the time left for diplomatic effort was short, but also the extent to which the emphasis of that effort had changed. No longer was the primary problem perceived to be that of persuading the white population to give up power, for power was in any case steadily slipping away; rather, the problem was now to seek some sort of unity among the competing black factions. But here too there was little success.

During the remaining months of 1978 the situation continued to deteriorate. In October Mr Smith, accompanied by the Reverend Sithole, visited the United States. Mr Smith had been invited by a group of conservative Senators. The question of whether to grant a visa to the Prime Minister of a government the United States did not recognize (indeed, supported sanctions against) was hotly debated in the State Department. In the end Cyrus Vance, the Secretary of State, authorized it. There was a precedent, in that Bishop Muzorewa, Mr Nkomo and Mr Mugabe had all previously visited the United States. There was also a domestic political consideration. The Senators and groups who wanted to hear Mr Smith had been sympathetic to the idea of internal settlement when it was first proposed. The Carter Administration saw no reason to alienate the political conservatives needlessly by keeping Mr Smith out, and it was judged that his presence would have little substantive impact on American public opinion as a whole. That judgement was largely correct, although the granting of the visa angered black African leaders, particularly the Front Line Presidents.

During his stay in the United States Mr Smith accepted the proposal of an all-party conference in principle. However, on the day he met Mr Vance, Rhodesian planes launched the first of a series of attacks against Nkomo's bases in Zambia (the camp at Chikumbi, 12 miles north of Lusaka, and other installations). These raids which came five weeks after the shooting down of the Air Rhodesian Viscount inflicted heavy casualties. Although the attacks may have been to a certain extent retaliatory, it would be simplistic to claim that is all that they were. The length and intensity of the attacks served to demonstrate how defenceless were both Zambia and Mr Nkomo's army. Moreover, the raids effectively scuttled any chance for the all-party conference to which Mr Smith had just agreed. As the raids continued, Mr Nkomo rejected the conference plan, as did Presidents Kaunda and Nyerere. Not only was the chasm between the opposing sides in the war wider than ever, but serious divisions were developing among the Front Line Presidents. President Kaunda's decision to re-open Zambian rail traffic through Rhodesia to South Africa in order to bring in desperately needed fertilizer angered President Nyerere particularly (he was already angry at Kaunda's role in the August Smith–Nkomo meeting). A summit meeting in Dar es Salaam was called by President Nyerere to re-establish unity among the Front Line Presidents, but it too ended in disarray.

In the following month, November 1978, Mr Smith warned that elections would not be held by the end of the year, as the Salisbury agreement had called for, but would instead be postponed until April 1979. In December he announced that seats in the new Cabinet would be allocated according to the number of seats held by each party in the new Parliament which meant that the whites, who would have 28 of the 100 seats in Parliament, would have 28 per cent of the seats in the Cabinet, could well constitute the largest single party in both Parliament and the Cabinet and might therefore end up forming the government. The internal settlement, which had little credibility to begin with, had virtually none at the turn of the year. The whites still controlled the Rhodesian government even if they controlled less of the countryside.

In early February 1979 legislation finally came into force outlawing racial discrimination, although that promised little actual change in Rhodesian life. For under the new constitution whites would not only continue to control the police, the armed forces and the civil service but would also be able to sustain large-scale, *de facto* discrimination in housing, schools and hospitals.

From 17–21 April 1979 the Rhodesian elections were finally held under security measures which included the mobilization of white males up to the age of 60. Neither the American nor the British government sent observers, although Britain's Conservative Party did. According to Rhodesian government figures, 64 per cent of the people of Rhodesia (white and black, over 18 years of age and resident in the country for two years) voted. Bishop Muzorewa's United African Nationalist Congress (UANC) was the clear winner, with 51 of the 100 seats in the new Parliament.

The Carter Administration viewed the election with trepidation. Although the voting appeared to have been carried out in an acceptable manner, the Administration had rejected in advance the legitimacy of the election results. It based its case on the fact that the voting was held under wartime conditions and without the participation of all the parties to the dispute. The primary concern of the Administration was that the voting would strengthen the growing sentiment in Congress for the lifting of sanctions and the recognition of the Salisbury government. The Case–Javits amendment of August 1978 had empowered the President to take such steps if it was found that the voting had been held under free and fair conditions. The implication was that if the President did not act, Congress might itself take action to lift sanctions and confront the President with a *fait accompli*. Indeed, on 6 May the Senate adopted a resolution calling for the removal of sanctions. The size of the vote (75–19) was especially worrying, since the Administration was not in a position to offer any alternative to the policy it was pursuing. The new British

Conservative Government, which took office on 3 May 1979, is currently attempting, at the Lancaster House Conference, to reach a settlement which will satisfy all the parties, internal and external. The new initiative followed the Commonwealth Conference in Lusaka. The American Government is now playing the role of spectator, although supporting British efforts to resolve the dispute.

Any examination of American policy and tactics in Rhodesia must start with the question of whether the goal (the peaceful transfer of power to a stable majority-rule government) was ever attainable. If the answer is 'probably not', it is not just hindsight which leads one to that conclusion. From the moment that Dr Kissinger entered into the politics of southern Africa, the obstacles to a peaceful, stable settlement were readily apparent. These were factionalism among the black nationalists and the attitude of white Rhodesians as exemplified by Mr Smith. Both sides had secure supplies of weapons, and the nationalist armies were in a position to wage their war indefinitely from bases in Zambia and Mozambique. Even if black leaders like Joshua Nkomo had been prepared, earlier in the 1970s, to seek some compromise with Ian Smith which would have allowed a gradual move towards black rule, by the spring of 1976 such accommodation was no longer acceptable to the more militant nationalist leaders whose power was growing. By the time Dr Kissinger arrived in Lusaka in April 1976, the goal American policy was seeking was already out of reach. That he recognized this fact can be seen in the ambiguous tactics he employed during the summer and autumn of 1976, when he tried to finesse the fundamental dispute over which side would control the security forces in a Rhodesian settlement. Subsequent events, as we have seen, have done nothing to settle that issue.

If the American policy goal in Rhodesia was always unattainable, what were the alternatives? There seem to be three possibilities.

One course of action (in theory) would have been for the United States to offer stronger sympathy and support to Mr Smith's government. Full support for Rhodesia's government was, of course, out of the question, given the British constraint. Beyond that, neither the African policy of the United States nor domestic political opinion (mainly black and liberal white opinion)

would have permitted such a course of action. However, when Ian Smith created his internal settlement in March 1978 the formulators of American policy had to come to terms with a new situation. Although there was some initial sympathy for the internal settlement among the globalists in the NSC, Mr Smith's creation was quickly branded by the Administration as too little, too late. Behind this was not only an appreciation of the inadequacies of the internal settlement as it was presented but also an awareness that overall American policy towards black Africa would not allow any backsliding towards even minimum support for Mr Smith.

Nevertheless, it is interesting to speculate about what might have been the result (at the time) of a more flexible American and British response to the internal settlement. Such a step would have given Washington and London a unique opportunity to exert considerable pressure on Mr Smith in the drawing up of the new constitution. He might have been prepared to sacrifice more of the 'entrenched' white powers (thereby making it easier to sell the new constitution) had the United States and Britain been prepared to offer the prospect of recognition and the removal of sanctions. Such a move might also have won new South African backing and brought additional pressure to bear on Rhodesia. Clearly, such a departure from established Anglo–American policy would have been a major risk. Even assuming that a new constitution might have been drafted which the United States and Britain could have supported, the fighting in Rhodesia would still have continued. Moreover, the United States and Britain would have had to mount a major campaign to convince others that they ought to recognize the new Zimbabwe. Even if recognition could have been won from countries like Botswana, Zaire and the francophone countries of West Africa (and, with real pressure, perhaps even Zambia), Mozambique and Tanzania would probably not have recognized the new state, which would have left the military contest unresolved.

Such a scenario involves many 'ifs'. For the United States to have attempted to sell such a policy would have meant a dramatic change from the role of middleman to that of an activist prepared to take a major gamble. It was a gamble she was not prepared to take.

If the option of increased support for white

Rhodesians was quickly dismissed, there was a second option. This was to support the liberation movements openly, even to the point of arming them. To the extent that this would have been the most effective way to pre-empt Soviet influence in Africa, theoretically such an action would have been in tune with American goals. Nevertheless, the arguments against this option were overwhelming.

Firstly, a British government would not have been able to support a policy of arming black guerrillas against Britain's kith and kin in Rhodesia. Similarly, an American President who supported such a policy would have faced severe questioning from middle-American whites, who would have asked why the United States was opposed to hard-working Rhodesian whites. It would have been a potent weapon for any right-wing opponent of the President. In domestic politics it has been important for a President not to lean too far to either side on racial issues but to occupy the politically important middle ground and to be perceived by the public as a leader trying to bridge the gap between the races. Certainly, a President could lean to the more liberal side of the fence (as Kennedy and Johnson did) or to the more conservative side (as Nixon and Ford did), but no President could afford to come down clearly on either side of the racial issue. American policy in Rhodesia had to be an extension of that attitude.

Apart from domestic political constraints, overt American support for the liberation armies would have elicited a strong reaction from American corporate interests in southern Africa – not because their interests in Rhodesia were large but because they would have seen the Administration's policy as establishing a precedent for the coming conflict in South Africa, where they do have important investments.

Finally, the soldiers of the Patriotic Front would have fought no more or less effectively with Western than with Soviet weapons. The war would have dragged on just as long, leaving the American Administration intolerably exposed to all the pressures noted here. In sum, therefore, this may perhaps have been an interesting theory, but it was an impractical policy.

If these two options were ruled out, there was one other possible course – to do nothing. The argument for abstaining from participation in Rhodesian events was that if the United States could not, or did not, want to support one side or the other in the dispute, and if a mediation effort was certain to fail, then it was best that she should not become involved in the first place. The role of middleman might be an honourable one but it also risked falling between two stools: it would fail to bring the contending sides together while alienating both. Certainly, until 1976 the United States had avoided getting involved.

However, what brought the United States into the southern Africa question was Dr Kissinger's perception of it as part of the larger East–West rivalry. Therefore it was incumbent on the United States to become involved in her capacity as a great power, particularly after her failure to act effectively in Angola. If the post-Vietnam United States was not in a position to respond to Soviet influence in the same military coin, she would have to do her best in the only currency at her disposal – diplomacy. Weak as that currency might be, in Kissinger's view its negotiation had to be attempted. As leader of the Western world, the worst thing the United States could do was to do nothing.

Having inherited the Kissinger policy, the Carter Administration could not disengage from Africa even if it wanted to. Like any new Administration, it had to demonstrate its capacity for leadership to allies as well as to opponents. Also Africa provided an opportunity for the Administration to demonstrate a new approach in policy-making. Whereas Kissinger had viewed the importance of American involvement in southern Africa in globalist terms, the Carter Administration considered it essential in regional terms; American participation in the Rhodesia question was important for the United States' standing in black Africa. Disengagement was unacceptable.

These options have been listed not only to show that they were unrealistic in political terms but also to illustrate what is readily apparent to policy-makers: that formulating a course of action is frequently less a creative act than a process of elimination – the elimination of those policies which are not (in the jargon of the trade) viable. It was this process as much as any other that dictated the United States' Rhodesia policy.

If the goal of American policy in Rhodesia (the peaceful transfer of political power to a stable majority-rule government) stands up to analysis, the same cannot always be said of the way that policy was conducted. What the Carter Administration did not realize until relatively late was that it was impossible to get the inner circle of competing Rhodesian factions (black and white, internal and external) to agree on a settlement until there was agreement and co-operation among the members of the outer circle – the Front Line Presidents and South Africa. It was this cohesion which was never established (indeed, never really attempted), since it was the policy of the Carter Administration to make no special effort to seek South African co-operation. The early decision by the Administration to divorce its policy towards South Africa from the Rhodesia question appeared with the passage of time to have been a tactical mistake. The United States gained little from such a move, which did not by itself appreciably raise American political stock among sceptical black African leaders. In fact, the results were mostly negative. Although there was certainly a limit to the pressure which South Africa was prepared to exert on Rhodesia, that limit was not reached during the course of the Carter Administration's peace efforts. The Administration's claim that it was in South Africa's own interests to work actively towards a Rhodesian settlement was not borne out in practice. The price of that misreading of South Africa's stance was not limited to its consequences in Rhodesia. It had even more serious repercussions in another key area of southern Africa – Namibia.

III. NAMIBIA

While American diplomacy with regard to Rhodesia commanded considerable publicity, similar efforts to resolve the problems of Namibia attracted less attention. The reasons for this are clear: Rhodesia was at war; a white minority was fighting with its back to the wall; the threat of a Communist take-over and the links with kith and kin ensured continuing public interest in the West; and Namibia was relegated to the inside pages of newspapers, few of whose readers could pinpoint her location on a map.

For American policy-makers, however, a close and important connection existed between the situations in Namibia and Rhodesia. The connection was South Africa. The thesis was that if the South African government could be committed to the peaceful transfer of power to majority rule in Namibia, it would be inclined to do the same in Rhodesia. It was another example of Pretoria's importance in southern Africa. The result was that Namibia occupied a position of high priority among American policy-makers, who recognized a set of circumstances (political and military) which not only could lead to a successfully negotiated settlement in that country but also could be a major step towards greater stability throughout southern Africa.

Formerly a German colony, South-West Africa was mandated to South Africa by the League of Nations in 1920. Following World War II and the dissolution of the League, South Africa refused to place the area under United Nations trusteeship. In 1966 the General Assembly, reflecting the growing influence of African and other Third World members, authorized the UN to assume responsibility for the territory until independence, whenever that might be. The UN resolution did not change the situation in South-West Africa or South Africa's control of the territory, but it did lay the foundation for international pressures which could be applied to Pretoria at every UN session. The pressures included UN recognition of the South-West Africa People's Organization (SWAPO) as the legitimate representative of the Namibian people.

SWAPO was founded in 1958. Its first President, Herman Toivo Ja Toivo, was first banned by the South African government and then imprisoned on Robben Island. Toivo's successor as SWAPO leader is Mr Sam Njomo. SWAPO launched its armed struggle against South African rule in Namibia in 1966. However, unlike the insurgent forces in Rhodesia, SWAPO has never been able to mount an effective military effort which would threaten the South African government's control. From its bases in southern Angola SWAPO has sent small raiding parties across the border into the fertile northern region of Namibia, the homeland of the Ovambo tribe which forms the basis of SWAPO's strength. However, the sheer size of Namibia and its open topography have prevented deeper penetration. Like the Patriotic Front forces operating in Rhodesia, SWAPO has received training and supplies from the

Communist world. Nevertheless, there is a fundamental difference between the two wars. In Rhodesia the insurgent army has demonstrated its effectiveness, although the extent of its support among the African population is still open to question. In Namibia, although SWAPO is relatively ineffective militarily, it does command extensive support, especially among the Ovambo.

There are only an estimated 900,000 people in Namibia, an area one-and-a-half times the size of France, and approximately half of these are Ovambos. The 100,000 whites form the second largest population group, followed by nine other communal groups, each one fearful of being dominated by the Ovambos.

If the mounting international pressure over Namibia posed a problem to the Pretoria government, the social fragmentation within the territory offered a possible remedy. In September 1975 a constitutional conference opened in the Turnhalle building in Windhoek, held under South African auspices. It was intended that representation at the conference (and in the proposed government of an independent Namibia) should be based on the various communities rather than on the principle of 'one man, one vote', which would have put effective power into the hands of the Ovambos and so of SWAPO. It was an attempt to bring about an internal settlement much like the one that Mr Smith would propose two years later in Rhodesia. It has had much the same results. When SWAPO's internal wing (which is legal in Namibia) was invited to join the talks it refused, and, without SWAPO's participation, it was soon evident that a Turnhalle solution would not win the necessary international recognition.

When Dr Kissinger met Prime Minister Vorster in Bavaria in June 1976 and again in Zurich in September of that year, Namibia was the major subject under discussion. Both men wanted to see a moderate solution to a potentially unstable situation. In addition, as we have seen, the United States wanted to involve South Africa more deeply in the peace efforts in southern Africa, and what better way than to draw her into discussions on Namibia, one of Pretoria's biggest unresolved problems?

The UN's deadline for the independence of Namibia was 31 August 1976. The threat to South Africa was less SWAPO's military strength than the UN sanctions prompted by South Africa's continuing rule in Namibia. By the time Dr Kissinger arrived in Pretoria in September 1976, only the final touches remained to be put to a plan for Namibian independence. On the surface the plan called for SWAPO to participate in a new conference, which was supposed to start by the end of October. As soon as he returned to the United States, Dr Kissinger met Mr Njomo in New York to try to persuade him that he had more to gain by joining the conference than by continuing his sputtering war. Mr Njomo was not persuaded. Perhaps he was aware of what appears to have been a co-ordinated American–South African effort to execute a rapid transfer of power to a moderate Namibian government. The leader being promoted by Pretoria was Clemens Kapuuo, Chief of the 75,000 Hereros who comprise the third largest community in Namibia. There is evidence of a major attempt by South Africa and the United States to build up Chief Kapuuo's international image as a valid leader of Namibia. Even with Dr Kissinger's backing, however, such a plan to hand over power to a moderate government lacked the essential ingredient of international (that is, UN) acceptance. To be acceptable internationally, the settlement had to include SWAPO, and since SWAPO was not to be given power, Mr Njomo saw no reason for joining the conference that Kissinger was trying to promote. The idea of the conference was abandoned. A few weeks later President Ford was defeated and, as in Rhodesia, it was time to wait for the Carter Administration.

The basic and significant innovation of the Carter Administration in dealing with Namibia was to recognize that the problem of the territory was legally a matter of the UN, which tactically should involve the United States' Western allies. Instead of staging a one-man show in negotiating with Pretoria and SWAPO, the new Administration organized a Contact Group comprising the five Western members of the Security Council (the United States, Britain, France, the Federal Republic of Germany and Canada). In addition to putting the Namibia question into a UN context, the Contact Group offered an important advantage: South Africa now found· herself facing a solid front of her principal trading partners. More important, as permanent members of the Security Council, the United States, Britain and France had the power of vetoing (or supporting) any economic sanctions the Council might vote against South Africa. It was with this leverage that the Contact Group held its first talks with the Vorster government in March 1977, less than two months after the Carter Administration had taken office. The American representative was Mr Donald McHenry, a career diplomat, and a deputy to Andrew Young at the UN. At first Mr McHenry, like many members of the new Administration, held out little hope that the Namibia initiative would succeed. All were convinced that South Africa was determined to promote her own internal settlement. However, after the initial contacts Mr McHenry and the rest of the Contact Group felt that a settlement acceptable to the UN was possible. On 31 March 1977 the Contact Group presented its first formal proposals to Pretoria and to SWAPO. Mr Njomo agreed to elections, and the South African government dropped its plans for an internal settlement. This was particularly significant, since on 18 March the Turnhalle conference had issued a draft constitution for an interim government leading to Namibia's independence.

As the Contact Group meetings continued through the year, considerable progress was made, and South Africa agreed to UN supervision of the elections and the presence of a UN force. But by early 1978 two points were still unresolved. The first was the number of South African troops which would be allowed to remain in Namibia during the transition period. SWAPO wanted them all withdrawn, or at least moved away from the border area, whereas Pretoria demanded that at least 3,000 soldiers be allowed to remain in the northern part of the territory, where SWAPO has most of its potential voters. The second contentious point was the status of Walvis Bay, the only deep-water port on the territory's 1,000-mile coast. South Africa bases her claim to sovereignty over the port on its annexation by the Cape Colony in 1884. Continued possession of Walvis Bay would give South Africa a powerful hold on the economic life of an independent Namibia. Beyond that, South African control of the facility would prevent the port from being used by the Soviet fleet, a factor which would be as much in the interest of the members of the Western Contact Group as in South Africa's. However, SWAPO insisted on the inclusion of Walvis Bay in an independent Namibia, a position certain to find backing in the United Nations.

On 22 March 1978 the Contact Group made its 'final' proposals to South Africa and SWAPO. It provided for the maintenance of 1,500 South African soldiers in two bases near the Angola border until one week after the elections. Walvis Bay was not mentioned. The issue was to be left to the new Namibian government and South Africa to negotiate.

The Western proposals came a week before President Carter's visit to Nigeria. Fearing that there was still strong support in South Africa for an internal settlement in Namibia, the President urged the Vorster government not to reach a hasty decision. Pretoria, however, was in no rush. On 27 March, while it was considering the proposals, Chief Kapuuo was assassinated in Windhoek. His murder was never solved, but the principal black figure in an internal settlement was dead.

In mid-April the American Secretary of State, Cyrus Vance, and the British Foreign Secretary, Dr David Owen, flew to Pretoria to offer 'clarifications' of the Western proposals. On 25 April South Africa accepted them. The announcement from Pretoria put SWAPO on the defensive. At the UN, journalists converged on Sam Njomo asking for his reaction to the South African decision. Flustered, he said, 'That's their problem.'

In fact, it was Mr Njomo's problem. He found himself in a position in which it would be difficult to reject a plan providing for UN supervision of the transfer of political power now that South Africa had accepted it. Moreover, his support among the Front Line Presidents was not as solid as it had been. The United States had been lobbying the Presidents to win their support for the Western plan, but it was already clear to them that the SWAPO struggle was not succeeding, and they were urging Mr Njomo to accept a political settlement (in this case, UN-supervised elections).

On 4 May 1978, just nine days after she had accepted the Western plan, South Africa launched a major attack against SWAPO's headquarters at Cassinga, 150 miles north of the Angolan border. The attack, carried out by several hundred airborne commandos, had predictable results. First, it elicited the scorn of the international community and a UN resolution condemning the raid. Second, it demonstrated SWAPO's military weakness, particularly to President Neto of

Angola, on whose territory SWAPO's bases are located, and to President Kaunda of Zambia, SWAPO's other principal backer. The South African attack gave Mr Njomo an excuse to break off talks on the Contact Group plan. However, it did not alter the position of the Front Line Presidents towards him. In May, shortly after the raid, Tanzania released Mr Andreas Shipanga and ten other SWAPO officials who had been held in custody for two years. Mr Shipanga, one of SWAPO's founders, led a faction within the movement which had challenged Mr Njomo's authority and had called for new party elections. Mr Njomo persuaded President Kaunda to arrest his opponents in Zambia; the President did this in April 1976. Mr Shipanga and his colleagues were later transferred to Tanzania, where President Nyerere agreed to hold them as a favour to Mr Njomo and in an effort to stop the factional fighting which was threatening to weaken SWAPO. The release of Mr Shipanga and his followers was an indication by the Front Line Presidents to Mr Njomo that their patience was wearing thin. In June the Presidents met Njomo in Luanda and told him that he had to accept the Western plan with two reservations: first, the position of the remaining South African troops (SWAPO wanted them pulled into the interior of the territory) and, second, Walvis Bay. The United States and the Contact Group told the Front Line Presidents and Sam Njomo that they would not move on the question of South African soldiers. As for Walvis Bay, it would have to be finessed. In early July Ambassador McHenry went to Luanda to meet Mr Njomo. Under pressure from the Front Line Presidents and with the promise of a special UN resolution on Walvis Bay, Njomo agreed to accept the Western plan.

On 26 July 1978 the Security Council adopted a Resolution formally approving the plan for Namibia as worked out by the Contact Group. Walvis Bay was treated separately in a second Resolution, which declared the port an 'integral part of Namibia' and called for its 'early re-integration' into Namibia. It did not, however, give a deadline for this re-integration. South Africa's reaction was to reject the Walvis Bay Resolution while conditionally accepting the first UN Resolution. The conditions were important for South Africa. This became evident when Mr Martii Ahtisaari, the UN Representative sent to Namibia to work out details of the planned UN presence there, submitted his recommendations to Secretary-General Kurt Waldheim. The report called for a UN presence in Namibia of 7,500 men, plus a special police force of over 300 men. In addition, whereas South Africa wanted a quick election, with the voting no later than 31 December 1978, the UN report called for an election date later in 1979. The extra time, South Africa feared, would give SWAPO a better opportunity to organize an effective election campaign.

On 20 September 1978 Prime Minister Vorster announced his resignation and, at the same time, stated that the South African government found the UN plan unacceptable and would proceed with its own elections in Namibia. The new Prime Minister, Mr P. W. Botha, shed further light on the revised South African policy by stating, shortly after his election by the ruling Nationalist Party (and before his first meetings with the Foreign Ministers of the Contact Group), that the planned elections did not close the door to future UN-supervised elections in Namibia. The South African strategy was to strengthen the *de facto* position of the Democratic Turnhalle Alliance (DTA), which was the party representative of Namibia's various ethnic groups, by allowing the voting for a constituent assembly to proceed. At the same time South Africa hoped to hold off UN action on sanctions by offering the prospect of further negotiations on a UN role in the territory.

South Africa's 'No, but – ' reaction to the UN brought the United States and the other members of the Contact Group closer to the situation they were trying to avoid – a vote on sanctions against South Africa, which many African governments were calling for. The result was an unprecedented visit to Pretoria by the Foreign Ministers of the five Contact Group nations. Three days later the two sides announced a 'tentative compromise plan' under which the December 1978 elections in Namibia would be held. After this Pretoria would 'urge' the new constituent assembly to accept elections under UN supervision to be held in 1979. It was also agreed that the conditions of the UN presence – specifically, the size of its military contingent – would be reviewed. More important, South Africa insisted that the date of the elections in 1979 should be maintained even if hostilities in Namibia had not been terminated.

South Africa's position was that she would not withdraw her troops from the territory until there had been a cessation of hostilities.

In essence, this compromise plan was little more than an agreement to keep talking. Since the alternative was a total breakdown of the negotiations and the certainty of a sanctions vote in the UN, it was in the interests of both South Africa and the Contact Group members to reach some agreement, however tenuous. The Pretoria statement also permitted Mr Vance to ask black African governments not to push the sanctions vote until the plan had had time to work.

The result of the December voting was, as predicted, a clear success for the DTA. The Alliance won 82 per cent of the votes cast, although, since SWAPO did not participate, the result cannot be called a true test of opinion in Namibia. Nevertheless, in late December the DTA agreed to UN-supervised elections in 1979. SWAPO's internal wing in Namibia also agreed, and the way to a UN-supervised resolution of the Namibia issue was clear once again.

Analysis of the Western effort in Namibia must start with the recognition of the significance of the issue. It is important not only in its own context, but also in terms of the future relationship between the United States (and her Western partners) and South Africa. The West, South Africa and the black African nations established a triangular relationship over the Namibia issue; in the latter part of 1978, following the Pretoria agreement between South Africa and the Contact Group, this relationship was strained almost to breaking point. Indeed, South Africa's decision to hold the December elections in Namibia was a clear test of the West's resolve to apply pressure. South Africa discovered that the Contact Group would go to almost any lengths to avoid a showdown over sanctions in the UN. By the beginning of 1979 the triangular relationship was still intact because of the coincidental, if distinct, interests of the three parties in seeking a Namibian settlement.

For South Africa these interests went beyond the settling of a long-running legal dispute and the avoidance of sanctions. It was necessary to have a stable and friendly Namibia as a buffer between South Africa and Angola, where Cuban forces were stationed, and it was also in South Africa's interests to demonstrate that at certain times and under certain conditions she was prepared to be a 'reasonable' member of the international community.

For the United States and the other members of the Contact Group the main concern was to avoid having to face a UN vote on economic sanctions. This was important not only because of the sanctions *per se* but also because, having once taken that first step down the path of economic sanctions, it was feared that sanctions would become the sole language in which the West's dialogue with South Africa was conducted, that positions on both sides would harden, that South Africa would grow even more intransigent, and that little room would be left for the diplomatic process. That the United States wanted to avoid a hardening of attitudes was demonstrated by the fact that when Mr Vance visited Pretoria in October 1978 he brought a letter for Prime Minister Botha from President Carter which emphasized that the United States wanted to have 'normal' relations with South Africa. Vance also indicated that Botha might one day be invited to visit the United States. The tone of the language used and of Mr Carter's letter was a far cry from that of the Administration at the Vienna meeting between Vice-President Mondale and Prime Minister Vorster eighteen months earlier.

If Pretoria had been testing the West on the sanctions issue, the United States was prepared to use Namibia as a test of South Africa's desire for 'normal' relations. Although the Western posture in dealing with Pretoria was seen by black African nations as at best a policy of ambiguity and at worst a policy of capitulation, they held off on their demand for a sanctions vote in the UN because they too had an interest in seeking an acceptable negotiated settlement.

The Front Line Presidents realized that, unlike Rhodesia, in Namibia black majority rule was not likely to be won through war, for South Africa could hold on militarily for a very long time. In particular, Angola was anxious to have a peaceful, friendly neighbour to the south, so that Namibia would no longer be used as a base for South African raids into Angola and as a conduit for supplies to the UNITA forces of Mr Joseph Savimbi which controlled a large part of southern Angola. With both of these problems removed, Angola would be less dependent on Cuban troops. Even Nigeria, the most important economic power in black Africa, saw the dangers she faced in a confrontation over sanctions. If the African nations called for sanctions and some or all of the Western nations voted against the Resolution in the UN, Nigeria would be forced to decide what action to take against them. The Contact Group included the principal purchasers of Nigerian oil. To cut off or limit oil sales to any of them because of their refusal to support sanctions against South Africa would only lead to a decline in Nigeria's much-needed oil revenues. Nigeria therefore played an active role in persuading her fellow African nations to hold off on their demands for a sanctions vote.

An important factor throughout the Namibian negotiations was the belief held by all sides that a settlement acceptable to all of them was possible. Nevertheless, the final step towards a successful agreement depended on South Africa, which controlled the territory. On several occasions Pretoria gave the impression that the talks were on the verge of breakdown. No doubt this was partly the result of tough negotiating tactics as South Africa fought for the best possible terms. However, it also reflected the continuing debate within the South African leadership over the fundamental question of whether South Africa's interests lay in seeking accommodation with the West through compromise (for a Namibia settlement would represent compromise) or in the continuation of a policy course which, although its aim was not confrontation, might be called 'rejectionist'.

The critical period of the Namibia negotiations occurred almost exactly at the point when Mr Botha succeeded Mr Vorster as Prime Minister and at the time of the revelations of irregularities in the South African Department of Information, a scandal which rocked both the country and the Nationalist Party. By April 1979 it appeared that the South African government was looking for a way out of the Namibian negotiations. While the talks had become bogged down (and the arrival of the UN contingents was delayed), the signals coming from South Africa turned decidedly negative. In April the South African Foreign Minister, Mr R. F. Botha, called Mr McHenry, the American negotiator, 'an enemy of South Africa', a charge which led to an official American protest. More ominous was the sudden announcement (on 12 April) that three American Embassy officials were to be expelled for taking photographs of classified installations from an Embassy plane, an action alleged to constitute espionage activity. The timing of the expulsions and the manner in which they were publicized led American officials to believe that South Africa was seeking a pretext to withdraw from the Namibia negotiations. Indeed, South Africa had laid the groundwork through an announcement by the Namibian Constituent Assembly that it intended to establish itself as an interim government.

It now appears that South Africa is leaning away from a solution to the Namibia question in co-operation with the Western powers and towards a unilateral solution based on a dependent relationship between Windhoek and Pretoria. This would seem to be the outcome of South Africa's internal debate on where to set her defence perimeter – as far north as possible to keep her enemies at arms length, or further south to conserve strength on borders which may appear more defensible.

IV. ANGOLA

Despite American diplomatic efforts to resolve the problems of Rhodesia and Namibia, it is in Angola that the full scope and conflicting currents of Washington's policy-making can be seen most clearly. From 1975 to 1978 Angola provided a stage on which globalists and regionalists could wage their policy struggle. The country posed real and not theoretical questions about intervention versus non-intervention. Events there prompted the strongest Congressional action limiting presidential power since the Vietnam war. Finally, in Angola, unlike Rhodesia, the possibility of direct Communist intervention became reality, with 19,000 or more Cuban soldiers on the ground.

What makes Angola particularly instructive, apart from the basic issues involved, is that the crisis in that country, and the challenge it presented to the United States, coincided with the delicate post-Vietnam period in America. In the summer of 1975 the final American evacuation from Saigon was still a living national trauma. Even if Dr Kissinger wanted to demonstrate American strength and resolve by opposing

Marxist influence in Angola, it was clearly a crusade in which American public opinion was not prepared to join. More recently, as the wounds of Vietnam have begun to heal in America, the presence of Cuban troops in Angola has touched sensitive nerve ends among some elements of the American public. This has helped to make Africa in general, and Angola in particular, a domestic political issue which the President cannot ignore with the election approaching in 1980.

Apart from American domestic considerations, Angola possesses enough of her own qualities to command attention in southern African affairs. A nation of six-and-a-half million people, Angola is rich in oil, diamonds, iron and other minerals. Beyond that, she has a significant geographical importance. Bounded by Zaire to the north and north-east, by Zambia to the east and by Namibia to the south, Angola is in a uniquely favourable position to promote stability or instability in much of southern Africa, as has already been demonstrated by the case of SWAPO, which mounts its raids into Namibia from base camps in southern Angola, and by the invasion of Zaire's Shaba province by *gendarmes* operating from Angola with or without the Angolan Government's knowledge and tacit support. The potential for similar destabilizing action against Zambia is evident, with serious consequences for a nascent, insecure and unstable Zimbabwe. In short, the Western and South African goal of a stable, relatively moderate, black southern Africa could always be threatened by a Marxist Angola bent on fomenting trouble. The theory, of course, is that a Marxist government is, by definition, determined to subvert its neighbours. It is a theory not borne out by Mozambique, the other Portuguese colony which gained independence at the same time. Despite one–party Marxist rule and the provision of support for the insurgents' war against Rhodesia's white rule, the government of President Machel has devoted its energies to domestic problems, even to the point of maintaining good relations with neighbouring South Africa. Recent developments indicate that Angola too is more interested in her domestic problems and in regional stability than in exporting revolution.

That Angola would assume an important position in southern African affairs became clear soon after the coup in Lisbon. Whereas Mozambique had had one dominant nationalist movement, headed by Mr Machel, Angola had three factions: the Popular Movement for the Liberation of Angola (MPLA), headed by Mr Agostinho Neto (a Marxist); the National Front for the Liberation of Angola (FNLA), headed by Mr Holden Roberto (based in Zaire); and the National Union for the Total Independence of Angola (UNITA), headed by Mr Jonas Savimbi. Not surprisingly, each movement had its own tribal foundation : the MPLA among the Kimbundu around Luanda, the FNLA among the Kikongo in the north, and UNITA among the Ovimbundu tribe in the southern third of the country.

In the summer of 1974, three months after the Lisbon coup, the United States chose sides in the pending struggle for power in Angola and began a modest funding of the FNLA – although it was not precisely an American policy decision, for the CIA paid out the money from its own funds without going to the Operations Advisory Group (still better known under its former name, the '40 Committee') which approves significant clandestine intelligence operations. The choice of the FNLA was almost automatic. The MPLA was the Marxist enemy, and UNITA was a relatively unknown quantity, whereas Mr Roberto had had contacts with the CIA in Zaire for many years.

Apart from the precedent it set, the initial funding of the FNLA was not particularly significant, for Angola was not at that time a preoccupying problem in Washington. There was still the hope that the three factions could join together and provide a peaceful transition to independence.

In July 1975 a transitional government was formed in Luanda, in which all three movements were represented. Elections were announced for October; independence was scheduled for 11 November 1975. Almost immediately it was apparent that the political process was not going to work. Fighting quickly spread, with the MPLA facing a two-front struggle against the FNLA and UNITA. On 22 January 1975 the '40 Committee' made what could be considered the first formal policy decision on Angola when it authorized the payment of $300,000 to the FNLA. In March the Soviet Union instituted large arms shipments to the MPLA in Luanda. That spring the Transitional Government disintegrated.

By July the MPLA had succeeded in driving FNLA and UNITA from Luanda.

In that month, as the situation seemed to be deteriorating for the West, the United States became seriously involved in Angola. During the spring the collapse of South Vietnam had dominated the attention of American policy-makers, particularly Dr Kissinger. By July not only did Dr Kissinger have the time to look at Angola but he was also determined to take action. His geo-political approach – founded on the view that Marxist expansionism had to be resisted in Angola (and particularly after the recent collapse of the ten-year American investment in Vietnam) – was not universally shared in the State Department. Mr Nathaniel Davis, Assistant Secretary for African Affairs, represented the regionalists who opposed intervention, arguing that the MPLA, though Marxist, was not necessarily anti-American and that a political settlement should be pursued. Mr Davis's argument was that a covert programme of military aid to the FNLA and UNITA ran a high risk both of exposure and of failure, which would leave the United States looking politically inept and militarily impotent. It was an argument that the regionalists were to lose, and in August Mr Davis resigned.

A candid record of US involvement in late 1975 is given by John Stockwell, ex-head of the CIA's Angolan Task Force.* On 14 July the '40 Committee' (headed by Dr Kissinger) asked the CIA to present its options for Angola. Two days later the CIA listed several, which ranged from limited financial help for the anti-MPLA movements to an investment of $40 million to equip and support the FNLA and UNITA for a year. The problem facing the Ford Administration was that given the post-Vietnam mood in the United States, Angolan intervention had to be conducted secretly. This meant that the Administration could not go to Congress to ask for funds. It knew these would be refused. Consequently, an initial $14 million (of an eventual total of $31.7 million) was authorized by the '40 Committee' towards the end of July. On 29 July the first aircraft-load of weapons was on its way to Zaire for delivery to the FNLA. The financial limits on American intervention also restricted its goals. The Administration had no illusions

about the possibility of defeating the MPLA – it merely sought to hold off its victory.

Up to this point the events in Angola had followed a familiar pattern: contending factions (one of them Marxist) fighting for power; the Soviet Union and the United States at first cautiously backing their respective 'clients' and then suddenly raising the stakes, with a corresponding commitment of each power's prestige as well as weapons. What was to change the Angolan scenario radically followed in autumn 1975 – the introduction of Cuban troops.

The chronology of events has been cited as evidence that the Soviet/Cuban involvement in Angola was a direct reaction to American initiatives there. It has been argued that American funding of the FNLA in early 1975 led in March to Soviet arms shipments to the MPLA, and that the American arms shipments to the anti-MPLA movements in July led to the introduction of the first major Cuban contingents in October. However, it was certainly clear to the Soviet leadership by early 1975 that a struggle for power among the three factions in Angola was inevitable, and that in such a struggle Soviet interests lay with the MPLA, regardless of any US action. Nevertheless, it appears that the acceleration of the Cuban build-up in the autumn of 1975 was at least, in part, a response to the increased American commitment that summer, as well as to the invasion of Angola by South African forces in October, which threatened Luanda before they withdrew.

It was the main-force units, that arrived in Angola in the autumn, which introduced a new element in African politics and a new and complicating factor in the East–West equation. It is not the purpose of this paper to discuss all the ramifications of the Cuban role in Africa. The Cuban troops have been viewed in the West as Moscow's mercenaries, and their presence as a cunning move by the Kremlin to have a third-world nation fight Communism's battles in the Third World. President Castro has denied that his army is for hire, claiming that Cuba is involved in Africa for her own imperative reasons – namely, to show solidarity with the Third World generally and, more specifically, with the Marxist movements in it. Indeed, in the early 1960s Cuba had been involved in the Congo as well as in Algeria and other African countries in a limited way.

---

*John Stockwell, *In Search of Enemies: A CIA Story* (London: Andre Deutsch, 1979).

Whatever the motivation for the Cuban escalation, it suddenly presented American policy-makers with a drastically altered challenge. The issue was no longer solely the political complexion of Angola but the fact that Moscow and Havana had called the United States' bluff.

On 14 November 1975 the '40 Committee', headed by Dr Kissinger, asked the CIA to develop a programme which would *win* the Angolan war. If the Cuban involvement presented the Ford Administration with a problem, it also provided a political weapon, for Angola suddenly constituted a Communist challenge to the West. It was a crisis which Dr Kissinger could hope to exploit publicly and in Congress to win support and money for a vastly increased American effort. The fact that Cuba was the 'enemy' in Angola added an extra element for many Americans who had a particular antipathy to Communist Cuba.

December 1975 was a pivotal month for American foreign policy, not only with regard to the specific question of Angola, but also in terms of the limits Congress then placed on the President in his execution of foreign policy. The lines in the debate were clearly drawn. On the one side, the Administration advanced the traditional argument that a Communist challenge demanded a forceful Western response, and Angola was the first post-Vietnam test of American resolve. Viewed from a different perspective, Angola was the United States' first opportunity since Vietnam to demonstrate resistance to becoming trapped in what appeared to be a similar quagmire, and public opinion was against an Angolan 'adventure', a mood quickly sensed in Congress. Moreover, when the Administration asked Congress for help, the Congressmen were not happy to discover that for a year the CIA and the '40 Committee' had been conducting a clandestine Angola policy behind their backs. A Congress which felt deceived and an American public which opposed a new foreign involvement was a formula for an Administration defeat.

The defeat was more serious and longer-lasting than was foreseen at the time. Congress was able to use Angola not only to block a specific Administration policy at a specific time, but also to assert its own role in the policy-making field. This was accomplished through the passage of an amendment to the Arms Export Control Act which banned indefinitely any military aid to the Angolan factions without Congressional approval. The amendment was passed by the Senate (54–22) on 19 December and by the House of Representatives (323–99) on 27 January 1976. The size of the votes was significant and on 9 February 1976 President Ford signed the Bill.

By early 1976 there was little the Ford Administration could salvage from the debris of its Angola policy. Its hands were tied by Congress. South Africa, who claimed she had been promised American backing for her entry into the Angola fighting in October 1975, pulled out her troops in January 1976 when it became clear that no American support, political or military, was forthcoming. By February 1976 the MPLA was rapidly winning diplomatic recognition from African governments as well as from most Western European countries, although not from the United States.

In July 1975 the Administration had begun a period of intensive policy formulation and execution in Angola. Seven months later, in February 1976, this effort had come to a halt. In July 1975 the MPLA had been on its way to winning power and international recognition. By the following February it had substantially gained both and, in addition, there was a Cuban army entrenched in southern Africa. The American policy had clearly failed. Indeed, it had led to a worse situation than at the outset.

The weakness of the policy was not its theory (that the United States should show resolve in the face of Communist expansionism) but the fact that in the prevailing domestic conditions in the United States it could not be implemented. The United States had started a process which she was not prepared to see to its conclusion. Militarily she was not prepared to become involved and politically she could not afford to associate herself with the South African incursion into Angola and hope to maintain the credibility of her overall Africa policy. Certainly, in Africa, the failure of this policy denoted a watershed, as it did in Washington, where Congress has since continued to assert its authority and independence from the White House in foreign policy matters.

Although the room for American manoeuvring in Angola was sharply limited by early 1976, developments still pre-occupied American policy-makers, who showed little desire to come to terms with the MPLA. If the FNLA in the north had become largely ineffective, UNITA in southern Angola had established itself as an effective and popular guerrilla movement among the Ovimbundu. In Mr Savimbi UNITA had a charismatic leader. Moreover, since it could be easily supplied through Namibia, UNITA offered the prospect of remaining a thorn in the side of the MPLA for a long time. In other words, the foundation for some future action against the MPLA still existed within Angola – and the desire to take that action existed outside the country. In Washington Angola continued to serve as a reminder to those policy-makers who advocated tougher action. In South Africa the government was licking its wounds after its Angola expedition and was still concerned about the Cuban military presence on the border of Namibia.

In June 1976 the United States vetoed Angola's application for membership for the UN. To many this appeared to be an act of petty spite; however, the veto made sense, not only because it withheld a certain legitimacy from the MPLA but also because if further action were to be taken against the MPLA, it would not be against a UN member state.

Some of the events associated with Angola in the late summer and autumn of 1976 remain unclear. However, there is considerable circumstantial evidence to suggest that some Western-backed military action against the MPLA was at least being contemplated. There was an increase in FNLA and UNITA activity in Angola in the autumn. Just as significant, the South African press devoted an unusual amount of space to descriptions of and praise for UNITA's successes. In December 1976 a UN report announced a significant increase in South African troops in Namibia. It seems clear that by late 1976 South Africa was at least contemplating renewed military action against Angola.

These events (or non-events) concerning Angola coincided with Dr Kissinger's strenuous personal efforts in southern Africa, including his meetings with Prime Minister Vorster and their agreement on a common approach towards Rhodesia and Namibia. It is hard to believe that the two men, who were trying to promote moderate, pro-Western black governments for Rhodesia and Namibia, did not discuss Angola as well. What course of action they may have

agreed upon is not known. However, another coincidence is interesting. After President Ford's election defeat in early November, the Administration withdrew its veto and Angola joined the United Nations. In Namibia the number of South African troops along the Angola border was reduced.

When the Carter Administration took office on 20 January 1977 the thrust of its policy-making process for Africa was focused on Rhodesia and Namibia rather than on Angola. This was not due to the evolving situation in these two countries, nor was it due to Congressional limitations on American involvement in Angola. It was because, in marked contrast to the Ford Administration, President Carter was disposed to live with the situation in Angola. Indeed, prior to the November election, Andrew Young had testified before the Senate Sub-Committee on African Affairs that the United States should recognize the MPLA and that recognition should not be delayed because of the presence of Cuban troops.

During the first ten months of the Carter Administration Mr Young set the tone of its policy towards Africa and Angola. This was a prime example of Young's (and the Administration's) 'cool' approach: the political complexion of the government in Angola (or Rhodesia) was not as important as its ability to provide leadership. In the end even a Marxist government (like the MPLA) would turn to the West for its economic ties. If the United States was not yet prepared formally to recognize the MPLA government, Young publicly insisted that she should not panic over the presence of the Cuban forces. Indeed, one of his earliest and most controversial statements was to call the Cuban forces a 'stabilizing influence' in Africa.

In Angola, as in Rhodesia, Young was actively opposing the globalist approach, arguing that African nationalism would triumph over Communist colonialism. The new American policy towards Angola found ready support among those African specialists in the State Department who had maintained all along that the MPLA desired good relations with the United States. Moreover, they believed that President Neto ran a government which was truly multi-racial and held out the promise of stable leadership. In contrast, Jonas Savimbi, despite his acknowledged capacity for leadership, was

27

considered less predictable and perhaps less interested in Western co-operation.

Further evidence that Angola did not fit any easy stereotype was the fact that throughout the civil war Gulf Oil had continued its pumping operations off the shore of the Cabinda enclave. With royalty payments of half a billion dollars a year, Gulf Oil was the main financial backer of the MPLA Government. Furthermore, no Washington policy-maker could ignore the existence of the 'Front for the Liberation of the Enclave of Cabinda' (FNLC), which was backed by Zaire, Gabon and France and was believed to be attempting to separate Cabinda from Angola, to expel Gulf Oil and to allow France to acquire the oil rights there. Other American multi-national corporations, including Boeing and National Cash Register, were doing business with the Neto Government. Angola therefore demonstrated that there was more than one way to define the United States' true interests. For the Carter Administration, the policy through 1977 was to allow the *status quo* in Angola to persist. Contact with President Neto was maintained through his role as one of the Front Line Presidents involved in the Rhodesian and Namibian negotiations.

Although the new policy approach to Africa had the personal support of President Carter, it had its critics, both in the Administration and in the White House itself. By November 1977, Mr Zbigniew Brzezinski, the President's National Security Adviser, began to mount a globalist's challenge to the policy which was being pursued by, among others, Andrew Young, Richard Moose, Assistant Secretary of State and Anthony Lake, Director of the State Department's Policy Planning Committee. Whereas under the previous Administration the globalists had dominated policy-making towards Africa while the regionalists suffered more or less silently, under President Carter the reverse was true. The globalists' challenge within the Carter Administration was of particular significance, and although it was not limited to Angola, that country loomed large in the debate.

Mr Brzezinski's conception of African policy was similar to that of Dr Kissinger and was dominated by geo-political interests: Africa had to be seen as part of the overall power balance. By late 1977 events were supporting his case. The Soviet shift of support from Somalia to Ethiopia

was cause for both alarm and temptation. The alarm arose because Soviet influence was growing in what had long been an important pro-American nation. This was followed and aggravated by the introduction of Cuban military units. The temptation was to leap into the vacuum in Somalia by supplying arms, a move which President Carter found attractive. A cooler appraisal, however, recognized that whatever Somalia's complaint might be, it was demonstrably the aggressor in the Ogaden, and it would be unwise for the United States to be caught on the wrong side of the fence by aiding Somalia.

Following the end of the Ogaden fighting, over 15,000 Cuban troops remained in Ethiopia. The adverse reaction of the American press and public opinion to the Cuban arrival in Angola was now compounded by events in Ethiopia. A Communist expeditionary force appeared to be moving at will through Africa. Foreign policy considerations aside, the spreading Cuban activity presented a growing domestic political problem to President Carter. A feeling began to gain ground that this was a test of his leadership and of his determination to stand up to Communist expansionism. These developments in Africa and in the United States tended to strengthen the globalists' position. In a speech in March 1978 President Carter warned that Soviet activity in Africa was harming East–West relations. On 1 April, during his visit to Nigeria, the President made a major policy speech on Africa which bore the clear imprint of Zbigniew Brzezinski and strongly condemned the presence of Cuban troops in Africa.

Following the President's return to Washington, Mr Brzezinski continued to promote some action against the Cuban presence in Africa. If there was little the United States could do in the Horn of Africa, there was still Angola. In April Brzezinski had told members of Congress that the United States should provide military aid to UNITA and that there was an opportunity for her to create a situation similar to Vietnam which would bog the Cubans down in the African quagmire. Though the imagery may have been attractive, this argument did not convince Congress that it should lift its ban on military aid to Angola. Accordingly, in early May 1978 CIA Director Stansfield Turner and a member of Brzezinski's staff visited Senator Dick Clark of

Iowa, who was both Chairman of the Senate African Sub-Committee and sponsor of the Angolan legislation of December 1975. Admiral Turner's question to Senator Clark was whether he would tacitly approve the Administration's desire to provide help for UNITA through a third country, believed to be France. Clark rejected the proposal.

At a news conference on 4 May President Carter said, 'We have no intention to intercede in any way in Angola.' That statement, made when the President's National Security Adviser and the Director of the CIA were actively trying to organize aid for UNITA, was in itself to prove to be an embarrassment for the President, who had pledged candour to the American people. The President's plight was to be aggravated by the tangle of events which followed in quick succession through the rest of May in both Africa and the United States.

On 11 May Zaire's Shaba province was invaded by anti-Mobutu forces which had fled from the old Katanga province in the 1960s and had taken refuge in Angola. It was the second invasion of Shaba by the 'gendarmes' in little more than a year. The news of the massacre of Europeans in Kolwezi horrified the world, and the international rescue effort mounted with Belgian and French troops was supported by 18 United States Air Force transports. The American role in the rescue operation was itself an indication of the ambiguous public position that the Administration assumed towards Africa.The airlift support was supposed to be seen as an example of swift, firm action on the part of the United States, closely co-ordinated with that of her Western allies, but at the same time the White House emphasized that American military personnel would be nowhere near the real action.

The invasion of Shaba province, more than any other single event, imprinted Africa and its problems indelibly on the consciousness of the American people. As a result, the timing of the Shaba invasion could not have been better for the Administration's globalists, who were trying to increase the pressure on the Cuban forces in Angola. The fact that the Shaba invaders had come from Angola immediately raised the spectre of a Cuban connection which was quickly exploited by Washington.

On 22 May President Carter met a group of Senators at the White House and complained to them about the Congressional restrictions on his ability to aid the anti-MPLA forces in Angola, a complaint which he had been making all week. On 24 May a top-level meeting was held at the White House to work out a position on African policy. The next day, at a news conference in Chicago, President Carter said that Angola bore a 'heavy responsibility' for the Shaba attack and claimed that Cuba was a conspirator in the invasion. Having made the charge, the Carter Administration had then to prove the Cuban conspiracy. Immediately after the start of the invasion, President Castro had sent a message to the State Department denying Cuban involvement. The denial was made public in Washington. However, there was more to the Castro message than was released. The Cuban leader also admitted that he had been aware of the pending invasion and said that he had tried to stop it, but had failed because President Neto had been in Moscow at the time for medical treatment. These further details were leaked to the press on 10 June, as the Administration was still trying to convince the Senate and the public of Cuban complicity in the Shaba fighting. The failure of the Administration to produce conclusive evidence, together with the disclosure of the full Castro message (and the fact that it had been kept secret), destroyed the Administration's case, at least in Congress. By mid-June the pendulum, which had swung far towards the globalists' side, began to swing away from them. Mr Brzezinski, who had been outspoken in his advocacy of stronger action in Angola, fell suddenly silent. In his commencement speech at the United States Naval Academy on 7 June President Carter, referring to events in Africa, said that the Soviet Union must choose between 'co-operation and confrontation'. It was, however, the globalists' parting shot, and a few days later Mr Vance softened the Annapolis rhetoric.

Throughout the policy debates between globalists and regionalists, Mr Vance had taken a middle path, reacting to the immediate problem rather than acting on the basis of an overall concept. In June he was finally able to reassert the State Department's authority in the White House. He had two cards to play. First, the NSC and the CIA had failed to prove that there had been a Cuban conspiracy to mount the Shaba invasion and, second, he could argue that the President badly needed a foreign policy success and that one was now possible in Namibia, where negotiations had reached a critical stage.

In its dealings over Namibia, the Administration was relatively slow to react to the fact that President Neto's position *vis-à-vis* SWAPO was similar to Prime Minister Vorster's role *vis-à-vis* Rhodesia. An understanding with President Neto was needed to persuade him to put much-needed pressure on Mr Njomo, whose SWAPO bases were in Angola. Mr Vance told the White House that President Neto was prepared for an accommodation with the United States. The White House accepted the policy.

On 20 June Mr Vance made a speech in Atlantic City, New Jersey. He announced that the United States wanted to increase contacts with the Angolan government. The statement came less than a month after the Administration had charged that Angola was an instrument for Soviet and Cuban adventurism in Africa. It was a dramatic *volte face* for American policy.

Even the most cursory analysis of American policy in Angola from 1975 to 1978 shows that consistency was not one of its hallmarks. In slightly less than three years the policy had veered from intervention to tacit acceptance of the MPLA, to intervention again, and then to tacit recognition of the MPLA. Indeed, the last three stages occurred under the same Administration in less than a year. Flexibility in policy decisions is, of course, admirable (and may even be necessary when changing conditions demand it), but the conditions in Angola remained essentially unchanged from late 1975, when Cuban forces began arriving in substantial numbers, until mid-1978, when the United States expressed interest in improving relations with the MPLA.

What caused the policy pendulum to swing so wildly between contradictory policies? Certainly, there was the continuing battle between the globalists, with their geo-political concerns, and the regionalists, with their particular expertise and different perspective. The globalist–regionalist conflict runs like an unbroken thread through American policy-making in southern Africa, with each side trying to gain the upper hand by winning the President's ear and support. However, there was more to the Carter Administration's zig-zag policy on Angola than bureaucratic in-fighting. There were clear signs that the President was unable to make up his mind about which policy to pursue. His vacillations may be partly ascribed to his inexperience in international affairs, but they also seem to have been related to the fact that in his conduct of foreign policy President Carter has tried to be two kinds of people. One might be called 'Mr Nice Guy', who has introduced a moral imperative into foreign policy (reflected most clearly in his emphasis on human rights) and who encouraged Andrew Young to articulate a new approach to foreign policy. The other is 'Mr Tough Guy', who wants to be seen as a strong, decisive leader. Like any President, Mr Carter is aware of the importance of appearing to act firmly in his dealings with the Soviet Union. Almost from the start of his Administration, public opinion polls have reflected two reactions to Mr Carter: the American people have continued to trust his personal integrity, for they feel that he is a moral man; however, the polls have shown a markedly lower support for the President's performance in office. Throughout 1977 the public's confidence in this performance showed a steady decline. By January 1978 most surveys showed that less than 50 per cent of the American people had confidence in the Carter Presidency. By May that support was down to approximately 33 per cent (and in some polls it sank even lower). Mr Carter was being called a "weak" President and there was considerable speculation over whether he would be elected for a second term. Political aides in the White House were urging the President to pursue a tough policy in Angola for domestic political reasons.

It was then that the Cuban entry into Ethiopia and the Shaba invasion occurred. Some commentators were seeing in Africa the makings of Carter's first real test, similar to that which President Kennedy had to endure in the Cuban missile crisis. The fact that a foreign policy problem in Africa could have domestic political importance was in itself unprecedented. Africa has generally had only marginal domestic political impact, even among American blacks, who are primarily concerned with government efforts to fight inner-city problems and unemployment, and to promote racial integration in schools, items which Democratic Presidents have traditionally supported. The black vote (small as it may be) was of decisive importance in Mr Carter's election victory. He won by sweeping the southern states (except Virginia), where he won between 85 and 95 per cent of the black

30

vote, and certain key northern states (New York, Massachusetts, Pennsylvania and Ohio), where the urban black vote was also heavily in his favour. Blacks could claim that they, as much as any single group, put Mr Carter in the White House. It came as no surprise, therefore, when the President appointed a black to a senior position in his Administration. As Ambassador to the United Nations, Andrew Young not only was highly visible but also held real power in the Carter Administration. His influence was due in part to the personal relationship between the two men and in part to Carter's support for the new policy approach towards Africa which Mr Young represented. Beyond that, however, was a political debt which the President owed the black community.

Nevertheless, the appointment of Mr Young and the new Africa policy did nothing to limit the criticism directed at the Carter Administration by the Congressional Black Caucus. It was based on the Administration's failure to make progress on domestic programmes which blacks felt they had been promised in the election campaign. In short, as far as blacks were concerned, there was no link between the Administration's Africa policy (which they supported) and its domestic policy (which they opposed). Consequently, when Africa did finally emerge as a domestic political issue in the United States, it was a concern not among the black minority but among the white majority; because it touched the American fear of weakness in the face of Communism, it became an issue of great importance to Mr Carter's political future.

In the end a combination of African developments and domestic political weakness was sufficient to make President Carter alter the policy course he had originally set in Angola. That he subsequently reverted to his original policy (of non-intervention) in June 1978, was due not so much to the fact that he recognized that the more activist policy advocated by Mr Brzezinski was intrinsically bad, as to the fact that it had failed – or, more accurately, had never been likely to succeed.

The Vance speech of 20 June, which indicated a pro-MPLA 'tilt' in American policy, was prompted by developments in the Namibia negotiations, which had reached a critical stage. It was clear that the United States and the Western Contact Group needed the help of President Neto to put pressure on Mr Njomo and SWAPO in order to persuade them to accept the proposed settlement plan. More than ever it was evident that the United States and the MPLA government could share political as well as economic and business interests in southern Africa.

When Ambassador McHenry visited Luanda a few days after the Vance speech it became clear that there were indeed common interests. He found President Neto eager to reach agreement on a new relationship with the United States. The pressures on President Neto were exerted by several issues: there was the continuing decline of the Angolan economy (diamond production was only 20 per cent of normal levels and iron-ore production had ceased) and there were serious food shortages; in May 1978 Neto had barely survived a coup attempt to unseat him which may have had tacit Soviet support; the fighting against UNITA was continuing inconclusively; and South African troops were still liable to invade Angola.

In such circumstances Angola and the United States were able to recognize common interests. The first step was to effect a *rapprochement* between President Neto and President Mobutu Sese Seko of Zaire, a move attractive to both leaders. For President Mobutu it meant further assurance that Angola would prevent raids into Shaba province from Angolan territory; for President Neto it meant a curb on the activities of the FNLA (with its headquarters in Zaire) in northern Angola. Although the FNLA had been defeated, with Zaire's backing it could still cause trouble for President Neto. The two governments agreed to re-open the Benguela railroad from Zaire to the Angolan port of Lobito, but this move clearly depended on the defeat of UNITA in the southern part of the country, for UNITA controlled the region through which the line ran. Unita's defeat could be brought about by the withdrawal of South Africa from Namibia, for it could then no longer be supplied via Namibia. South Africa's withdrawal would follow the establishment of an internationally recognized government in Namibia elected under UN supervision, a government which would pose no threat to Angola's security. However, for all this to happen, SWAPO had to take part in the elections. In this context it is not surprising that President Neto was prepared to put pressure on Mr Njomo to accept UN elections.

In return the United States offered a better relationship between the two countries. American policy was still to seek a reduction in the Cuban presence (hopes of a total Cuban withdrawal were no longer entertained) before formal diplomatic recognition would be extended, but American policy-makers now recognized that the best chance of bringing about a reduction in Cuban force levels lay in reducing the perceived threats to the MPLA from UNITA and South Africa, which had brought in the Cuban forces in the first place.

In the end, the twisting path of American policy towards Angola followed the course that Mr Young and the Africanists in the State Department had been advocating all along. Policy-makers accepted the assumption that African governments born of liberation movements would seek a working relationship with the West to help solve their economic problems, not only because of the established pattern of their commercial ties with the West but also because the Soviet Union was neither prepared nor able to bear the economic burden of countries like Angola.

The new American approach to Angola, however, extended beyond her borders. It was also in a position to make an important contribution to stability in Zaire and to advance the chances of a peaceful and stable solution to the Namibia problem. Although barely one month earlier, the Carter Administration's policy had been to support UNITA and to subvert President Neto, it was now realized that stability in three African countries could follow from a policy of active support for President Neto.

The American experience in Angola has raised many questions about the policy-making process, about the relationship between the Executive Branch and Congress and, indeed, about the influence of domestic politics on foreign policy. Angola, in the spring of 1978, also raised broader questions regarding the policy of detente with the Soviet Union. Events showed that the United States and the Soviet Union had never agreed on the rules of detente. Here again the question of linkage arose. Dr Kissinger had insisted that

events in Africa were linked to detente. The Soviet Union, however, has never accepted the American definition of the word, insisting that detente is nothing more (and nothing less) than the sum of negotiated agreements. The Carter Administration's decision to follow a regionalist approach in southern Africa in effect marked the abandonment of the principle of linkage.

In the latter part of May 1978, following the invasion of Shaba province, Mr Brzezinski tried to resurrect linkage by charging that the Soviet Union was violating the 'code of detente' but because the Soviet Union and the United States had not agreed on what the 'code' was supposed to be, or even if such a thing existed, Mr Brzezinski's claim was weak. The Soviet Union, which understood the limits of American action in Africa, seemed unflustered by such charges. When the Administration turned in the following month from tough East–West rhetoric to an accommodation with the MPLA, Mr Vance was making it clear that the United States was not asserting any specific linkage between African events and detente. He was particularly interested in preventing the SALT talks from becoming contaminated by events in Africa.

The policy differences between Mr Vance and Mr Brzezinski over linkage reflect the basic differences between the globalists and the regionalists. It is clear from any reading of what has happened in the past few years in Africa in general, and in Angola in particular, that there is a serious conflict between these two schools of policy-making. It is a question not only of different priorities but, more fundamentally, of different conceptions of what is happening in southern Africa. There is no obvious solution to the global-regionalist conflict in policy-making towards southern Africa, for it has by now become institutionalized in successive Administrations. What will be required in the future will be a firm Presidential hand to clamp down on any sudden swings from globalism to regionalism or vice versa. That will be essential in the coming years as the United States is forced to turn her attention towards the Republic of South Africa.

CONCLUSION: POINTERS TO SOUTH AFRICA

Although developments in Zimbabwe-Rhodesia, Namibia and Angola have been of inherent importance to the West, as the active involvement of the United States testifies, they are merely the prologue to the ultimate issue in Africa – that of South Africa.

South Africa promises to become a major foreign policy problem facing the United States and her allies. The importance of this problem will not be limited to Africa; it could have broader repercussions within the Western Alliance as well as in domestic American politics.

It is, of course, impossible to forecast precisely what American policy towards South Africa will be. But the events set out in this paper can help to identify likely patterns of behaviour, the interaction of pressures and the priorities which will define policy, or will at least establish the limits within which policy is formulated.

Certainly, the dominant behavioural trait in American policy has been to avoid choosing sides in southern Africa's disputes, for that would mean choosing between black and white – or, to put it the other way, it would mean an irrevocable break with one side or the other. There is every likelihood that the United States will persist in this approach to South Africa for as long as possible; such a policy is an example of making a virtue of necessity. The necessity is to identify the United States with the aspirations of black Africa, while maintaining access to the mineral wealth and investment possibilities of South Africa. The virtue of this ambiguous policy – ambiguous because there are discrepancies between American declarations and actions – is that it permits the United States to assume the honourable role of middleman in the search for a peaceful, stable settlement.

The early statements of the Carter Administration were unequivocal in their opposition to South Africa's political system. Events, though, have revealed American reluctance to apply serious pressure on South Africa; indeed, American investment in that country has continued to grow. While the Vienna declaration made by Vice-President Mondale in April 1977 was unmistakably firm, by early 1979 events had moved the United States to seek a more flexible relationship with South Africa, if only for the immediate tactical purpose of reaching a settle-ment on Namibia. The inherent conflict of American interests posed by South Africa dictates an *ad hoc* policy of reaction rather than one of initiative – a policy which will be frequently contradictory and which will allow the United States to postpone, for as long as possible, the final choice between black and white. It is a premise of this paper that such a choice will have to be made one day if present policies and attitudes of South Africa's white population are not modified to permit effective black political participation.

In approaching the South Africa problem American policy-makers will have to take into account American priorities, both geo-political and regional. Africa, as we have seen, has provided numerous examples of conflict between these two schools of policy-making. Conflict will continue as long as the Soviet Union chooses to be involved in the South Africa issue. If there is substantial Soviet involvement, as there has been in Angola and in Ethiopia, the proponents of a geo-political approach will probably have the dominant voice in American policy-making. If Soviet involvement is restrained, the regionalists will have a greater opportunity to demonstrate their skills. Consequently, the American approach to South Africa will be determined primarily neither in Pretoria nor in Washington but in Moscow.

It is in regional African considerations that the United States will face challenging and difficult decisions. If there is a desire to make the American attitude towards South Africa a magnified version of the position of the United States in Rhodesia (that of middleman, trying to get all the parties around a conference table), there must be considerable doubt about whether the policy can succeed.

One interesting aspect of the Rhodesian experience was that the Front Line Presidents were not particularly vociferous in their criticism of the United States for not giving full support, including arms, to the liberation movements. Their attitude ('You can't do it, and we know that') suggested a recognition of the realities of the moment. Such tolerance, however, is unlikely to be extended to the case of South Africa, where white rule is not an instance of crumbling colonialism (as it was in Rhodesia), over which

33

time and a degree of insurgency would seem likely to triumph. South Africa will be a much tougher nut to crack. White rule is already a very emotional issue for black Africans across the continent and it will become even more emotional as the conflict in South Africa sharpens. In the coming years opposition to South Africa could become an important cohesive element in black African politics. As this happens, African pressure on the United States to side openly with blacks will increase. Initially, this pressure will be exerted in the United Nations on such matters as sanctions, but it could eventually grow into demands for overt military backing against South Africa's political system.

Recognition that a conflict over South Africa will come must be accompanied by the understanding that a Western response to that conflict cannot be avoided. The formulation of that response, however, must acknowledge the potential for serious disagreements between the United States and her industrial allies over the appropriate course to steer in dealing with South Africa, disagreements which could lead to tensions within the Western Alliance. The United States and her industrial allies have not invested equally in South Africa, nor are they equally dependent on her. To the degree that their dependence differs, there will be differences of opinion over what steps (if any) need to be taken against South Africa. For example, the United States' investment in South Africa is far less than Britain's and American dependence on South African minerals is less than that of Japan, West Germany and Britain. In theory therefore it would be easier for the United States to apply pressure (including sanctions) against South Africa than for her allies to do so. But there can be little comfort in that. Unilateral American action against South Africa would be ineffectual without solid support from South Africa's other principal trading partners; and pressure on the United States' allies to enlist this support could lead to serious dissension within the Western Alliance as each industrialized member looked to its own national interests and priorities.

Recognition of this danger was one of the motivating forces in the creation of the five-nation Contact Group for Namibia. Although the main purpose of the Contact Group was for those nations who held the power of decision over sanctions in the United Nations Security Council to present a solid front to South Africa; it also introduced an institutional structure for the harmonization of policies towards Namibia. It is clearly a mechanism which can be used in the coming years in dealing with the South African Government over the future of South Africa herself. Admittedly, such a team operation would limit the flexibility of American policy towards South Africa, since it would proceed only as rapidly and as forcefully as its most reluctant member would allow. But that would be the price of maintaining harmony in the Alliance. In addition to ensuring that harmony, a combined approach would also make it difficult for critics of Western policy towards South Africa to focus their wrath and reprisals (if any) on any one country. In this sense, the Contact Group offers a degree of collective security.

The formulation of foreign policy in a democracy can rarely, if ever, be carried out without reference to domestic pressures. This will be particularly true of American policy towards South Africa. Among the pressures any administration will have to face, the most immediate will be applied by American commercial interests in South Africa. In time, however, serious racial pressures could also develop. The result is that any American President will find his field of manoeuvre limited by various constituencies. No President will be able to support South Africa because of the domestic opposition that would be generated among American blacks, white liberals and Church groups. This would be particularly true if the racial power struggle in South Africa led to sustained violence. Although the plight of South Africa's blacks has not been a prime issue among American blacks, it could become so one day. The racial violence in American cities in the 1960s has been forgotten neither by whites nor by blacks. Events in South Africa would probably not be enough to set off renewed violence on the part of American blacks, but they could be an important factor if other black frustrations (over unemployment and the lack of government concern for their inner-city problems) were to explode again. That prospect alone is enough to limit an Administration's support of white South Africa. But an American President will also be prevented from coming out solidly behind black aspirations at the expense of white South Africans. That would elicit a reaction from conservative, white Middle America,

34

as well as from American business interests in South Africa – a combination which could carry considerable political weight.

The Range of Options
There are in theory (if not in practice) four options facing the United States in South Africa. One is to offer strong support to the white South Africans and the *status quo*. A second is to pledge solid American support for the blacks. Both are non-starters for reasons which have been described. The two remaining options are to do nothing and to engage in preventive diplomacy. It is here that careful decisions will have to be made.

The 'do nothing' option (that is, minimimal American involvement in the events in South Africa) would be based on the assumption that if the racial conflict in South Africa is inherently insoluble without a lengthy blood-letting, then it would be better to abstain as much as possible and to let nature take its course. The frustrations and failures of American diplomatic intervention in Rhodesia might make this an attractive option. Such an approach would have to try to separate Western economic interests from political considerations. The United States' policy which neither 'encourages nor discourages' investment in South Africa would continue. American statements of abhorrence towards South Africa's racial policies and declarations of support for black aspirations would, however, not be followed up by effective action which might accelerate change. In short, this would be a continuation of the present US relationship with South Africa – trying to have it both ways.

Certainly, such a policy would win support within the Western Alliance. Indeed, of the options facing American policy-makers, this is probably the most attractive, if only because it presents the fewest immediate problems. Nevertheless, the implications of such an approach in the longer run cannot be ignored. Racial tensions in South Africa will increase; violence will grow; and there is a real possibility that the West will one day lose access to South Africa's minerals through prolonged internal instability. If that possibility is unacceptable to the West, so must be any policy of disengagement which would allow it to develop.

The United States could adopt the fourth option – preventive diplomacy. The premise is that some form of outside action will be needed to head off unacceptable instability in South Africa. This is the familiar path down which the United States wandered in Rhodesia. There is, however, an important difference. In Rhodesia American diplomatic intervention came late in the day. The insurgency was already well under way and power was unmistakably (if slowly) shifting from the Salisbury government to the Patriotic Front. It was too late for diplomacy to alter the course of events. By comparison, these are still early days in South Africa. If the Soweto riots were a sign of things to come, they did not in themselves mark a shift in the basic power relationship between blacks and white. There is still no sign of sustained, organized black South African insurgency. White South Africans may see this as confirmation that there is no need to change attitudes or policies, but this is surely a misreading of the situation. The present stability should not be viewed as justification for complacency but rather as an opportunity to instigate peaceful change, particularly as the present established black leadership will, with time, be replaced by younger, more militant blacks with whom it will be much more difficult to maintain a dialogue or to negotiate.

If there is still time for negotiation over South Africa's future, it must be admitted that the situation is not viewed that way by the Government in Pretoria. Given the racial imbalance in the country, white South Africans see no way in which the granting of black demands could be compatible with the maintenance of white privilege. Moreover, there seems to be no room for compromise. The South African government may make cosmetic changes in the area known as 'petty apartheid', but the white nation has offered the blacks no political power except within the sharply circumscribed limits of their tribal homelands. Even if South Africa were to accept the principle of gradual enfranchisement of blacks during a lengthy transition period (of a decade or more) leading ultimately to majority rule, it is doubtful whether this would satisfy the increasingly strident demands of blacks both in South Africa and elsewhere on the African continent.

The conclusion must be that there is no mutually acceptable formula for resolving South Africa's problems on the basis of the principle of 'one man, one vote'. Although South Africa has advanced her own solutions (for example, the homeland scheme and separate parliaments for coloureds and Asians), these are clearly inadequate.

Is there, then, any prospect for a peaceful resolution of the South African dilemma or any scope for preventive diplomacy? If true power in South Africa cannot be shared, then power may have to be divided in a manner acceptable to both sides. Numerous plans have been put forward over the years, ranging from federal or confederal solutions to outright partition. It is not the intention of this paper to analyse specific solutions to the South Africa problem, even if they could be identified. Nevertheless, it should be pointed out that as American policy towards South Africa develops, it will be necessary to look beyond the rhetoric of 'one man, one vote' and to search for other solutions which might be acceptable to both whites and blacks. Indeed, there is evidence to suggest that the United States has recognized this. Although supporting the concept of 'one man, one vote', the Carter Administration has frequently used less precise language, calling simply for the 'full participation' of blacks in the political process. Given that, is there any possibility that blacks and whites might accept a solution based on some form of partition of their country? It is difficult to gauge black opinion, although one prominent black leader, Chief Tasha Buthelezi, has said that he would not reject the idea out of hand. As for white South Africans, it must be remembered that the entire policy of apartheid or separate development is itself based on parting the races. The campaign to turn the tribal homelands into 'independent' states is another step in this direction, if an inadequate one. Although the jump from the present homelands policy to a more substantial partitioning of the country (acceptable to blacks) may appear today to be impossible, it should not necessarily be discarded. The Afrikaners see themselves as an African nation, whose top priority is to maintain its identity. Their struggle has been to avoid being submerged – first by English-speaking whites and now by blacks. If their survival is paramount, then the Afrikaners can be expected to pay a high price to ensure it. At present they see that price as having to be prepared to fight. It is not impossible that with time, and under increasing internal pressure from blacks, they may see the price as another sort of sacrifice. It will be a prime task of American and Western diplomacy to try to move white South African thinking in this direction.

Yet while the United States will not be able to escape her international responsibilities in the South Africa dispute, there are clear limits to the extent to which she can influence South Africa's behaviour. These limits are set by American domestic considerations, by the differing priorities of the United States' allies and, not least, by the attitudes of the South African government and of the white population which supports it.

South Africa promises to be a foreign policy problem which the United States can neither solve nor ignore. It has the makings of a quagmire, which American policy-makers will have to approach carefully to avoid being sucked in too deeply as they deal with a white nation confident of its supremacy and a black population which is only starting to recognize the full potential of its power.

2 South Africa's Narrowing Security Options

ROBERT JASTER

INTRODUCTION

From the standpoint of Western security interests, South Africa is rapidly becoming a major problem. The white minority government is under mounting world pressure to make fundamental changes in its social and political system. The industrial democracies, which are the only countries with substantial economic leverage over South Africa, have also come under increasing pressure, both from Afro-Asian states and from limited but growing constituencies at home, to start exercising that leverage, even though it would have adverse effects on Western business, trade and investment.

As pressures on South Africa have grown and the West has distanced itself from the government in Pretoria, South Africa's leaders have been turning to hard-line, often dangerously belligerent, responses. Both the elusive peace in Namibia and South Africa's gradual slide towards domestic tragedy seem likely to involve the West in some increasingly messy and hazardous situations. Hence a study of South Africa's security strategy – her changing threat perceptions, her responses and her likely moves during the coming decade – is of direct relevance to international security.

The ultimate goal of national security policy is national survival: the perpetuation of a people with its cultural institutions and national identity intact. To the Afrikaner people (the authentic white tribe of Africa) the issue of national survivial has dominated national life for almost 150 years. Indeed, national survival, as described in 1942 by a future Prime Minister, has come to be imbued with a divine mission:

> It is through the will of God that the Afrikaner People exists at all. In His wisdom He determined that on the southern point of Africa . . . a People should be born who would be the bearer of Christian culture and civilization. He surrounded this

People by great dangers . . . . God also willed that the Afrikaans People should be continually threatened by other Peoples. There was the ferocious barbarian who resisted the intruding Christian civilization and caused the Afrikaner's blood to flow in streams. There were times when as a result of this the Afrikaner was deeply despairing, but God at the same time prevented the swamping of the young Afrikaner People in the sea of barbarianism.[1]

The over-riding and ever-present threat perceived by the Afrikaner people has, of course, been precisely this *swartgevaar:* the fear of being overwhelmed by the black majority. Hence the essential mandate of successive South African governments has been to demonstrate the will and capacity to meet this threat effectively and to maintain white supremacy. But in the years since World War II, and particularly since the official advent of apartheid, South Africa's leaders have faced the new and growing threat of outside interference in their domestic race policies.[2] This threat, which government spokesmen have attributed to radical black nationalism and Western liberalism in the unwitting service of world Communism, has intensified fears of an internal black uprising supported by an external power.

With the National Party (NP) electoral victory in 1948, the fears of the Afrikaner community began to be translated into the domestic and foreign policy initiatives which their leaders thought necessary to ensure national survival. Since then the Government has had virtually a free hand in the area of security policy.

In part this reflects the safe and growing parliamentary majority which the Party has enjoyed since 1958. At a deeper level it is a function of the Afrikaner community's interlocking leadership. Members of the numerically small Afrikaner élite are well known to one another through former student contacts and membership of the National Party, the Dutch Reformed Church, Afrikaans cultural and business organizations and, of course, the *Broederbond*.[3] The corporate character of Afrikaner leadership 'has facilitated the formulation of collective goals for Afrikaner organizations and introduced a unity of purpose into corporate Afrikaner action (e.g., "the church" supports the government, "the universities" support "the church" and *vice versa*)'.[4]

Through this corporate network the Government has been able to build up a consensus among the Afrikaner élite on the nature of the security threat and the appropriate policies for dealing with it. There is thus a close congruence between rhetoric and action, perceived threat and response. Moreover, this informal system of consensus-building among the élite is reassuring to the Afrikaner public, which sees that its ministers, educators, editors and Members of Parliament (MPs) are supportive of government policy. This, together with the Afrikaner's general lack of interest in politics, has led to far more public trust in Government and a less critical electorate than in the Western democracies. It remains to be seen, of course, how far this almost blind faith may have been shaken by the 'Muldergate' scandal, which exposed a substantial degree of corruption among the ruling élite.

A second notable feature of the South African system has to do with the notion of 'strategy'. Although South Africa is a remote, third-ranking country in terms of the influence she

can bring to bear on great-power politics, her leaders have consistently viewed South Africa as having significant military, economic and political roles to play in global, as well as regional, affairs. This may reflect simply the Afrikaner élite's sense of a God-given purpose and design to all events, or it may be due to some deep-seated psychological need to link South Africa to the European mainstream. Whatever the cause, the result has been the formulation of security policies to accord with the leadership's current perspective on global trends and their implications for South Africa. This is not to say that the assessments have necessarily been correct; indeed, as argued in this Paper, defective security policies have resulted from distorted perceptions of threat and misreadings of the motives and likely behaviour of foreign actors. The point here is that South Africa's policies, domestic and foreign, have *generally* been formulated as part of the leadership's comprehensive strategy at the time, rather than as isolated, *ad hoc* responses to particular events.[5]

This Paper will analyse South Africa's security strategies under National Party rule. The factors informing the leadership's changing perception of internal and external threats will be identified, and the strategy and policies adopted in response will be discussed. Particular attention will be given to the marked shift in threat perception after 1975 and its impact on policy. The concluding section will assess South Africa's security options in the 1980s and their implications for the West.

I. THE CORE STRATEGY

In 1948 the National Party, the major party of the Afrikaners, came to power on its platform of *apartheid:* racial separateness. This was understood to mean much more than mere 'park bench' segregation or white job preference, both of which have been features of South African society for over a century. It meant the social, political and territorial separation of the races. Its most radical aspect, of course, was the proposal to create tribal 'homelands' or Bantustans, for each of South Africa's major tribal

groups. Blacks would be allowed political expression and permanent residence rights only within their assigned tribal areas.

This concept of separate development, often called 'grand apartheid', provided National Party leaders with a long-sought ideology for unifying the Afrikaner nation.[1] On the ideological level it offered a solution to 'the native problem', which the Afrikaner people could accept as being ordained by God and resonant with their own national experience. This aspect of apartheid was summed up by the Government when it introduced the Bantustan legislation in Parliament:

> God has given a divine task and calling to every People in the world, which dare not be destroyed or denied by anyone. . . . Every People in the world, of whatever race or colour. . . has an inherent right to live and develop. Every People is entitled to the right of self-preservation. . . . It is our deep conviction that the national ideals of every individual and of every ethnic group can best be developed within its own national community.[2]

Afrikaners recognized this as the means by which they themselves came to survive and prosper as people in the 1930s and 1940s. It also seemed to provide the Government with a morally defensible answer to the outside world's growing demand that blacks be given a political voice in South Africa (until 1959 blacks had a small indirect representation in Parliament). It would at the same time direct black nationalist aspirations into the presumably safe channels of Bantustan politics.

On the pragmatic level, too, apartheid had a strong appeal. The notion of physically removing millions of blacks from white areas to often remote tribal territories might seem a ridiculous scheme to outsiders. But to most South African whites, who had watched with alarm the rapid growth of black shanty towns around South African cities during World War II, the idea was very attractive. The influx of blacks was a visible reminder to whites that they were a small minority surrounded by a large and potentially explosive black majority.

Moreover, apartheid meant additional protection for white workers. This was particularly important to the several hundred thousand poor whites, the majority of whom were unskilled Afrikaners, who had drifted off farms into urban areas during the 1930s and who found themselves in competition with blacks for the lowest-paying jobs.[3]

While at the ideological end of the spectrum apartheid appealed to the Afrikaner conscience, at the other it appealed to instinctive white racism.[4] J. G. Strijdom, who served as Prime Minister from 1954 to 1958, encouraged this latter strain in Afrikanerdom:

> If the European loses his colour sense, he cannot remain a white man . . . . You cannot retain your sense of colour if there is no *apartheid* in everyday social life, in the political sphere . . . and if there is no residential separation . . . . South Africa can only remain a white country if we continue to see that the Europeans remain the dominant nation.[5]

Apartheid thus promised something to whites, and particularly to Afrikaners, at almost every level of their concern: ideology, politics, economics, physical security and national survival. Moreover, the white stake in apartheid grew rapidly with the introduction of implementing legislation, especially in the late 1950s. By 1977 a poll of white South Africans showed 76 per cent agreeing that: 'We should fight to maintain South Africa as it is, whatever the risks.'[6]

The essential element in apartheid, however – the feature that has made it an indispensable strategy to successive National Party Governments – is its ingenious formula for the nominal devolution of political power to blacks, while effectively denying them a voice in South Africa's political affairs. Since the only alternative would have been some form of power-sharing in white political insitutions (anathema to the electorate), separate development has remained the core of government policy, the castle keep of white survival for more than 30 years. The pursuit of the separate development ideal has also served to legitimize, in the eyes of most whites, the increasingly harsh coercive measures promulgated by the Government from the 1960s.

The brief sketch above is not intended to be an assessment of separate development, which is outside the focus of this study. The purpose here is to point out the crucial importance of separate development to the goals and values of white South Africans and their leaders. Indeed, apartheid has been the major factor defining and constraining South Africa's policy options in other areas. The question of how this strategy has interacted with other strategic objectives of the National Party informs a substantial part of what follows.

II. THE FIRST DECADE: THE SEARCH FOR SECURITY

Seeking the Levers of Power

During roughly the first decade of National Party rule (1948–58), domestic issues overshadowed those of foreign policy. The prime task for the new leaders was to strengthen their tenuous hold on power. They had won only 70 of 150 Lower House seats in 1948; to get legislation through Parliament, they had to form an alliance with the small Afrikaner Party and its nine House members. Mutual antipathy between the English-speaking and Afrikaans communities ran high, and the Nationalists were obsessed with the fear that 'the English', with their liberal notions of race and their suspected lack of patriotism, might again come to dominate South African politics.

To forestall this, the Malan Administration almost immediately initiated a series of apartheid measures designed to consolidate behind the Party the support of the entire Afrikaner electorate. Executive action established legal segregation of public accommodation, ordered that poor whites be hired in preference to blacks and withdrew medical scholarships for blacks at white universities. In 21 South African cities and towns residence was closed to blacks in all but a few job categories.[1] By 1950 Acts of Parliament had outlawed marriage between whites and non-whites, made inter-racial sexual relations a criminal offence and formally established residential and territorial separation by race.

Simultaneously, actions were taken to weaken the role of English-speakers. Immigration, most of which had been from Britain, was discouraged. The two-year waiting period, a statutory requirement before immigrants could acquire South African citizenship, was extended to five, thus reducing the future voting potential of English-speakers. The Defence Minister, who openly expressed his mistrust of English-speaking officers, was accused of politicizing the armed forces through wholesale dismissals of English-speakers and arbitrary appointments and promotions.[2] The Chief of the General Staff resigned in protest.[3] Not until 1961 was an English-speaker appointed to the Cabinet.[4]

The rapid proliferation of apartheid legislation, while it went a long way towards uniting Afrikanerdom, soon led to widespread dissidence and protest, particularly (but not solely) among South Africa's non-whites. In the year following the accession of the National Party to power, racial violence – which has never been far beneath the surface in South African society – broke out in Durban, taking the lives of 136 blacks and Indians and injuring more than a thousand.[5] Typically, this spontaneous protest quickly sputtered and died.

Much more serious for the new leadership was the organized non-white resistance to apartheid which began in 1950–51. The African National Congress (ANC), the dominant and most enduring political organization of South African blacks, abandoned its long-standing policy of working within the law and organized a well co-ordinated campaign of boycotts, strikes and civil disobedience. Joining the campaign of defiance in a loose association were the Indian National Congress (INC), a newly formed Coloured Congress and the Congress of Democrats, a white leftist group formed after the Communist Party was outlawed in 1950. During this period the ANC remained essentially liberal, nationalist and non-violent. Its underlying strategy was to use mass protest to frighten the Government into withdrawing its apartheid policy. Its members entered racially restricted areas without permits, joined white queues in public places and spoke in public in defiance of bans. The Government's counter-strategy was to apply whatever force it judged necessary to maintain internal security and to make no concessions to what its leaders saw as Communist-instigated unrest among non-whites. Thus the stage was set for an upward spiral of non-white protest against apartheid and white repression in the name of anti-Communism.

Anti-Communism

Anti-Communism has deep roots among Afrikaners. In white South Africa, as in other non-Communist industrial societies, there is an abiding ambivalence in the 'Communist threat'. It is at once something which both the leadership and the public perceive as real (though each may see it in different terms) and something in which the leaders see potential for mobilizing or manipulating public opinion. Thus in the 1930s, as Afrikaner leaders were trying to unify the people and build a distinct Afrikaner nationalism, they feared that the appeal of Communism among Afrikaner workers – most of whom were unskilled migrants from the countryside – would have a seriously divisive impact on Afrikanerdom.

A more powerful and enduring element of the Afrikaners' fear is Communism's advocacy of racial equality. A leading authority on Afrikaner nationalism writes: 'for all Afrikaners the Communist disregard for racial differences [is] a thrust at the very heart of their ethnic existence.'[6] This fear was reinforced by the fact that the white leaders of South Africa's small Communist Party were among the most outspoken champions of black rights. And since English-speaking liberals, Afrikaner heretics, and black nationalists advocated the same thing, it was easy to class them all together as Communists or Communist-inspired.

This loose definition of Communism was reflected in. the Suppression of Communism Act (1950), which gave the police greater power to arrest, detain and ban.[7] Communism was defined extremely broadly to include 'any doctrine or scheme which aims to bring about any political, industrial, social or economic change within the Republic by the promotion of disorder, by unlawful acts or omissions, or by the threat of such acts' or 'which aims at the encouragement of feelings of hostility between the European and non-European races of the Republic'. Similarly, a Communist was anyone defined as such by the President on the basis that he was involved in encouraging 'any of the objects of Communism'.

Maintaining Internal Security

Police forces were rapidly enlarged to cope with the resistance, and three successive National Party Administrations made it clear that the *primary* responsibility of the Defence Force was to maintain internal security.[8] Arrests and detentions were occurring on such a large scale in the 1950s that the Minister of Justice found it feasible to open a series of Convict Labour Stations in rural districts to supply prison labour for white farms.[9]

As mass resistance grew, the Government found that existing legislation prevented it from dealing with the problem in the quick and peremptory way it would have liked. Learning from its growing experience with dissidents and the courts, in a few years the Party's Parliamentary majority[10] had enacted a succession of tough new internal security laws to close the loopholes and strengthen the authority of the executive, particularly the police. This learning process was reflected in a deadly game of challenge-and-response between the resistance and the Government:

1953: During a massive protest organized by the ANC and the INC to defy petty apartheid, riots took place in several cities, resulting in some deaths. The Government responded with the passage of the Public Safety Act, giving the Minister of Justice sole authority to declare a state of emergency and to carry out summary arrests and detentions. Also the Criminal Law Amendment Act (1953) made it a criminal offence to advocate resistance to *any* law or to give financial aid to any organization defying the law. Strikes by black workers were made a criminal offence under the Native Labour Act.

1954: The ANC and other groups planned a Peoples' Congress to draft a freedom charter. The Government staged an advance security sweep, arresting 156 people, including ANC leaders, on treason charges – later dismissed by the courts after trials lasting several years. The Government preferred pre-emptive arrest and detention of leaders to the more cumbersome and uncertain process of banning entire organizations.

1958: Mass protests and a 'stay-at-home' by black workers were scheduled on the eve of the 1958 national elections. The Government acted in advance by banning meetings of ten or more blacks without special permission, and the Defence Force was put on the alert.

These are a few examples of the growing security crisis of the 1950s. The defiance campaign of 1952–53 alone led to the gaoling of 8,000 non-whites. In spite of the Government's coercive measures, however, sporadic organized protests continued throughout the decade. The most successful were those with bread-and-butter goals such as the strike for the 'pound-a-day wage' in 1957, which affected industry in several cities and led to some remedial wage

41

action on the part of the authorities. Yet while the protest flickered into life from time to time, it failed to ignite into anything like a nationwide protest movement in this period. This may have been due less to police action than to weak leadership and poor organization of the resistance, together with the fragile financial state of black workers, who could not withhold their labour for long. Moreover, up to this time the major resistance groups had not opted for violent confrontation. The really serious disturbances were yet to come.

Military Alliance with the West
While struggling to get a permanent grip on the levers of power and to suppress internal protest, South Africa's new leaders also charted a basic strategy for external defence. They saw no immediate threat of outside attack. But they were much concerned by the growing political and social upheaval as black nationalism spread across Africa, a development which they saw as a direct result of Communist agitation and as part of a global Communist plan to weaken the West by wresting Africa and its riches from Western control. (Perhaps because of their pre-occupation with race issues at home, South Africa's leaders were also seized with the notion that India, and later China, sought to colonize Africa.)[11]

Hence an over-riding objective of the Malan and Strijdom Governments was to keep radical black nationalism from spilling southwards over South Africa's borders and infecting her non-white population. To this end they adopted a three-pronged strategy. First, the Government determined that in the event of war against Communism, the enemy must be engaged as far away as possible from South Africa. Second, the leadership attempted to become involved in a formal Western defence alliance. Third, the Government tried to commit the Western powers to the defence of Africa.

In pursuing this strategy, however, the Malan and Strijdom Administrations operated on a number of key assumptions, several of which proved false. Above all, they assumed that South Africa, by virtue of her white, Christian, anti-Communist Government and her dominant economic and strategic position in Africa, would be a welcome and valued ally of the West in the struggle against Communism. The 1950s

were, indeed, a period when the cold war and containment of Soviet expansionism were the dominant concerns of Western statesmen; but their attention was focused on Europe and the Western democracies. Africa was far from the main arena of the East–West struggle – a point which South Africa's parochially disposed leaders failed to perceive at that time.

It was also assumed in Pretoria that the colonial powers would acknowledge a major role for South Africa in African regional affairs. A further assumption – like the others, held onto for far too long – was that Britain and other colonial states would defend the *status quo* in Africa. Decolonization, if it occurred at all, was therefore expected to be a piecemeal and selective process, stretching over many years.

South Africa nevertheless found the cold war era an opportune moment in which to implement the strategy outlined above. While banking on the Western powers to counter the threat of general Communist aggression, South Africa quickly demonstrated her willingness to play a role in Western defence commensurate with her size and capabilities. Sixty South African airmen were sent to take part in the Berlin airlift, and a fighter squadron joined UN forces fighting in Korea. When Britain tried to organize a Middle East Defence Organization (MEDO) in the early 1950s, South Africa accepted an invitation to join, and purchased 68 British *Centurion* tanks plus aircraft, between 1955 and 1959, as evidence of her commitment to send forces to the Middle East in the event of Communist attack.[12] Thus the Government carried out its policy of preparing to meet the enemy far from South African shores and at the same time took an active part in Western military operations.

South Africa, of course, hoped that such co-operation would pave the way for her admission to a Western military alliance. Her chief interest in an alliance was to gain a formal Western commitment to Africa's defence. Prime Minister Malan said, 'South Africa's aim is to take responsibility, *insofar as agreement can be reached with other countries*, for territories to the north of South Africa. We want to *help* in the protection of our neighbours' (italics added).[13]

Mr Malan's ultimate goals, first set out in his 'Africa Charter' in 1945, were to 'retain Africa as a reserve . . . for the further development of

West European Christian civilization'[14] .To keep Africa from falling into Communist hands, he was adamant that the colonial powers – particularly Britain – should not relinquish control over their African territories. He also urged them to agree that Africans 'will not be given military training nor be armed, so that they will not constitute a danger to each other and to other nations in Africa'.[15]

As early as 1951 Prime Minister Malan and his Defence Minister were promoting the idea of an African Defence Organization – a southward extension of NATO to include South Africa and the colonial powers in Africa.[16] In 1951 they also joined Britain in sponsoring a conference in Nairobi to discuss the defence of East and Central Africa. The Conference, which was attended by South Africa, Southern Rhodesia and all the colonial powers in the area, was limited to discussing logistics and the problems of communications in the event of war: strategic planning was not on the agenda, nor were any decisions taken. A similar conference to discuss West African defence took place in Dakar three years later, where a similar lack of progress was made. Of the five participating states (Britain, France, Belgium, Portugal and South Africa), only South Africa came away claiming that she had undertaken substantial commitments in the event of Communist aggression in Africa.

South Africa nevertheless continued to agitate for an African defence alliance throughout the 1950s. The closest she came to achieving this was the conclusion of the Simonstown Agreement with Britain in 1955. Under the accord the British naval base at Simonstown, near Cape Town, was turned over to South Africa, and both governments agreed in general terms to contribute forces for the defence of southern Africa against external aggression. It was noted that southern Africa's defence 'lies not only in Africa, but also in the gateway to Africa, namely in the Middle East'. Britain gained the right to use Simonstown during the course of hostilities in which South Africa was not involved, thus putting South Africa's future neutrality in jeopardy. Internal security was explicitly excluded from the terms of the Simonstown Agreement.

The two Governments further resolved to sponsor a conference aimed at making suitable Western defence arrangements for Africa. South Africa saw this, too, as leading to a Western military alliance, but Britain viewed it in much looser terms, emphasizing that it did not contain any substantive obligations. Indeed, no such conference took place; and although the Simonstown accord led to joint British–South African naval exercises and British arms sales to South Africa, it did not result in the military alliance sought by South Africa.

Promotion of the Status Quo

Throughout this period South Africa continued to urge the colonial powers to remain in Africa. In 1953 Prime Minister Malan said it would be 'generations' before the Gold Coast (soon to be Ghana) would gain independence. His successor, Mr Strijdom, also favoured co-operation with the West in order to maintain European control in Africa. While paying lip service to the need to win the friendship of emergent black states, Mr Strijdom declared (in 1954) that close collaboration with other white communities in southern Africa 'is what we generally mean when we talk about an African policy'.[17] Even as late as 1959 South Africa's Foreign Minister warned that it would be 'unwise for a colonial power to withdraw its guiding hand, and to grant full independence to a country where the people are not fully mature and ripe for independence'.[18]

The question is not why South Africa was hoping to see the colonial *status quo* maintained in the early 1950s – she was not alone in failing to foresee how rapidly decolonization would occur – but why she hung on to this policy for so long and did so little to adjust to new conditions, even in the last years of the decade. In speeches, it is true, the Strijdom Administration offered the hand of friendship to new African states and begrudgingly acknowledged that 'points of contact will have to come and [in time] normal and even diplomatic relations will have to come.'[19] But no significant initiatives were undertaken before 1960.

Indeed, South Africa rebuffed repeated friendly overtures from Ghana in 1957–60, including offers to exchange High Commissioners and an invitation to a conference of independent African states. According to an inside observer of South African Government affairs during this period,[20] when Foreign Minister Louw proposed in May 1959 that he visit the new black-ruled states and that South Africa consider permanent representation in some of them, the entire Cabinet was against him. Thus even at the end of the decade South Africa had not adjusted her strategy to take account of the radically new situation that she faced in Africa.

The African Role

A further early setback for South Africa was the unwillingness of the Western powers to concede her an important role in African affairs, including defence. Soon after taking office in 1948, Mr Malan asserted:

> South Africa also has the right, by virtue of its position as a white man's country and its experience during the course of years in connection with the native problem and the coloured problem, to aspire to leadership in this matter and to act as adviser to the peoples of the Northern territories.[21]

In the late 1950s the Foreign Minister spoke of South Africa's 'vocation' in Africa, where 'it must play its full part as an African power.'[22] He also saw South Africa as a bridge between Africa and the West, since his country was 'the West's most reliable ally in the struggle against Communist penetration in Africa'.[23]

But South Africa's perception of her importance to the West differed sharply from that of the Western powers. As apartheid was implemented and protest, both domestic and foreign, intensified against her policies at home and in South-West Africa, South Africa became a growing liability to the West. Moreover, the threat of Communism was perceived differently by Western and South African leaders. In particular, South Africa's over-riding concern with the Communist threat to Africa was not matched in the West.

Hence South Africa – to her leaders' outspoken annoyance – was not consulted about such matters as Britain's decolonization moves in Africa. Most important to South Africa was the disposition of the three British High Commission Territories (HCTs) in southern Africa: Basutoland (now Lesotho), Bechuanaland (Botswana) and Swaziland. All three dependencies shared long borders with South Africa, and

Basutoland was an enclave territory totally within South Africa. All three were heavily dependent on the South African economy, to which they were closely bound by trade, a common currency and participation in a customs union.

Since the 1910 Act of Union provided that the ultimate disposition of the HCTs would be decided by Britain and South Africa, the latter assumed that it was only a matter of time before the territories would be incorporated in South Africa. The issue was a touchy one for Britain. She sought to avoid a showdown with Pretoria over this issue; yet to hand these territories over to apartheid-dominated South Africa would have been totally incompatible with Britain's post-war colonial policy – particularly as the people in the HCTs were making clear their strong opposition to incorporation in the Republic.[24]

The issue was also a serious one for South Africa, particularly from the standpoint of security. If the HCTs remained British protectorates, it was feared that a liberal British 'native policy' on South Africa's very doorstep would become a source of friction in her domestic race relations. Were they to become independent, they might become bases for subversion against South Africa. Prime Minister Malan asserted that South Africa's defence could not be effectively organized unless she controlled the Territories.[25] His Defence Minister called them 'blind spots' in South Africa's radar defences. About this time (the mid-1950s) National Party newspapers began reporting the tiny Basutoland enclave to be a hotbed of Communist intrigue, and some National Party right-wingers urged the Government to seize all three HCTs.[26]

While ignoring such extremist positions, the Government nonetheless continued to press its claim to the Territories, though with diminishing vigour, until Verwoerd came to office in 1958. A year later he signalled a change in policy, asserting that Britain was the HCTs' 'governmental guardian', but that South Africa was 'the greater guardian: the economic guardian'.[27] It was only in 1964, however, that the Government 'adopted the realistic attitude that South Africa no longer claims the incorporation of these territories'.[28] Mr. Verwoerd subsequently expanded on the proposition that South Africa's economic power could be con-

44

verted into political power in the region – a theme which has since become a major element in South African security strategy in southern Africa:

> Once Britain is out of these protectorates ... and these peoples' own governments are faced with the demands of survival ... then they will judge their actions and their relationships in terms of their economic interests. ... *I believe that the one thing that really counts in international relations is common economic interests.* So far as the government of these protectorates is concerned, political interests will be dominated by their economic interests.[29] (Italics added).

Response to the External Threat

In reviewing the external security threat perceived by the South African leadership during the 1950s, at first glance it is difficult to reconcile the high level of rhetoric with the low level of concrete action taken to enhance South Africa's real defence capabilities. Between 1946 and 1960, for example, no new equipment worth mentioning was acquired by the army or the air force, except for *Centurion* tanks and *Sabre* aircraft bought in 1955 as a consequence of South Africa's commitment to the abortive Middle East Defence Organization discussed above. Major naval purchases were limited to two 'comparatively modern' destroyers.[30] Defence spending in 1950 came to just over £8.25 million – less than 1 per cent of national income. Two years later the Defence vote was still less than £17 million (1.6 per cent of national income), and something like one-fifth of this sum went on

tank and aircraft purchases for MEDO and South Africa's operations in Korea. Even as late as 1960–61, defence spending totalled only 44 million rand, and came to less than 1 per cent of GNP.

A partial explanation of this discrepancy is the nature of the perceived security threat. As argued earlier, the chief and immediate danger in the 1950s was that of an internal black uprising; the menace of Communist aggression appeared both vague and remote and was viewed as a threat for which the leading Western powers must bear a large proportion of defence responsibility, with only token aid from South Africa. Seen in this light, South Africa's major armaments outlay for her MEDO and Korean obligations was consistent with the security strategy outlined above. Moreover, for a small country starting with a small defence force concerned mainly with internal security and a small (white) manpower pool on which to draw at the beginning of the decade, South Africa's arms acquisitions during that period were not insignificant. As noted in a South African defence publication, the purchase of the two destroyers 'heralded a new era in technical complexity for the Navy ... hitherto ... a comparatively uncomplicated small-craft Navy'.[31]

While the Government thus appeared to have internal security under control by the end of the 1950s, it was still groping unsuccessfully for a defence pact with the West and for a recognized leadership role in Africa. With the 1960s – and particularly after Sharpeville – both the threat perception and response began to change.

III. FROM SHARPEVILLE TO LISBON

The Immediate Danger

Internal security was the dominant concern of the early 1960s.[1] Indeed, the decade opened with the emergence of a suddenly militant internal black resistance. In 1960, the Jubilee year of the Union of South Africa, this resistance, which had been flickering feebly for several years, was suddenly fanned into flame. The immediate issue was the hated pass laws. Robert Sobukwe, head of the Pan-African Congress (PAC), called for a massive appearance of Africans at police stations, where they were to demand arrest for

being without their passes. When 20,000 turned up at a remote station in the township of Sharpeville on 21 March 1960 the police panicked and fired on the crowd, killing 67 and wounding 186.[2] Demonstrations quickly spread to all four provinces, continuing into April. In Capetown 30,000 Africans marched to the city centre: in Durban 10,000 marched on the city gaol to demand the release of prisoners. An organized 'stay-at-home' succeeded in closing down much commercial and industrial activity for several days in major cities.

45

Whites were frightened, and the Government reacted quickly and with force. On 24 March all meetings of blacks were prohibited. A few days later the ANC and the PAC were banned. Pass laws were temporarily relaxed, as the Government claimed that blacks had been intimidated into going without their passes. On 30 March a state of national emergency was declared, and more than 11,000 people, including leaders of the banned organizations, were detained. Troops were called up to surround and seal off black townships.

By mid-April order had been restored, but the troubles were not over. Blacks continued to schedule meetings to plan future actions. The Government responded by arresting the leaders, often well in advance of the meetings. Police also raided the black townships to arrest *tsotsis*, the young thugs and drifters from among whom the ANC – which had by then gone underground – recruited its armed 'enforcers'. In conjunction with industry, the Government announced that employees taking part in 'stay-at-homes' would be dismissed.

Umkhonto we Sizwe ('Spear of the Nation') and *Poqo* ('We Alone'), violent offshoots of the ANC and the PAC respectively, turned to sabotage. From August 1961 to July 1963, 193 acts of sabotage were reported. Since the Government had earlier put the major installations (for example, oil storage depots, dams, power stations) under wartime security protection, and since neither explosives nor training in sabotage was easily available, most sabotage was of a low order (placing burning matchbooks in post-boxes, for instance). But in some instances serious damage was done.

By mid-1963 the Government had begun to penetrate and destroy the feeble underground resistance. The increasing effectiveness of the police was due in part to improved tactics: for example, generous payments were offered to informants.[3] Police work was greatly facilitated by a succession of harsh security laws, passed between 1961 and 1967. A General Laws Amendment Act in 1961 widened the definition of 'intimidation' and extended the Justice Minister's right to hold trials without jury and to prohibit meetings. By 1962 an organization could be banned indefinitely. Subsequently magistrates were authorized to refuse bail, and the Minister of Justice could detain an individual for

a year beyond his original sentence if it was thought that release might promote Communist aims. A police lieutenant could, on his own authority, detain for 90 days anyone suspected of crimes against state security, and unco-operative witnesses could be gaoled for successive 12-month periods. The Terrorism Act of 1967 provided for indefinite detention of prisoners for interrogation and permitted summary trial by a judge sitting alone.

Thus in barely half a dozen years South Africa had moved away from British law, with its protection of individual rights, to a series of draconian regulations in which the powers of the state were overwhelming. Only the courts remained independent and effective in protecting individual rights – although the National Party's growing parliamentary majority frequently enabled it to over-ride court decisions. The National Party knew that the vast majority of whites would support almost any measures taken in the interests of maintaining the *status quo* – particularly as it was understood that few whites would be directly touched by the security apparatus. This has remained an operative principle of South African political life.

Finally, police work was made easier by the hopelessly amateurish character of most attempts to organize violence. A typically inept effort to establish a 'munitions factory' at a remote farm was doomed to failure. It was uncovered when the new owners neglected to make their initial mortgage payments.

By 1964 incidents of sabotage had dropped from about 100 a year to ten. By 1965 internal resistance was virtually crushed.

Shifting Threat Perceptions

The years 1960–63 were a watershed for South African defence policy. Strategic judgments and decisions made in that period led to a new defence posture, which remained essentially unchanged until the mid-1970s.

On the basis of a 'military appreciation of the world situation' and of its implications for South Africa which was framed in 1960 the General Staff concluded that it was vital for South Africa 'to enhance its military capability and state of readiness'.[4]

A later Defence Review stated that the decision was based on assessments of such global considerations as the nuclear stalemate, and that the goal was to enable South Africa to counter any act of aggression 'within its capability'.[5] Parliamentary debates in 1961, however, suggest that the external threat was not particularly clear or menacing at the time; indeed, the threat of *internal* disturbances was clearly the Government's paramount concern. The Defence Minister in 1961, Mr Fouche, listed four objectives of the South African Defence Force (SADF):

To preserve effectively internal safety;

Within its limits, to be able to cope with any invasion from outside;

To have something to offer when South Africa wanted to enter agreements or military alliances with other countries;

To act as a deterrent, 'so that no insignificant little state can believe it can invade South Africa'.[6]

The Minister concluded by saying, 'We do not know what threatens us . . . Anything might happen, and South Africa must prepare herself for it as fast as possible.'

In spite of the Minister's generalized definition of the threat, much of the defence legislation which he introduced early in 1961 was explicitly directed towards tightening internal security. In cases of internal disorder, rail services were to be made immediately available to the SADF, which was also given authority to commandeer vehicles and to move people from one area to another. Mr Fouche raised the prospect that the SADF might have to suppress large-scale riots or engage in street fighting.

At the same time new developments outside South Africa were also alarming. In April 1961 South Africa was forced to leave the Commonwealth.[7] Soon thereafter 24 African states introduced a UN resolution urging the severance of diplomatic ties with South Africa, which became a republic on 31 May. Disturbances in the Congo were discussed in Parliament, and the Angolan uprising of 1961 prompted South Africa to initiate naval and air patrols of the South-West African coast and to enlarge her garrison at Walvis Bay.[8] In addition, the Western powers were starting to vote against South Africa in the UN. In 1960 the United States supported a Security Council resolution that apartheid might endanger world peace and security. In 1963 Britain endorsed a General Assembly resolution favouring anti-apartheid actions by member states, and a year later both

the United States and Britain subscribed to a UN arms embargo.

By 1962 Mr Verwoerd was able to delineate more clearly what he saw as the approaching external threat.[9] He discounted the likelihood of a global conflict in the near future and dismissed the possibility of international intervention under UN auspices in South Africa. The major threat – and even this he regarded as 'boastful talk' – was Afro-Asian aggression against the Republic. But should it come, he warned, South Africa could not count on help from the Western powers, which would 'look to their own interests as they see them. *Therefore they will not conclude any alliance with South Africa*' (italics added). Hence, he claimed, to prevent other states from 'imposing their will' on South Africa, she must have her own striking power and must be able 'to stand upon her own feet'.

The Defence Minister elaborated on this theme but added a note of ambivalence.[10] A few years ago, he said, when 'we found ourselves in the midst of the West, the SADF was intended only as a complementary force', but in the changed conditions in which South Africa finds herself, she 'cannot do anything else but build up a defence force able to stand on its own feet'. Then, while reiterating Mr Verwoerd's theme that 'the West is abandoning Africa', he added a footnote of his own: 'If we have to fight a major war on the side of the West, we will also be much more valuable to the West if we have built up our defence force as an independent unit.' These apparently contradictory notions (that of an isolated South Africa forced to battle against hostile forces alone, and that of a South Africa seeking and needing the protection of a Western military alliance) have persisted in South African strategy and policies right through to the present day.

As South Africa's defence forces grew during the 1960s, the threat of direct, conventional attack across the border faded rapidly, and the chief emergent threat was seen to be 'small wars', such as guerrilla incursions. The SADF's first reported large-scale military exercise, *Operation Sibasa*, took place in the northeastern Transvaal in 1968, against a force of mock terrorists presumed to be coming from Portuguese Mozambique. The following year, in the Eastern Cape, a combined force of land,

47

air and naval units was involved in *Operation Enterprise*, in which it was assumed that guerrillas entering the Republic from a privileged sanctuary (perhaps Lesotho) had exhausted the resources of local police. By 1973 the army was reported to be training all its forces in counter-insurgency warfare. Some of the troops were being trained in the area along the Limpopo valley border with Rhodesia.[11]

As one observer noted,[12] once the real military threat was seen to be guerrilla attack, it was clear this was something which South Africa could handle by herself; hence the need for military alliances diminished. In 1971 Mr P. W. Botha, who had become Defence Minister in 1965, analysed this revised threat perception in terms of global strategy.[13] Because of the great powers' fear of nuclear confrontation, he said, South Africa was faced with a new situation – a neutralization of power. This in turn had forced the Communists to adopt new methods in their drive for world domination. The first phase of the 'Communist onslaught' had been to create internal unrest, and South Africa had been a target of this in the 1960s. But now the Soviet Union had adopted an 'imperialistic, militaristic policy', and her new tactic was to instigate local wars and to provide the arms and personnel to sustain them.

In the same speech, however, Mr Botha said that Moscow and Peking had abandoned 'the direct strategy' only temporarily. 'It is a total, indirect strategy which is directed at us, and if and when it has achieved sufficient success, the *final conventional confrontation will take place*' (italics added). The implications of this eventual showdown were outlined in a major strategy speech by Admiral Bierman shortly after his appointment as Commandant-General of the South African defence forces in 1972.[14] He said that South Africa must first of all ensure law and order and the inviolability of her territory. However, since South Africa could not exist in isolation, she must strive for 'the highest degree of co-operation' among states with common interests in the region. But even this would not be enough, because 'the combined maritime capability of these countries is inadequate to withstand a large-scale enemy infiltration or invasion.' He thus saw the 'need for a super-power to be involved'. He added, 'In the final analysis it is a prerequisite for the successful defence of the Southern Hemisphere that the deterrent strategy based on nuclear terror and the fear of escalation should also be applicable in this region.'

In short, to ward off the final confrontation between South Africa and the Communist world anticipated by Mr Botha, South Africa and the southern hemisphere must seek refuge under the Western nuclear umbrella. (Alternatively, this may have been the Admiral's indirect way of suggesting what no South African official might express publicly – that South Africa should acquire her own nuclear deterrent.) In accordance with this view, the twin goals of achieving an independent military capability, while at the same time taking steps to enhance South Africa's military value to the West, have been reflected in the South African military build-up.

The New Defence Programme
Development of a Modern Defence Force
In view of the threatening developments within and outside South Africa, even the parliamentary opposition supported the Government's decision, taken in 1961, to enlarge the Permanent Force (PF) – the 'regulars' – as a command and training nucleus for an accompanying expansion of the Active Citizens' Force (ACF), the citizens' army on which South African defence is based.[15] The PF grew from 9,000 in 1960 to 15,000 in 1964. Almost 20,000 national servicemen were in training in 1964 – a tenfold increase over the number trained in 1960. At this time the Commandos numbered 51,000 and the police around 34,000. Thus during this period the total number of men in uniform had risen to 120,000. Towards the end of the decade this total had grown by another 10,000,[16] and the annual intake of trainees levelled off at about 26,000. (See Table 1.) But by then South Africa had a trained citizens reserve of 45,000 and police reserves of 15,000.[17]

Throughout the 1960s and 1970s, manpower remained the most critical constraint on defence planners. Forced to draw almost exclusively on the white community of some four million for its rapidly growing requirements, the SADF soon found that it was failing to compete successfully with South Africa's burgeoning private sector, which also relied heavily on whites to supply its skilled personnel. In response to a serious shortage, particularly of technical personnel, salaries in the PF were raised by 11–50 per cent in 1967, and the training of technical apprentices was expanded. The following year saw the introduction of a compulsory national service system for all white youths – including aliens of five years' residence – to replace the previous system of selection by ballot. The total (lifetime) period of service liability for the ACF was extended from four to ten years and the initial training period from nine months to a year (maximum). To help relieve a chronic shortage of PF personnel, the initial training of national servicemen was combined with service, and they were used both as instructors and to fill out PF combat formations and headquarters.[18]

Table 1: National Servicemen Trained Annually, 1960–70

1960	2,000	1966	23,100
1961	7,000	1967	22,600
1962	11,800	1968	22,500
1963	14,600	1969	25,400
1964	19,800	1970	26,400
1965	19,500	[1978	27,000]

SOURCES: *Review, op. cit.*, in ch.II, n.30 p.6; *WP 64/65, op. cit.* in note 16 (for 1960); for 1978 figure *South Africa 1978* (Johannesburg: Perskor, 1978). The periods of continuous training varied from 3–12 months and their number changed several times.

But the manpower problem persisted. In 1971 an MP questioned the Minister about the shortfalls in planned levels of PF personnel of 338 majors, 299 captains and lieutenants, 1,628 sergeants, and 1,296 corporals. The national service system was modified in early 1974 to permit more effective operational deployment of the SADF. The Defence Minister argued that it was imperative that a force-in-being be established, because in order to challenge the terrorist and other threats well trained, mature and experienced troops were required who could operate in small groups or as individuals. Manpower in the PF was inadequate, he said, for this task. Therefore volunteers from among national service trainees would undergo a single, continuous period of training and service of 18 to 24 months. This force-in-being would eventually amount to almost 6,000 in the 18-month group and 2,400 in the two-year group. He acknowledged that a well trained PF brigade would be more effective but that it would be difficult to find the personnel for such a force. Hence South Africa would have to settle for a middle-of-the-road solution – voluntary extended service.

Another solution, of course, would have been large-scale recruitment of non-whites. But, as discussed in Chapter II, the arming of non-whites (particularly of blacks) has been an extremely sensitive issue for South Africa's whites. At about the time that the Government had managed to suppress the internal black resistance, it faced the mounting threat of black insurgency from outside. The leadership has therefore moved slowly and cautiously. The (coloured) Cape Corps was re-established in 1963, with white officers and coloured NCOs. It was intended to serve in a non-combatant role alongside regular PF units. In 1973 the Government created the Cape Corps Service Battalion, which began to train coloured volunteers at the rate of 200 a year, and plans were announced to form an Indian Service Battalion.[19] (Since non-whites are not accorded citizenship rights, they are not subject to national service but are accepted as volunteers.)

The question of arming blacks was far more difficult. In 1972 Defence Minister Botha dismissed an MP's suggestion that a Bantu (black) military corps be formed. 'We are proud of the service blacks are rendering the SADF as civilians', he said, 'but we cannot create such a corps. I think that would be wrong.'[20] Two years later, in February 1974, he was still opposed to the scheme, though not as adamantly. He said the history of South Africa, which was 'full of tragedies', argued against arming blacks '*unreservedly*'; the Opposition's pressure on this was, he said 'reckless' (italics added). Curiously, he treated the issue in terms of the Bantustans, noting that the Government had been approached by homeland leaders wanting to combat terrorism in their own territories. Negotiations were going on, he said, but it all took time. He then touched on the key issue for white sensibilities:

It would be foolish of me to announce a policy here today concerning something with so long a history in South Africa *without being able to tell the country that there are guarantees and firm agreements.* (Italics added).[21]

49

In short, whites would have to be assured that Bantustans' weapons would not be turned on South Africa proper.

Within a year, as discussed in Chapter IV, the Government's growing concern over the threat to its borders, and particularly to Namibia, led to a quick (but apprehensive) reversal in policy, and blacks were finally admitted to the SADF on a small scale.

New Weapons

Along with the expansion of the SADF, the General Staff's review in 1960 also called for a rapid modernization of the army's equipment to cope with the emerging threat of guerrilla incursions and possible ground attack from the north.

Table 2: Arms Expenditure 1960–69

Equipment	million rand
Aircraft	254·6
Ships	54·7
Armour	26·5
AA guns	21·6
Rockets, guided missiles	18·3
Radio, radar, sonar, navigational equipment	102·1
Ammunition	114·6
Vehicles	67·9
TOTAL	660·3

SOURCE: *White Paper on Defence 1969*. (Pretoria: Government Printer, 1969).

The navy – previously no more than an appendage of the Royal Navy charged with coastal defence – was to be converted into an effective, *independent national* force. Over the next nine years South Africa spent 660 million rand on arms, allocated as shown in Table 2.[22]

The navy's main purchases were the modern frigates delivered by Britain in 1963 and 1964 under the Simonstown Agreement at a total cost of 25 million rand and three *Daphne*-class submarines bought from France and delivered in 1971–72. The acquisition of these submarines, together with the earlier purchase of 15 *Buccaneer* aircraft from Britain and the refitting of two destroyers to carry helicopters, gave South Africa a creditable maritime strike capability.

But ground defence accounted for the lion's share of arms purchases. Aside from some tanks and troop carriers acquired in the 1950s, the majority of the army's equipment in 1960 dated back to the 1940s. Major purchases for the army reflected the growing emphasis on developing a counter-insurgency capability as well as enhancing the means of deterring a conventional land attack. The arms import list of the 1960s included 'the latest semi-automatic rifle, light machine-gun, pistol, sub-machine-gun, flamethrower, heavy and light mortar, guided anti-tank projectile, cargo vehicles, and anti-tank gun'.[23]

Aircraft purchases, too, were directed towards the landward threat. As one observer noted:

the role of the air defence, built around the *Mirage III*, is to deter any threats that might in the future occur in the event of hostile countries to the north receiving quantities of modern aircraft capable of reaching South African or 'friendly' targets.[24]

The same analyst concluded that the large number of aircraft (125 at that time) marked for interdiction and close support, together with the considerably enlarged transport capabilities of the air force and army, gave the South African Defence Force highly mobile air and ground forces with which to repel ground attacks.

Later programme budgets indicate that landward defence continued to receive the highest priority. Table 3 covers the *total* defence budget, including those of all Government departments, for the years shown. The landward defence share of the budget rose from 17 per cent in 1969 to 25 per cent in 1972 and 31 per cent a year later. This rapid rise reflected mainly the expansion and upgrading of the army which was begun in 1968–69 and carried out over several years. The 'protracted war of low intensity' in which South Africa was engaged led the army, in the early 1970s, to review its tactical doctrine in order to adapt it better to local conditions. This review pointed to an ever-increasing need for mobility and striking power and more extensive training to a higher standard. This explains the sharp rise in expenditure in 1973–74.

Table 3: Budget Programmes for Military Expenditure (mill. current rand)

	1969-70	1972-73	1973-74
Landward defence, of which	52·2	89·5	150·8
(1) conventional	(29·7)		
(2) counter-insurgency	(22·5)		
Air defence	17·2	25·2	44·0
Maritime defence	28·8	29·9	28·9
Transport	33·6	15·8	19·0
Training	73·7	68·7	77·5
Command and control	33·2	53·7	58·0
Technical & Logistic support	22·1	69·9	75·9
Personnel services	7·3	7·4	11·5
Civil defence	1·2	1·0	0·5
General SADF support	49·7	14·5	15·0
TOTAL	319·2	357·9*	481·1

*Minus 17·7 million available from previous year. SOURCES: for 1969–70 from *WP69, op. cit.*, in ch. III, n.18, p.4; for the two later years from *WP73, op. cit.*, in ch. III, n. 19, p.8.

In conjunction with its procurement efforts abroad, the Government undertook a costly and comprehensive programme designed ultimately to achieve near self-sufficiency in arms production. It was initiated in response to growing UN pressure for punitive action against the Republic's apartheid administration, leading to a voluntary arms embargo, voted by the Security Council in December 1963. The United States had already announced a unilateral arms ban, but both Britain and France made a distinction between weapons for internal and external use, agreeing to embargo only the former. In 1964, however, the new Labour Government in Britain announced that no arms of any kind would be sold to South Africa.

This last move was an immediate spur to South Africa's domestic arms drive. Within weeks of the British announcement, the Verwoerd Government suddenly presented and rushed through Parliament a Bill creating a Munitions Production Board with sweeping authority to enter agreements, at home or abroad, for the development, manufacture or supply of any sort of weapons or munitions.[25] Its initial budgetary authority ran to 100 million rand annually. The Board was also to run the several weapons- and munitions-producing facilities which already existed under the Department of Defence. The Armaments Development and Manufacturing Corporation (Armscor) was established as a state corporation in 1968, and this subsequently assumed the dominant role in the local production of arms and munitions.

By 1967 South Africa was producing the Panhard armoured car, various types of ammunition and explosives and (allegedly) a 'wide range' of electronic equipment.[26] In 1971 the Defence Minister gave Parliament the following indicators of South Africa's production capability:

Explosives: Self-sufficiency was such that exports were under consideration.

Ammunition: Some 100 types, representing 'the largest part' of all conventional ammunition, were being produced. Only a start had been made in quick-firing ammunition, but South Africa was self-sufficient in heavy calibre and close to that state in infantry and naval ammunition. Ammunition for aircraft was either in production or under development.

Weapons: Mortars, submachine-guns and an automatic service rifle were being manufactured. Production of a 90mm anti-tank gun had begun.

Armoured Cars: Facilities existed for turning out 'practically any armoured vehicle'. (By 1972 the *Eland*, a South African offshoot of the French Panhard, was equipped with a locally produced engine and was manufactured almost entirely in South Africa.)

Missiles: The *Cactus* surface-to-air missile was soon to be 'on display'.

Aircraft: The *Impala* trainer was being produced; 'only the sophisticated components' were still acquired abroad.

Electronic equipment: Local manufacture of integrated electronic circuits was receiving 'high priority'. South Africa had an independent design and production capability for aircraft and manpack radios, mine detectors and line communications.[27]

In spite of these impressive results of South Africa's decision to force the pace of her arms output, serious deficiencies remained. A seasoned military analyst observed in 1974, 'Except for small arms, mortars, etc. much of the Army's equipment is of World War II vintage.'[28] The Defence Department claimed in 1973 that 50 per cent of the total amount spent on arms production was being paid to 200 South African contractors and sub-contractors.[29] Presumably, a large part of the remainder was spent on imports. South Africa today remains dependent on foreign suppliers for tanks, aircraft, helicopters, advanced naval vessels and sophisticated electronics. And, as shown in the summary progress report above, key components in a number of locally produced weapons continue to come from abroad.

Indeed, foreign suppliers have been essential to South Africa's weapons modernization programme since its inception in 1960. Openly acknowledged exports of arms and arms technology from Western countries, particularly Britain, France and Italy, continued into the 1970s, but supplies from Israel and several less likely sources (e.g., Jordan and India) have also been important. As one analyst noted:

> the Western embargo . . . is only as strong as its weakest link. Weapons can be moved without much difficulty within the 14 nations of NATO, and the South Africans can thus concentrate on the weaker members, notably Greece, Italy and Portugal, and Belgium; while Spain, though not within NATO, shares its equipment.[30]

As Western governments have come under increasing pressure from, and scrutiny by, black African states and domestic groups opposed to the arming of South Africa, the acquisition of weapons – heavy weapons, in particular – has become more difficult and more costly. This has been especially the case since the UN imposed a mandatory arms embargo on South Africa in 1977. The involved and circuitous arrangements to which South African arms purchasers are obliged to resort have been well documented. In one recent case, according to Anthony Sampson, 11 Bell helicopters, built in Italy under American licence, were exported to Israel[31]; from there they were shipped to an American-owned company in Singapore, then to South Africa, ultimately ending up with the Rhodesian armed forces. And, as Mr Sampson noted, arms suppliers are tempted by bribes, commissions and 'South Africa's willingness to pay twice the market price'.

Rising Defence Costs in a Growing Economy
As shown in Table 4 defence costs rose rapidly in the early 1960s and (as discussed in Chapter IV)

again in the latter half of the 1970s. In defending the virtual doubling of the arms budget for 1962, the Minister of Finance called the national budget that year 'a budget of national security'. He added, 'defence is its dominant theme and its ultimate justification.'[32]

Table 4: Defence Vote 1960/61 to 1979/80*

Financial year	Defence Vote (million current rand)	As % of budget	As % of GNP	% increase over previous year
1960/61	44	6·6	0·9	—
1961/62	61	10·0	n.a.	38
1962/63	120	n.a.	n.a.	96
1963/64	120	n.a.	n.a.	0
1964/65	230	21·0	n.a.	92
1965/66	219	n.a.	n.a.	n.a.
1966/67	248	19·0	n.a.	13
1967/68	256	n.a.	n.a.	3
1968/69	252	16·1	2·5	n.a.
1969/70	272	16·8	2·4	8
1970/71	257	13·0	n.a.	n.a.
1971/72	317	12·0	2·6	23
1972/73	335	12·0	2·3	6
1973/74	472	13·7	2·6	41
1974/75	692	16·0	3·2	47
1975/76	948	18·5	3·7	37
1976/77	1,400	17·0	4·1	48
1977/78	1,526**	19·0	5·1	9
1978/79	1,682	n.a.	n.a.	10
1979/80	1,857	n.a.	n.a.	10

*Amounts include only sums voted for the Department of Defence on the main, or Revenue, account. This covers the bulk of defence spending, but excludes expenditure by the DoD on Loan Account and defence spending by other ministries.
**Budget revised downward, due to French cancellation of a 128 million rand shipbuilding contract; this sum was added to the 1978/79 budget.
SOURCES: from official Government White Papers, yearbooks and Hansard. Since these often conflict some judicious selection has been necessary.

At the middle of the decade the terrorist threat seemed no greater, while the danger of a conventional attack across the northern borders had diminished. The Defence Vote remained fairly constant from 1964 to 1973, averaging roughly 285 million current rand a year. In terms of constant rand, according to Defence Department data, defence spending actually declined until 1970.[33] It is clear that the Minister of Defence was under pressure to reduce his spending in line with the generally perceived fading of the immediate threat. The Defence White Paper of 1969 referred to the general needs of the country in non-defence areas and claimed that the Department was making its contribution by limiting expansion and improvements 'to the absolute minimum'. A later White Paper noted that defence spending was held down in the late 1960s to help fight inflation, and that this had adverse effects in 'deferring replacement and expansion programmes and reducing stock levels.'[34]

Yet this very period was one of record-breaking growth for the South African economy. Between 1960 and 1970 GNP increased 140 per cent, and South Africa shared with Japan the world's highest growth rates: never less than 5 per cent a year, and in several years more than 10 per cent.[35] As shown in Table 4, the Defence Vote remained less than 3 per cent of GNP until 1974; thus defence cannot have been an excessive burden on the economy. South Africa's economic planners were probably most concerned over two aspects of defence spending: the large bite out of the total budget which it represented, when domestic programmes were being expanded, and its inflationary impact on an over-heating economy. In particular, it contributed to the serious shortage of skilled labour which was the major factor in inflation towards the close of the decade.

It seems very likely, however, in the absence of an economic boom and the associated heavy influx of foreign funds, that such a rapid growth in defence capabilities could not have been achieved without severe strains on the economy and a decline in the living standards of the white population.

A New Aggressiveness in Foreign Relations

Until the mid-1960s South Africa's foreign policies were largely passive and dependent on the acquiescence or active co-operation of Western powers. In large part this reflected the country's essential weakness. When South Africa became a republic in 1961, she had a small and weak defence force. Moreover she was almost totally dependent on foreign arms and at the same time was struggling to get a grip on internal security.

As discussed above, the internal situation changed dramatically during the Verwoerd and early Vorster Administrations. The apparent end to internal resistance, the country's increasing armed might, the economic boom and the growing unity of the white community all contributed to the security of white rule and led to a new self-confidence among the leadership in the late 1960s. Moreover, at about that time Britain was withdrawing from her southern African territories, and South Africa suddenly found herself the dominant power in a region of weak new states (Botswana, Lesotho, Swaziland, Zambia, Malawi and post-UDI Rhodesia) and two colonies, Angola and Mozambique, under ineffectual and crumbling Portuguese rule.

South Africa quickly took advantage of this situation to offer economic aid to the newly independent mini-states, and these – unlike earlier South African overtures to Africa – were warmly received by Lesotho, Swaziland and Malawi. This encouraged Pretoria's leaders to attempt a broader initiative.[36] Prime Minister Vorster announced in mid-1967 that the time had come for an 'outward movement' to build good relations with neighbouring states and later with those in the north, 'as saner attitudes prevailed.'[37]

But there was more to the decision than economic power, political opportunity and South African goodwill, although the South African leadership did not spell out all its motives. First, of course, there was the question of external security. Though the threat of a conventional attack against the Republic by African states had virtually evaporated by the late 1960s, the guerrilla threat was growing. In 1965 the South-West African People's Organization (SWAPO) made its first raids into Namibia from Angola. By 1967 members of the Zimbabwe African People's Union (ZAPU) and the old (and banned) South African nationalist group, the ANC, had launched a serious guerrilla campaign inside Rhodesia. The alarm with which these developments were viewed in Pretoria was indicated by the Government's extension of its own draconian security laws to Namibia in 1966 and its decision to send troops into Rhodesia in 1967. In that year ANC and ZAPU formally appealed to the Organization of African Unity (OAU) for recognition and support.

The fear that guerrilla activities might be launched from bases in neighbouring Botswana and Swaziland was undoubtedly an important factor in South Africa's efforts to build strong and lasting economic and technical ties with these states. In more general terms, South Africa's new Prime Minister, John Vorster, saw advantage in projecting South Africa's new-found power 'outwards to influence and improve the external environment in which the Republic's foreign policy was shaped'.[38] More pragmatic and far less doctrinaire than his predecessor, Mr Vorster was better able to take advantage of *ad hoc* opportunities as they arose.

Symbolic of this shift was Mr Vorster's decision to exchange ambassadors with Malawi in 1967, a move which contributed to the separation of the right wing from the National Party and which meant that special suburbs in Pretoria and Cape Town had to be created for visiting foreign diplomats. Only a few years earlier the Verwoerd Administration had rejected similar offers from Ghana, because its Embassy might become a centre for agitation against apartheid, and from Zambia for much the same reason. Mr Vorster later told Parliament that he had established diplomatic ties with Malawi because of the danger that the Communists, who, he said, had infiltrated into Tanzania, might extend their influence from the East to the West coasts, cutting Africa in two.[39]

The so-called 'outward policy' was implemented primarily through trade and aid. As explained in a leading National Party newspaper:

> It is possible that the Afrikaner may attain his rightful place all the sooner if he takes the lead in the formation of an economic bloc extending north of the Zambesi and Cunene. . . . With an eye to the security of the Republic and its economic welfare, such a bloc is of the utmost importance.[40]

In 1968 the Government established a five-million-rand fund for low-interest loans to friendly African countries, and organized a modest technical-assistance programme. The customs union agreement between South Africa and Botswana, Lesotho and Swaziland (the BLS states) was renegotiated in 1969, giving the three smaller members free access to the South African market but at the same time making them more heavily dependent on the dominant member state.

South Africa has also attempted to use the Bantustans and their leaders as builders of good will in black Africa. From time to time there was official talk of an eventual merger of frontier Bantustans with neighbouring BLS states; for example, the incorporation of Bophuthatswana into Botswana to form a greater Tswana nation was mentioned. No steps were taken to implement these ideas, however. Meanwhile, some Bantustan leaders – notably Chief Gatsha Buthelezi, leader of the Zulu homeland and a long-established opponent of apartheid, who nonetheless tries to work within it – have made 'official' visits to African states, thereby giving at least some credibility to the notion that the Bantustans are separate political entities.

That the 'outward policy' was also intended to enhance South Africa's position outside Africa was made clear in a speech by Foreign Minister Muller, in which he said:

> The West is becoming aware of our fruitful co-operation with other countries in Africa, its attitude and disposition toward us are improving, and I believe this will happen to an increasing degree. We must simply accept that *our relations with the rest of the world are determined by our relations with the African states.* (Italics added.)[41]

Viewed in this light, the 'outward policy' was a failure. Malawi remained the sole African state to establish diplomatic ties with Pretoria. South Africa's exports to Africa increased but, by 1972, totalled only 300 million rand (15 per cent of her total exports) and much of the rise appears to have been accounted for by South Africa's 'captive' trade partners, Rhodesia and the BLS states. The major black African response to the 'outward policy' was the Lusaka Manifesto of 1969, in which 13 African states rejected compromise with apartheid and called for the liberation of southern African blacks. But an olive branch of sorts was held out. 'If peaceful progress to emancipation were possible, or if changed circumstances were to make it possible in the future, we would urge our brothers in the resistance movements to use peaceful methods of struggle even at the cost of some compromise on the timing of change.'[42]

But not every black African leader was ill-disposed towards the Republic. In 1970 the Ivory

Coast's President Houphouet-Boigny declared that force was not the answer to apartheid and that he proposed to organize an African dialogue with South Africa. Pretoria naturally welcomed his proposal, which elsewhere in Africa led to strident debate and serious differences of view before finally being rejected by the OAU summit a year later (the vote was 28 to 6, with 5 abstentions).[43] Although little is known about why several Francophone states put forward the dialogue proposal, one analyst[44] notes that three of the strongest advocates – the leaders of the Ivory Coast, Madagascar and Mauritius – were among the few African leaders who shared South Africa's frequently voiced fear of the Communist threat and the need for preventive measures. Madagascar and Mauritius, in particular, would have been sensitive to the Soviet Union's growing presence in the Indian Ocean at that time.

In any event, by 1974 South Africa's Foreign Minister acknowledged that dialogue, though not dead, had 'gone underground'.[45] But the proposal had had two favourable consequences for South Africa: it had caused serious divisions over relations with the Republic to surface within black Africa, and it had led to some occasional bilateral (and unofficial) exchanges with at least three friendly OAU member states. Even as late as 1972 (that is, after the OAU vote against dialogue) South Africa's Defence Minister had been urging African states to join South Africa in establishing an anti-Communist bloc.

Of greater interest, vis-à-vis security strategy, was the aggressive, or interventionist, aspect of the 'outward policy'. Despite protestations to the contrary, South Africa has, in fact, adopted a highly interventionist policy towards nearby African states since the latter half of the 1960s. In one way or another she has intervened in Lesotho, Rhodesia, Portuguese Angola and Mozambique, and has been suspected of intervening in Malawi, Swaziland and (earlier) in the Belgian Congo.

South Africa intervened politically in Lesotho when the 1970 election returns indicated a narrow victory for the Opposition party. The incumbent Premier, Chief Leabua Jonathan, was encouraged to thwart the election results by staging a coup. Mr Vorster backed this move, asserting that the Opposition leader was undeniably a 'Peking Communist'. More to the point, South Africa is said to have recalled Lesotho's Chief Justice (a South African national), to help block any judicial challenge to Chief Jonathan's coup.[46] And South Africa moved quickly to shore up Lesotho's security force.

Economic intervention is more difficult to document. There have been, reports, however, of official South African pressure on Swaziland to prevent the establishment of industrial plants likely to compete with South African industry.[47]

Cases of military intervention are, on the whole, well documented. South African military forces, officially claimed to be police seeking to intercept terrorists headed for the Republic, were active in Rhodesia from 1967 until late 1975. According to newspaper reports, between 2,700 and 4,000 South African troops, supported by armoured cars, helicopters and spotter planes, were engaged in the Rhodesian fighting in 1968–70.[48] An additional 1,000 South African troops were reported to be helping the Portuguese in Mozambique.[49] Under a Portuguese–South African agreement of 1968, a joint command centre was established inside Angola to direct South African air-reconnaissance and troop-transport activities against Namibian and Angolan guerrillas.[50] There were also reports (never confirmed) of a secret South African military pact with Malawi[51] and of unofficial South African military support – 'white mercenaries recruited by private agencies' – for the short-lived Tshombe regime in the Congo in 1964.[52]

A candid statement of South Africa's non-intervention policy was made by Mr Vorster in 1967: 'South Africa has never interfered in the internal affairs of other nations, *except where her interests have been directly touched.* [But] I must keep in mind that her interests can be touched.' (Italics added.)[53]

In her quest for friends and allies South Africa also has looked beyond the African continent. In the latter half of the 1960s the leadership began to cultivate political and economic links with Latin America as part of a new interest in establishing closer associations among countries in the southern hemisphere. This led to a flurry of business transactions between South African firms and enterprises in a handful of Latin American states. Within a few years diplomatic relations had been established with five Central American and three South American states. In Parliament South Africa's Foreign Minister stressed Latin America's importance to South Africa, noting the continent's landmass and population; the fact that the states played an important role in the UN; were moderate on the whole and 'very aware of the Communist menace'.[54] Expanded military ties may eventually result from the visit to Latin America in March 1978 of South Africa's Air Force Chief, General Rogers.

But it is uncertain what South Africa foresees as the broader political consequences, if any, of her southern hemisphere initiative. The leadership recognizes the difficulty that other countries face in dealing with the South African 'pariah'; hence South Africa seems content to move slowly and, since she remains an economic determinist in assessing other countries' likely actions, to hope that the seeds of trade and investment will ultimately bear fruit in the form of more formal political and military co-operation. She also appears to believe, or at least to hope, that other non-Communist states will eventually come to share her own appreciation of the dangers of Communist expansionism, and that when this occurs she will be seen as a valuable potential ally.

South Africa's relations with Israel are a different matter. The two states share the status of international outcasts, and each is acutely aware that its national survival is at stake. Moreover South Africa's large Jewish community has extremely close links with Israel. Both Governments have shown concern over the advent of radical, pro-Soviet regimes in Africa. It is not surprising, then, that political, economic and military collaboration between Israel and South Africa should have flourished. Joint efforts in the military area have been particularly important to South Africa and have involved the supply and manufacture of naval vessels, aircraft and other weapons, as well as extensive ties with Israeli military technicians and advisers. There have been unconfirmed reports of collaboration in the development of counter-insurgency tactics and in nuclear technology.[55] In mid-1979 Israel appointed as her Ambassador to South Africa Joseph Harmelin, former Director of her Security Service.

In spite of her oft-expressed belief that the Western powers should be written off as potential allies, South Africa has continued to woo them. In 1972 the Defence Minister told Parliament that the Government was seeking military agreements with 'like-minded' countries, and that its defence facilities were available for 'our friends' defence as well'.[56] He mentioned, in particular, the vast expansion planned for the Simonstown naval base, which will eventually be able to handle some 50 warships, including nuclear submarines – a capacity clearly far beyond the future requirements of the South African navy alone. On another occasion he said that despite Western activities on Diego Garcia and elsewhere, Simonstown remained 'of the utmost importance' to the West, and 'in this regard we must go on making our voices heard.'[57] As part of this initiative, South Africa made office space available specifically for Western military personnel at her automated Silvermine communications centre on the Cape, which processes data on surface ships and submarines in the area.[58]

South Africa's attempts to win Western approval and friendship led to what her leader at the time considered a major concession in domestic policy (a concession which he later regretted). The issue was separate development – in this instance, the political development of the Bantustans. The Verwoerd Administration's original notion was to establish these as remote rural settlements to which the Government would send blacks whose labour was not required, or was no longer required, by the South African economy. There was some commitment to limited self-government in the Bantustans, but the Government did not plan to grant them formal independence.

In the early 1960s, however, all this changed. According to an inside observer of South African politics at the time,[59] Mr Verwoerd had been convinced by his Foreign Minister that South Africa must do something dramatic and spectacular to show the world that she was serious about political rights for blacks; otherwise, he feared, damaging international action would be taken against the Republic. Thus when Verwoerd announced to Parliament that the elective system would be introduced into the Bantustans, he saw this as an overwhelming concession to foreign pressure. 'The Bantu will

56

be able to develop into separate Bantu states. . . . It is a form of fragmentation which we would not have liked, were we able to avoid it. *In the light of pressure being exerted on South Africa*, there is no doubt that eventually this will have to be done.' (Italics added).[60]

The following year the Government formally granted the Transkei's request for immediate self-rule. This move led to serious divisions in the Party and in the Cabinet. At first Verwoerd was convinced that this 'diversionary move' had succeeded; later he acknowledged privately that it was not succeeding as he had hoped, and

he had doubts whether any countries had been impressed. He would move more slowly on the Bantustan issue in the future.[61]

The points to note here are, first, that South Africa made what to her were substantial concessions in domestic policy in response to foreign pressure; second, that since these moves were completely out of line with outside critics' perceptions of the scope and the sort of change needed in South African race policies, they were bound to fail. And this failure, in turn, led to a hardening of official South African attitudes towards future concessions.

IV. TOWARDS 'FORTRESS SOUTHERN AFRICA'

The Shrinking White Redoubt

The Lisbon coup of April 1974 brought an end to the Portuguese empire and a dramatic shift in the balance of power in southern Africa. Suddenly Rhodesia and South Africa were the only remaining white-ruled states in sub-Saharan Africa. No longer would South Africa's or Rhodesia's borders enjoy the protection afforded by a co-operative Portuguese Adminis-tration (faltering though it was) in the vast northern buffer zones of Angola and Mozam-bique. Particularly worrying to Pretoria's leaders was the prospect that self-declared Marxist regimes in these territories would provide sanc-tuary and passage for guerrillas operating against South-West Africa, Rhodesia and South Africa herself. But above all South Africa feared a repetition of the bloodshed and chaos of the 1960 Congo crisis, with rival factions seeking outside help in their battle for power and the high risk of spill-over into South Africa, either through the spread of the fighting or as a con-sequence of its exemplary effect on South Africa's blacks.

The Vorster Administration made a clear dis-tinction, however, between the Angolan and Mozambican dangers. Mozambique's heavy economic dependence on South Africa was seen as an important factor in securing the 'friendly co-operation' of her new leaders: economic self-interest, it was felt, would restrain her from undertaking hostile action against the Republic. Hence when the Machel Government came to power in June 1975 South Africa quickly arranged

to renew the long-standing agreements for tech-nical aid to Mozambique's railways and main port, as well as the special convention under which Mozambicans working in South African mines had 60 per cent of their earnings remitted in gold at the official rate.[1] In addition, Mr Vorster saw little chance of political turbulence following the transfer of power in Mozambique, since there was only one unchallenged national liberation group, Frente de Libertaçao de Moçambique (FRELIMO), claiming the right to power. Indeed, Mr Vorster passed up the chance to support a short-lived *putsch* attempt by dis-gruntled whites, although it has since been alleged that Mr P. W. Botha had tried (without Vorster's knowledge) to supply weapons to Mozambican counter-revolutionaries.[2]

Angola was a different story. South Africa had very little economic leverage over her. Nor did the growing strife among competing nationalist groups promise an orderly or peaceful transition there. Not the least of South Africa's concerns was the likely support which a radical Angolan government would provide to SWAPO.

In the autumn of 1974, however (that is, some six months after the coup in Lisbon) Mr Vorster was offering South African co-operation to both new states, and he expressed the hope that sound, stable governments would come to power – a clear indication that Pretoria was already resigned to living with black-ruled Marxist neighbours, provided they got their houses in order and avoided becoming a de-stabilizing influence in the region.

Detente

These gestures towards Mozambique and Angola were part of a broad initiative launched in June 1974 under the label 'detente'. Coming in the immediate aftermath of the Lisbon coup, detente was Pretoria's response to the new situation in southern Africa. The essence of the policy was that South Africa should assert vigorous leadership in regional affairs and should win the co-operation of black African states – conservative states, in particular – in order to bring stability to the area and to prevent the further spread of radicalism and chaos.

Rhodesia was the major test for detente.[3] Between September 1974 and February 1975 South Africa conducted high-level, secret talks with African leaders to find a peaceful solution to the growing Rhodesian crisis. Mr Vorster himself assumed a major role in the discussions. The importance he attached to a peaceful settlement was shown by his willingness, for the first time, to apply pressure on the Salisbury regime. To force the intransigent Mr Smith to the bargaining table and to demonstrate to sceptical black African leaders South Africa's *bona fides* as an honest broker, Mr Vorster announced in February that South African forces would be withdrawn from Rhodesia, where they had played an active counter-insurgency role for some seven years. Other, more subtle pressures (for example, slowing down the vital through rail traffic to Rhodesia) were not lost on Mr Smith, who tried to appeal, over Mr Vorster's head, to pro-white Rhodesian sentiment inside South Africa. Following a showdown between the two white leaders in March 1975, Rhodesia agreed to Mr Vorster's demand that she release the nationalist leader, the Reverend Sithole, from gaol, so that he could take part in the forthcoming settlement talks. In April, President Kaunda – whose representatives had held more than 15 secret meetings with South Africa – announced that Pretoria had agreed to remove its forces from Rhodesia by 31 May.

The point to note is that Mr Vorster put himself and his Administration at some political risk through his Rhodesian initiative. Among South African whites there was, and still is, a residue of sympathy for 'Smitty' and the beleaguered white minority inside Rhodesia. Indeed, Mr Eschel Roodie, South Africa's disgraced ex-Secretary for Information, has charged the then Defence Minister, Mr Botha, with secretly planning to reintroduce South African troops into Rhodesia, a plan which was allegedly thwarted only when the scheme was reported to Mr Vorster.[4] Many English- and Afrikaans-speaking South Africans have close family ties with the whites in Rhodesia. Had the Smith Government collapsed or a slaughter of whites occurred following South Africa's troop withdrawal, Mr Vorster might well have been forced to drop both his detente policy and his Foreign Minister to placate white criticism, particularly from the hardliners on the right wing of his own party.

Even as Pretoria was preparing to remove its forces from Rhodesia, President Nyerere was drumming up support among African states for a formal rejection of detente with South Africa. Apparently fearful that South Africa's shift in her policy towards Rhodesia, together with her offers of technical aid to black states, would weaken the OAU's anti-apartheid stance, Mr Nyerere drafted a firm statement, the 'Dar Declaration', which was signed by 16 states in April 1975. It did not reject consultation with Pretoria on the Rhodesian problem or other matters, but it ruled out any concessions towards South Africa herself, where (it was stated) black Africa must be prepared for armed struggle if peaceful means failed to bring about majority rule.

Mr Vorster told Parliament that such declarations would not deter him from holding discussions with those African states which wanted to do so, and he went so far as to predict a period of more open diplomacy ahead. By then, however, even the most conservative African leaders were reluctant to establish any closer ties with South Africa. Indeed, in the subsequent disclosures of Mr Roodie's secret projects it was alleged that South Africa had paid 'substantial' sums to leaders in Gabon, Liberia and the Ivory Coast to win their co-operation on diplomatic, trade and economic issues.[5]

In the event detente finally died in late August 1975, in a railway carriage on the Victoria Falls Bridge over the Zambesi, where Premier Vorster and President Kaunda had finally brought together Ian Smith and Rhodesia's top black nationalist leaders, Joshua Nkomo, the Reverend Sithole, Bishop Abel Muzorewa and Robert Mugabe. Serious dissension among the nationalists enabled Mr Smith to hold out against making any concessions. Nor could South Africa apply heavy pressure on him, since the nationalists offered no credible grounds for assuming that they could provide a stable and orderly alternative to the Smith regime. The Victoria Bridge meeting – the high-water-mark of detente – led to a formal split in the two main Rhodesian nationalist groups. Joshua Nkomo left the ANC and Robert Mugabe formed his own militant wing of the Zimbabwe African National Union (ZANU). By the autumn President Nyerere had persuaded the other Front Line presidents that peaceful change in Rhodesia was no longer attainable and that the Lusaka Manifesto's 'alternative strategy' – that is, intensified guerrilla war – must be invoked. It would be three years before a new South African Administration would again launch an African initiative, and then the Botha initiative would represent a new, more militant approach. Meanwhile, the deteriorating situation in Angola began to overshadow the problems in Rhodesia.

The Angolan Venture

By March/April 1975 the eruption of heavy fighting among rival national liberation groups in Angola signalled the collapse of the Alvor accord and the beginning of foreign military intervention in Angola on a large scale. In late March Frente Nacional de Libertação de Angola (FNLA) units, trained and armed largely by China and Zaire, began arriving in large numbers in Luanda, where they challenged the Movimento Popular para a Libertação de Angola (MPLA)'s bid for power. To build up the MPLA against the better armed FNLA, the Soviet Union sent in several plane-loads of weapons via Congo-Brazzaville during March, to be followed by six ship-loads of arms, which were unloaded in Luanda between April and June.[6] In late July the United States decided to supply $60 million worth of arms to both the FNLA and the Uniao Nacional para a Independencia Total de Angola (UNITA).[7]

South Africa's initial involvement in Angola was modest. In June, leaders of both the FNLA and UNITA came secretly to South Africa, seeking aid.[8] By July, she was supporting both groups.[9] Apparently this early assistance was limited to the supply of small arms and other military and non-military goods.

From press reports and official South African sources it appears that South Africa did not have any advance master plan for her Angolan involvement. Rather, like other intervening countries, she seems to have been drawn into a step-by-step escalation, over the next six months, mostly through a series of *ad hoc* responses to growing fears and perceived tactical opportunities. During July South Africa watched with alarm the collapse of order and the spread of chaos in southern Angola, in the wake of the Portuguese withdrawal. SWAPO raids into Namibia increased, and 11,000 Angolan refugees fled across the border. According to South Africa's Defence Minister, the MPLA had deployed as far as the southern border and now harboured SWAPO guerrillas in its ranks.[10]

South Africa first became directly involved in early August, when her workers at the joint Angolan–South African Calueque Dam, inside Angola, were allegedly 'threatened by foreign soldiers'. A platoon of South African soldiers went to investigate; a skirmish followed, and South Africa informed Lisbon that she would occupy Calueque until order and control were re-established. She later acknowledged that she had also participated in 'hot pursuit' and 'other engagements' in response to SWAPO attacks on South-West African tribal administrators and police near the Angolan border. Moreover, to stem the flow of refugees, South Africa established and administered two refugee camps *inside* Angola. Thus by midsummer southern Angola had become a no-man's-land, where South African forces found they could move about freely, guarding hydro-electric installations, running refugee centres and seeking out SWAPO camps in the hope of delivering the organization a crippling blow.

From there it was but a short jump to the decision to play a far more active role by helping UNITA and the FNLA to block the MPLA's efforts to gain control of the country. This course was the more attractive since the United States, and apparently several African states as well, were already helping the two anti-MPLA groups.

The immediate South African objective was to help UNITA to clear and hold southern Angola, and to assist FNLA to do the same in the north, by the forthcoming independence date, 11 November 1975.[11] At the very least Pretoria hoped that

59

this would lead to an OAU-inspired political solution, giving the two non-Marxist nationalist movements a decisive voice in the new government. The South African leadership may even have hoped for a partitioned Angola, the vast southern half of which would be a friendly buffer state under the control of Mr Savimbi's UNITA.

In late September a South African liaison officer and 18 instructors, together with three anti-tank weapons and some machine guns, joined a UNITA company, which then halted an MPLA advance against UNITA in central Angola. As Cuban troops reinforced the MPLA in mid-October, South Africa's involvement quickly accelerated. In the south, a South African-led combat group (code-named 'Zulu') of about 1,000 FNLA and UNITA troops, augmented by South African armoured cars and mortars, moved rapidly west. In two weeks it had advanced 400 miles, overcoming MPLA–Cuban defenders in several towns, to reach the sea at Mocamedes. This drive effectively cleared the MPLA from the southern third of Angola. A week later this group captured Benguela and Lobito, important coastal towns at the terminus of the Benguela railroad. At that point the South African forces added four 88mm guns to 'Zulu'.

In central Angola South Africa organized a second combat group ('Foxbat'), originally comprising South African-trained UNITA forces and a squadron of South African armoured cars. In the last ten days of October 'Foxbat' recaptured five cities from MPLA–Cuban forces and advanced more than 500 miles north towards Luanda.

According to the official South African account, some sort of 'mediation by go-betweens' took place at about the time of the Angolan Independence Day (11 November) and led to expectations of a political settlement. When this effort collapsed South Africa and her allies faced stiffer resistance, as Cuban troops and large numbers of Soviet weapons had begun moving into Angola. The introduction of 122mm Soviet rockets prompted South Africa to bring in 140mm artillery for her combat groups. As fighting intensified in November and December, South Africa ultimately had 'just under' 2,000 troops involved. At the time that it inflicted the heaviest defeat of the war on a Cuban–MPLA force at 'Bridge 14' (otherwise unidentified),

'Foxbat' consisted of a company of South African infantry, an armoured car squadron, 12 heavy artillery pieces, a platoon of mortars and an engineer element, in addition to three FNLA–UNITA companies. In the battle – which Communist Press sources admitted was a disaster for Cuba – South Africa claims to have killed 200 Cuban soldiers and an equal number of MPLA.

The combined South African–UNITA–FNLA forces continued fighting through December, apparently without suffering any military reverses. Indeed, according to South Africa, they were poised for an assault on Luanda and 'could have conquered the whole of Angola'. But on 22 January 1976 South Africa withdrew all her forces, except those patrolling the border, back to 50 kilometres inside Angola.

Why did South Africa withdraw? South African spokesmen have not been forthcoming on this question. Political factors were crucial. Contrary to Pretoria's expectations, the OAU failed to support South Africa's intervention in mid-January. About half the member states condemned South Africa's action but not that of Cuba or the Soviet Union, while the more conservative half called for a cease-fire and the withdrawal of *all* foreign forces. Moreover, on 19 December the American Senate had overwhelmingly passed an amendment barring aid to any Angolan faction without Congressional approval. South Africa thus found herself politically in an extremely exposed position, with virtually no prospect of further international support for her intervention. Beyond this it is by no means clear what would have happened, or what the South African leadership thought might happen, if South Africa had occupied Luanda. It is doubtful, for example, whether she would have wanted to remain as an occupation force to support and defend a UNITA–FNLA government against growing Soviet–Cuban support to the MPLA.

The widely accepted view that the South African decision was a purely political one is not satisfactory. Soviet weapons and Cuban soldiers had been arriving in Angola at an increasing rate since October. Some of the December engagements had been much tougher than the easy sweep through the south a few months earlier. Shortly before the withdrawal Mr Vorster told the Press that the Soviet Union was sending in 'sophisticated weapons: tanks, 122mm rockets mounted in clusters of 50 . . . infantry-borne SAMS. *Only big powers* can affect this arsenal. . . . *It is certainly beyond our limits*' (italics added).[12] Moreover, supply was a growing problem, as the South African forces had moved 1,000 kilometres or more from the South-West African border. In sum, withdrawal was prompted by important military, as well as political considerations. Without broad international support and military co-operation, South Africa faced a bleak future in Angola.

The Angolan venture was, in the event, a costly one for the Vorster Government. It wiped out Mr Vorster's carefully nurtured (though never widely accepted) image of South Africa as a benign and non-interfering force in southern African affairs. It led to widespread international condemnation and put additional strains on South Africa's relations with the West and with friendly African states. Most important, it gave the Soviet Union and Cuba a pretext for massive Cuban military intervention, thereby bringing about the very situation which South Africa has always most feared – a strong, conventional Communist military presence of some 20,000 Cuban forces on her borders. In addition, South Africa's withdrawal was seen by some in Africa as a military defeat.

Domestically, too, there were costs. Although South African casualties were light – 43 killed and about a hundred wounded – these came as a shock to South African whites, who had been told nothing about the invasion of Angola until after the South African troops had been removed. Furthermore, in spite of the low-level counter-insurgency in which South Africa had been engaged for a decade, there had been almost no casualties until the Angolan episode. In early 1972, for example, the Defence Minister reported to Parliament that counter-insurgency warfare had claimed no South African soldiers' lives. The white public was therefore unprepared for the Angolan campaign's casualties. Indeed, parents of young national servicemen complained to Parliament that their sons had been sent to fight in foreign lands without parental approval. As a result – and, since future cross-border operations remained an option – in early 1976 Mr Botha pushed through Parliament an Act allowing SADF personnel to 'perform service against an enemy at any place outside the Republic.'[13]

Surprisingly, however, the Government survived the Angolan disaster with relatively little public outcry. No ministers were sacked, nor were any special commissions of inquiry constituted. This would have been almost inconceivable in a Western democracy. But the South African Government was able to keep the whole operation secret for six months, thanks in part to an extremely tough Official Secrets Act. By the time potential critics knew about the intervention, it was all over. In addition, the Government (particularly the Defence Minister) was apparently successful in shifting the blame elsewhere. Dark hints emanated from Government leaders (sometimes to be retracted later) about alleged American perfidy, the failure of some (unnamed) African states to rally to support the South African initiative and the strong desire of UNITA leaders to limit the operation to clearing and holding only their own tribal territory. Perhaps the most candid explanation was Mr Vorster's statement to Parliament in January 1976 that South Africa had gone in 'to chase Cuba and the MPLA away from the dam. . . . It is rather difficult, Sir, when you chase a man to decide when to stop.'[14]

The Angolan venture also had important implications for future South African plans. The fighting, aside from giving the SADF its first experience in conventional warfare, demonstrated a need for longer-range artillery and armoured fire-power. It may also have led military leaders, who allegedly opposed the deep military penetration, to seek a greater voice in central decision-making. But most important was the heightened threat which South Africa's leaders perceived in the presence of 20,000 Cuban troops, armed with sophisticated Soviet weapons, stationed within easy reach of South Africa's borders – thus bringing the Communist threat much nearer.

The Legacy of Soweto

In June 1976 South Africa was suddenly and unexpectedly struck by her most serious racial disturbances of this century – the so-called 'Soweto riots'. Between June and November, when serious protest finally died out, demonstrations, boycotts, arson and rioting had occurred in almost every non-white township and university in South Africa, leaving some

600 dead (including four whites) and thousands injured, as well as widespread damage to property. Moreover, the disturbances had spilled over into some white areas of Cape Town, Johannesburg and some smaller cities.

The immediate issue that touched off the protests was the continued use of Afrikaans as a medium of instruction in social sciences and mathematics in black high schools, but there is impressive evidence to suggest that the underlying discontent ran much deeper. The burden of public testimony before the Cillie Commission – the official commission of inquiry chaired by Chief Judge of the Transvaal Justice Cillie – pointed to generalized frustration among non-whites and antagonism towards 'the system' as the root problem. This is consistent with the results of a painstaking survey of urban black attitudes in the Durban area which was undertaken in 1972.[15] For more than half of those interviewed the major areas of discontent were economic conditions, general race discrimination and resentment of whites. Almost 70 per cent clearly identified the source of their problems as white policies, laws and discrimination.

The Government responded to Soweto with a massive security clamp-down, as well as some token concessions to non-whites. In the 15 months following the outbreak of disturbances the police detained 2,430 people under various security laws. During 1976 and 1977 over 1,000 whites were added to the South African active police force, bringing its total strength to roughly 35,000 (19,000 whites and 16,000 blacks), while another thousand swelled the police reserve to more than 18,000.[16] Security laws were further tightened; the prohibition on open-air meetings was kept in force; and bannings and preventive detention were widespread. In October 1977, as student protest and school boycotts continued to plague the Government as it prepared for a general election, security police carried out a wave of arrests and bannings of journalists, Churchmen, black community leaders and various organizations, all of which were outspoken opponents of apartheid.

Soweto was a serious setback for the Government. The world was forcefully reminded yet again of the inequitable nature of apartheid and of the depth of black resentment and frustration. In early 1977 the Western powers drafted their Declaration on Southern Africa, calling on South Africa to take steps, *inter alia*, towards the elimination of apartheid and the granting of equal rights to all population groups. Internal events undoubtedly helped to win support for the UN's mandatory arms embargo of November 1977.

But Soweto has come back to haunt South Africa in a more direct way – and with more serious implications. During the troubles of 1976–77 roughly 3,000 South African blacks, most of them young and many of them students, fled the country.[17] Most hoped to continue their education elsewhere, according to a survey taken at the time, but it was estimated that seven per cent committed themselves to military training under the banners of the ANC or the PAC.[18] The proportion may have grown, particularly as the Soweto refugees found more attractive options denied them. In June 1978 the Chief of South Africa's security police alleged that 4,000 black South Africans were then undergoing guerrilla training in Mozambique, Angola, Tanzania and Libya.[19]

Whatever the number, the Soweto refugees seem to be in large part responsible for the recent increase in armed guerrilla incidents inside South Africa. Indeed, the security police have explicitly linked the Soweto exodus with a rise in urban terrorism.[20] During 1977–78 the police reported 19 separate 'notable incidents' of terrorism inside the Republic, in which there were 11 deaths (including those of seven terrorists) and 33 wounded (of which one was a terrorist). According to a press analysis, the terrorist campaign had 'reached the stage where well armed groups with sophisticated Communist-made weapons [were] crossing the borders trying to reach South Africa's urban areas'.[21] The incidents include a number of skirmishes between infiltrators and police. Although the 19 incidents occurred in eight general areas of South Africa, six took place in the Johannesburg region and four along the Botswana border. By May 1978 police had announced the capture of 'scores' of foreign-trained terrorists, and 66 separate security trials were going on in various parts of the country.[22]

Far from playing these incidents down, the Government has given them full publicity, probably to alert the public and to win its active support in the counter-insurgency campaign.

But the threat seems real enough. Of particular concern is infiltration through the sparsely populated areas along Botswana's border with the nominally independent Bantustan, Bophuthatswana, from which it is only 160 kilometres or so to Johannesburg. In January 1979 South Africa announced the capture of an ANC terrorist in this area and warned Botswana that further incidents could lead to 'hot pursuit' across the border. South African farmers in this area have been abandoning 'front line' farms, 60 per cent of which are now deserted. Both security and economics are responsible for this abandonment.[23] Official concern is reflected in a Defence Department study proposing that demobilized servicemen be given financial inducements to settle on farms along the border.

The potential for serious trouble from infiltrators in the future was suggested by an audacious attack on a Soweto police station in May 1979. Three men armed with AK-47 automatic rifles and grenades killed a guard and wounded others, then hurled grenades into the station's archives and offices, starting a fire which badly damaged the building and destroyed 'hundreds of police dossiers'. They scattered ANC pamphlets as they left.[24]

Towards a Garrison State

The years 1975–79 witnessed the cumulative militarization of South African society. Although South Africa's leaders have denied that this has occurred, the evidence is persuasive. It includes:

A dramatic change in the perceived threat and in South Africa's response to it;

Sharp increases in defence spending and a rise in the defence share of the budget and GNP;

An enlarged military 'presence' in South African life;

The growing role and involvement of the military in policy-making;

A broad mobilization of the population.

Mr P. W. Botha, when Defence Minister, told his provincial Party Congress in 1977, 'We are moving more and more in the direction in which the state of Isreal has already been since 1948. And that country already spends more than 50 per cent of its budget on defence.'[25] Even by early 1975 – before the Angolan venture and the influx of Cubans into southern Africa – the sweeping changes that were occurring in neighbouring states were already having a considerable impact on South African defence policies. The biennial White Paper on defence issued in March 1975 spoke darkly of 'undesirable influences and tendencies' in Angola, Mozambique and Rhodesia and warned that Portuguese developments:

will undoubtedly encourage the radical elements in revolutionary organizations inside and outside [South Africa] and incite them to greater efforts. *They regard Angola and Mozambique as new allies and potential new operational bases for action against Rhodesia and the [Republic].*[26]

At that time the only 'actual physical' threat to South Africa was seen to be the guerrillas: specifically 'armed elements of [the ANC and the PAC] accommodated in neighbouring states... attempting to infiltrate South Africa to conduct terrorism, sabotage, and subversion with a view to overthrowing the existing order'.[27]

To meet the new conditions no radical changes were proposed, but rather a shift in emphasis among strategic priorities. First was a need for greater vigilance and improved technology in order to guard against surprise attack. In meeting this requirement South Africa had decided a few months earlier to expand coastal surveillance through the acquisition of patrol vessels, short-range maritime patrol aircraft and coastal radar stations, as well as to establish anti-sabotage units in her ports. Orders were placed for minesweepers and submarines to counter the threat of a limited commodity blockade. Ground forces were split into a Conventional Force and a Force for Counter-Insurgency and Terrorism, and officers in charge of the latter were upgraded in rank.

A second proposed shift was to enhance the credibility of South Africa's conventional forces, because 'our capability . . . to counter-attack *or to take preventive action* against bases supporting aggression against us . . . requires adequate conventional capability on land, in the air, and at sea.' (Italics added.)[28]

Since South Africa claimed that the only real threat at that time came from the guerrillas, and since conventional weapons are not particularly suitable for counter-insurgency, the need for an enhanced conventional capability probably reflected South Africa's intention to conduct

63

large-scale pre-emptive and punitive raids against guerrilla bases in neighbouring countries and her fears that those raids might invite conventional strikes in retaliation. Thus in mid-1974 South Africa is believed to have bought 54 *Tigercat* surface-to-air missiles and 41 *Centurion* Mark V tanks[29] – weapons that were not at all appropriate for dealing with SWAPO raiders or ANC infiltrators but were suited for meeting ground attack from, for example, Zambia. In fact, there was virtually no risk of such attack, since the military weakness and domestic troubles of nearby states meant they were in no position to take on South Africa, even with her newest weapon purchases.

A year later, however, the Defence Minister said that the presence of Cuban troops and sophisticated weapons in Angola has 'introduced a completely new factor ... virtually overnight'.[30] He reminded Parliament that South Africa was a middle-rank power which could not take on the whole world:

> South Africa can establish a balanced defence force to defend itself firstly against terrorism . . . and this we are fully able to do. . . . Secondly, *we must have a deterrent to be able to resist a fairly heavy conventional attack* on South Africa. (Italics added.)[31]

The Minister then described South Africa's growing conventional capability. He noted that she was 'better off' as far as heavy artillery was concerned ('the goods are here') She produced her own armoured battle vehicle ('on display soon') and was strengthening her modern anti-aircraft equipment. She had also acquired large numbers of anti-tank projectiles, was 'improving' her air-to-air projectiles and was buying naval attack craft. In 1977 he noted the acquisition of new long-range strike aircraft.[32]

South Africa responded in other ways as well. A State Security Council was established in 1977 to formulate a 'total national strategy' – that is, a co-ordinated and comprehensive programme to tighten national security planning.[33] The Defence Amendment Act of 1977 legalized for the first time the deployment of SADF personnel 'at any place outside the Republic', suggesting that the Angolan episode had by no means dampened the Defence Department's commitment to pre-emptive attack.[34]

Most revealing of South Africa's heightened threat perception, however, was a large-scale military exercise conducted in September 1977. Unlike previous manoeuvres, which had been concerned with counter-insurgency, the aim of *Exercise Blitz One* was to test a mechanized combat group in conventional warfare. The South African forces used artillery, armoured cars, tanks and mortar units against the 'enemy' – an armoured division supported by aircraft – which had entered South Africa *via* Namibia and had reached the Upington area, some 135 kilometres inside South Africa.

In 1978 South Africa announced the establishment of a school for conventional combat training, where brigade-size exercises could be held.[35] It was also announced that paratroop strength would be increased, and a parachute brigade headquarters was formed at Bloemfontein.

Defence expenditure in the last half of the 1970s was consistent with South Africa's heightened threat perception. After remaining stable at 300–400 million rand a year in the early 1970s, the Defence Vote rose steeply to almost 700 million rand in 1974/75, and a five-year programme to expand and modernize the SADF was initiated. Two years later the Vote had doubled, to 1,400 million rand. Even the cancellation of major arms deliveries following the 1977 arms embargo failed to reduce the Defence Vote, which amounted to 1,600 million rand in 1978/79 and over 1,800 million rand in 1979/80. Only part of this increase was due to inflation. From 1976 the Defence Vote accounted for almost 20 per cent of the budget and roughly 5 per cent of GNP – substantially above the corresponding figures of 12–13 per cent and 2.5 per cent of the early 1970s.

The Growing Role of the Military

The military presence in South African society has grown markedly, particularly since the Angolan crisis of 1975. Major industrial installations have been designated 'national key points', to be defended by local militia units in case of emergency. In 1977 Mr Vorster announced plans to double the number of school cadets (to 300,000). A year later the decision was taken to train the cadets during regular school hours and school holidays and to make obligatory their attendance at 'adventure camps'.[36] The initial period of continuous military service for draftees was doubled from one year to two in January 1978 [37] In 1977 the army's women's college began to admit 500 entrants a year as against 150, its previous intake.[38] In 1977 local authorities throughout the country established committees whose function was to facilitate adjustment of national servicemen to civilian life. At the same time the SADF was seeking improved pension benefits for the war-disabled. A new military hospital was opened in 1979; by then, too, a second one was half-finished.[39] By the end of 1977 723,000 white South African civilians were licensed to carry fire-arms; 150,000 licences had been issued in 1977 alone.[40]

The military establishment has assumed a more prominent role in the policy-making process since the Angolan venture. Symbolic of its emergence as a political force was the conspicuous part it played at the celebrations when Mr Vorster was inaugurated as President in October 1978. His swearing-in was followed by the biggest jet fly-past ever seen in the southern hemisphere. In addition, as the official SADF journal noted, 'when the time came for Mr Vorster to take the oath, top Defence Force officers rose to flank him.'[41]

But the military has assumed a political role beyond that of mere symbolism. In October 1978, when five Western Foreign Ministers arrived in Pretoria to take up the Namibian issue with the new Prime Minister, Mr P. W. Botha, the South African side was joined for the first time by its top military official, General Magnus Malan, Chief of the Defence Staff.[42] The General has since come to play a major role in the Namibia negotiations, and in September 1979 he was reported to be strongly opposed to the West's proposal for a demilitarized zone along the Angolan border.[43]

At the inter-departmental level, too, the military has recently become broadly engaged in the planning process. A new study of South African decision-making states: 'SADF representatives now take part in all inter-departmental meetings, regardless of their subjects or whether direct SADF interests . . . are involved.'[44] With increasing intrusion of military matters into the national life of the Republic, the role and influence of South Africa's military establishment seem likely to continue to grow in the next few years.

Manpower

As South Africa has moved towards a war footing, the problem of manpower has continued to be the greatest constraint on Government actions. Since only whites can be drafted, the SADF must draw heavily on the country's pool of 750,000 white males between the ages of 18 and 35.[45] Moreover, this same group accounts for some 40 per cent of South Africa's economically active whites: hence the continuing tension between the manpower needs of the armed forces and those of the private sector. From the SADF's standpoint, the essential problem is that of retaining skilled personnel – technicians and instructors, in particular – in the face of attractive offers from commerce and industry. The rate of attrition in the PF has been about 15 per cent in recent years, and the average length of stay is only 6.5 years.[46] As a result, the Defence Minister has been unable to form a PF brigade to serve as the SADF's basic force-in-being, nor is the PF able to provide all the training cadres needed for the planned expansion of the SADF. In 1977 the PF comprised only 7 per cent of total SADF strength, as against the 1981 target of 13 per cent.[47]

Prior to 1977 South Africa could count on a substantial number of white immigrants each year to meet her growing manpower requirements. Indeed, the Government's earlier economic growth target of 5–6 per cent a year was based on an assumed annual (net) inflow of 30,000 whites. But in 1977, following the Soweto riots of the year before, South Africa suffered a net loss of about 1,200 whites. In 1978 the net outflow rose to 2,500.[48]

The Defence Department has recently taken a number of steps to ameliorate the manpower crisis, with both the SADF and the economy in mind. With the extension of the initial service period from 12 to 24 months for draftees, the SADF is able to use them as instructors and in regular line units after their initial year's training. In 1978 27,000 national servicemen were in training. The civilian sector also benefits, since the burden of service now falls on young school-leavers, rather than on experienced men drawn from civilian jobs for extra tours of duty. In a move to encourage national servicemen to stay on after their two-year mandatory tour, their pay was approximately doubled in 1979.[49] In addition, a recent citizenship Bill declared every white male up to the age of 25 a South African citizen liable for military duty.[50] Since 1970 a total of 100,000 immigrants have registered for national service.

The Government has also taken steps in the past few years to expand the participation of other population groups in military service. This is particularly the case with regard to coloureds, who have been serving in naval, infantry, anti-aircraft and other units since the Cape Coloured Training Corps was re-activated in 1963. By 1977 the Government had accepted, in principle, the recommendation of a special commission on coloured affairs which called for a national service and a cadet force for coloureds.[51] With the creation of an Indian Training Battalion in 1975, Indians, too, were being admitted into the SADF.[52] By 1979 coloureds and Indians together made up 20 per cent of the navy's PF personnel.[53] Women are also playing a growing role in the SADF; increasing numbers are enrolling in military training schools, and 6,000 are now serving in non-combat roles in the Commandos.[54]

The arming of blacks remains a sensitive issue among the white electorate; hence the Government has moved with great caution. In 1975, a year after the army had begun the training of black volunteers, it was disclosed that only 35 blacks were involved.[55] By 1978 the army's black complement had grown into a battalion, the 21st, numbering 515 blacks up to the rank of corporal. The 21st Battalion has served on the Angolan border, where it won its white officers' praise for its performance in combat. The army plans to train at least four other black battalions, but this is likely to take a long time. Mr Botha's plan to arm blacks has almost certainly met with resistance and serious misgivings within his party. Moreover, the selection and training of black volunteers will pose problems. These include the all-important question of loyalty, the shortage of training cadres, black language and educational deficiencies. Clearly a combat failure (or, worse still, a mutiny) would spell the end of Mr Botha's scheme to augment the army with black volunteers.

Meanwhile, the SADF has trained six ethnic battalions of Namibians, which have been serving on the Angolan border and which will form the backbone of an independent Namibian army, to be formed some time in 1980.[56] The SADF also trained an independent military force for the Transkei and is training similar forces for the other nominally independent Bantustans – for Bophuthatswana since 1977 and for Venda since September 1979.

The SADF appears to have encountered some serious opposition to military service among whites. In 1977 an SADF colonel, writing on combat leadership, warned:

> we are losing much of the quality among our junior leaders. The number of good young men who avoid a military career *because of current social attitudes* cannot be known, but *is undoubtedly large* . . . the day is past when we can expect a great supply of bright young men from whom we may pick our leaders. (Italics added.)[57]

The Government has consistently followed a hard line on conscientious objectors, who now are jailed for the maximum period of their service liability. Similarly, in an obvious attempt to silence the South African Council of Churches, which has condoned resistance to military service, the Government has sought to make it a criminal offence to advise anyone not to bear arms in defence of the country.

The 1973 White Paper noted a generally unsatisfactory public attitude towards national service and military preparedness, as well as a declining interest in voluntary duty.[58] Since subsequent White Papers and parliamentary debates no longer identify this as a problem, it may well be that government efforts over the past few years to put the country on a military footing and to engender in its citizens a siege mentality have been effective in dampening opposition to military service. Moreover, the large white exodus in the past few years has undoubtedly included many of those seriously opposed to service in the armed forces.

Deteriorating Relations with the West

The high-water-mark in South Africa's recent dealings with the West occurred in the spring of 1976, when Dr Kissinger sought South African co-operation and support for his peace initiatives in Rhodesia and Namibia. By the end of the year, however, Pretoria's Western ties had suffered a sharp deterioration, which has persisted into the new decade. The repercussions of South Africa's invasion of Angola and the eruption of black frustrations in Soweto were, of course, major factors. But there were others. By the end of 1976 the Geneva Conference on Rhodesia had collapsed, and the Namibian negotiations had reached an impasse. The defeat of Gerald Ford in November heralded the advent of the Carter Administration and a new, tougher American policy towards South Africa.

In Pretoria Defence Minister Botha was already expressing doubts about the usefulness of contacts with the West. Prime Minister Vorster elaborated this theme in a sombre New Year's address to the nation. Because, he said, the West had 'lost the will to take a firm stand against the increasing [Communist] menace', the Communist states knew from the Angolan experience that they could attack any country in Africa with impunity.

> If therefore a Communist onslaught should be made against South Africa, directly or under camouflage, South Africa will have to face it alone, and certain countries which profess to be anti-Communist will even refuse to sell [us] arms . . . This is the reality of our situation.[59]

Nor did subsequent events inside South Africa do anything to soften Western attitudes or deflect outside attention from the iniquities of apartheid. In September 1977 a popular and much-respected black leader, Steve Biko, died in detention. The inquest revealed to the world not only the beatings and neglect that caused his death but also the appalling arrogance and callousness of South African prison officials towards black prisoners. In October, when hundreds of prominent black opponents of apartheid were rounded up and gaoled in a sudden security sweep, the world was reminded again of the important role accorded to the security police in maintaining the system. In November 1977 the UN adopted a mandatory arms embargo against South Africa.

A further source of strain emerged when South Africa was suspected of preparing to explode a nuclear device in the summer of 1977. This development, which is analysed in the next chapter, led to some tough, mostly low-key exchanges between South Africa and the Western powers, particularly the US, which left each side suspicious of, and uncompromising towards, the other.

The only important area of continuing co-operation between South Africa and the West since the collapse of the Kissinger initiative has been the Namibian problem. Yet this, too, contributed to strained relations towards the end of 1978. A new Namibian initiative was launched early in 1977 by the five permanent members of the UN Security Council, the United States, Britain, West Germany, France and Canada. In working for an internationally acceptable settlement, the so-called 'Contact Group', made up of the Ambassadors of the five Western powers, made it clear at the start that a South African walk out or refusal to negotiate would mean that the Western states would no longer be able to veto UN calls for sanctions.

While the Front Line states (Angola, Mozambique, Botswana, Zambia and Tanzania) nudged SWAPO towards concessions, the Western Five applied pressure on South Africa. In 1977 Pretoria agreed to halt the internal settlement process it had set in motion two years earlier. As the talks with the Western Contact Group dragged on into 1978, South Africa agreed in principle to universal suffrage and a UN role in the electoral process. South Africa also accepted the idea of one-man, one-vote elections in a unitary state, in contrast to her previous plan for a federation of semi-autonomous tribal and racial groupings.

In the spring of 1978 South Africa announced her qualified acceptance of the Western Five's plan. But by the autumn Western negotiations with the SWAPO side had resulted in several modifications which the South Africans found unacceptable. Therefore in December Prime Minister Botha gave the go-ahead for organizing internal polls to elect a Constituent Assembly. The Western Five were eager to salvage their plan, which by then had formal UN approval, and to avoid a final collapse of talks – particularly as that would force the UN show-down vote on sanctions which they hoped to postpone. South Africa was persuaded to declare that the December elections were an 'internal' matter, and that she would encourage the new constituent assembly to take steps to gain international acceptance. Under this fragile, face-saving formula South Africa continued to discuss the modalities of a second, UN-supervised election; yet Pretoria also upgraded the Constituent Assembly into a National Assembly with certain legislative powers.

Early in 1979 negotiations with the UN broke down completely, as South Africa accused the Western Five of bad faith and the UN Secretary-General of 'drastic departures' from the proposals to which she had already agreed. South Africa's Foreign Minister accused the chief American negotiator of trying to instal SWAPO in power, and Prime Minister Botha said South Africa had been 'left in the lurch' by the West.

The most serious issue in contention, and the one that probably led to South Africa's denunciations of the talks, was the UN's monitoring of bases during a transition period. The original understanding, to which South Africa had agreed, was that the UN would monitor both South African and SWAPO bases (the latter were located in Angola and Zambia). But the later UN proposal called for establishing SWAPO bases or gathering-points within Namibia herself, while SWAPO bases outside Namibia were not to be monitored.

South Africa's bitter denunciation of the process may reflect, above all, the different negotiating modes of South Africa and the Contact Group. The latter sought, with considerable success, to develop broad areas of agreement between Pretoria and SWAPO. It tried to play down the most contentious issues and to find vague and inoffensive language which could be clarified later, once general agreement had been reached. But for the South African side the process was a sensitive one in terms of domestic politics. Important constituencies within South-West Africa and within the Party and Cabinet – almost certainly including the Prime Minister himself – were suspicious of the Western Five, hostile to the UN (which recognizes SWAPO as the sole spokesman for the Namibian people) and not at all convinced of the need to include SWAPO in a settlement. Hence South Africa's Foreign Minister apparently had little room for manoeuvre, and the Government little patience with suggested changes to terms already agreed upon. Indeed, the Foreign Minister may have been instructed to stay in the talks as long as there was a chance of getting a settlement on favourable terms, but to opt out if that chance was seen to evaporate.

In any event, the South African side seemed to be convinced that the West had capitulated to SWAPO and had connived at the deception of South Africa. Thus early 1979 found South Africa more suspicious of, and more hostile to, the UN negotiations than she had been at the start of the process two years earlier. Yet the issues dividing the two sides had been substantially reduced.

Implications of 'Fortress Southern Africa'

During 1979 official South African attitudes towards the West, particularly the United States, hardened abruptly. In the spring of 1979 American military attachés in Pretoria were expelled for alleged spying. In a number of major policy statements by the Prime Minister and the Foreign Minister the West was depicted as unwilling to stand up to Communist expansionism and as sly and dishonest in its dealings with the Republic. From this it followed that South Africa could not look to the West for help in solving southern African problems, but must herself take the lead in seeking peaceful solutions and in preventing further Communist inroads in the region. Indeed, it was asserted that South Africa stood to gain so little from the West that she should adopt a neutral stance between East and West.

The opening salvo in this apparent policy shift was delivered by Foreign Minister Pik Botha in a speech to the Swiss-South African Association in March.[60] The speech contained a harsh and detailed condemnation of alleged Western and UN perfidy in the Namibian negotiations. But at two points he spoke of a new dispensation for southern Africa, in the implementation of which Pretoria would:

Follow a road of *greater neutrality* between East and West; work at its own regional problems with its own leaders, *black and white, Coloured and Asian*;

Consider a *constellation of seven to ten southern African states*, with up to 40 million people south of the Cunene/Zambesi line (in a subsequent statement to Parliament he spoke of the possibility of '*international secretariats*' being established to regulate the affairs of the people in these states);[61]

Set up targets of its own, including the achievement of peace and stability in the region and the establishment of a *sub-continental solidarity* which could form the basis for close co-operation in all the important spheres.

68

What is the significance of this new policy – if, indeed, such general statements add up to a policy at all? Is it merely the latest in a long line of futile South African overtures to Black Africa? Is it, rather, an angry reflex action provoked by the collapsed Namibian negotiations? Or is it, as some suspect,[62] an elaborate bluff aimed at extracting better terms in the next round on Namibia? The answer seems to be that it is an amalgam of all these, plus some dangerous new factors. But official statements contain a number of disparate elements; to assess the policy, the 'soft' elements must be separated from the 'hard'.

First, neutrality is not a serious option for South Africa. She depends on the West for capital, technology, manpower and fuel. No Communist state would believe a South African declaration of neutrality, let alone adopt a less hostile policy towards Pretoria because of it. The white minority's best hope for survival – as its leaders have always acknowledged in more reflective moments – is to win Western support, whether in the form of secret arms deliveries or restraint in imposing punitive economic measures. Threats to remain neutral thus appear no more than an angry gesture of defiance – a way of demonstrating to the electorate that its leaders have been tough and uncompromising in the Namibian negotiations, even though they have failed to gain their objective.

Table 5: Possible Southern African 'Constellation'

Countries	Population (million)
South Africa (including 3 Bantustans)	27·0
Zimbabwe-Rhodesia	6·3
Namibia	0·9
Botswana	0·7
Lesotho	1·2
Swaziland	0·5
Malawi	5·0
TOTAL	41·6

The notion of a southern African 'constellation' of 40 million people, with South Africa at its centre, also looks less than credible. The suggested seven to ten states (presumably counting the three nominally independent Bantustans as separate states) would include the countries

mentioned in Table 5. The addition of any other regional countries would raise the total by some nine million (Mozambique), over six million (Angola) or about five million (Zambia). It seems highly unlikely, however, that Pretoria consulted any of the proposed member states about joining a constellation. Apart from Namibia, Zimbabwe-Rhodesia and perhaps Malawi, the others have been making strenuous efforts to *reduce* their economic dependence on South Africa. They all reject apartheid and have refused to recognize the Bantustans as independent countries. Hence the notion of their forming a closer association with South Africa and the Bantustans, and particularly the idea of their relinquishing sovereignty to 'international secretariats' in which Pretoria would have the dominant voice, flies in the face of what these states have been trying to achieve – some for the past 15 years.

Indeed, both Botswana and Lesotho have already rejected this latest South African vision of their future.[63] And in July 1979 the Front Line states led by Botswana, initiated their own long-term plan for a regional transport and communication network to reduce their dependence on South Africa.[64] Other countries in the area will be invited to join. South Africa may, of course, be anticipating that these states will face deepening economic problems which might drive them into closer political and economic association with Pretoria. (There is undoubtedly weakness in certain of these states, as Zambia's re-opening of her Rhodesian rail links demonstrated.) But to pass from that pre-supposition to proposals for a formal political or economic association is a leap of fantasy.

If neither neutrality nor a broad regional constellation is a viable policy, why were they proposed? Are South Africa's leaders so out of touch with outside developments that they really believed in what they were suggesting? This is possible, of course: the deepening crisis in the Party and in the Botha Administration as the 'Muldergate' scandal unfolded undoubtedly absorbed much of the leaders' attention. But it seems unlikely they were as naive or unaware as that.

A more likely explanation is that the Government wanted to confer an aura of grand strategy and larger purpose on a policy which, in fact, was based on narrow, pragmatic self-interest.

For what remains of the policy, once the 'soft', rhetorical parts have been excised, is a tough plan for tightening the *laager*, but a *laager* re-drawn to include Namibia and Zimbabwe-Rhodesia. Some of this was implicit in the Foreign Minister's talk of establishing 'sub-continental solidarity'. In November 1978, within a month of becoming Prime Minister, Mr Botha told Parliament of the need for the 'free nations' of the region to plan a joint strategy based on their resistance to Russian imperialism and militarism.[65] This revival of the regional security idea was made more explicit in the 1979 White Paper in which Mr Botha des-cribed his Government's vision for southern Africa, including 'the concept of mutual defence against a common enemy' – the latter defined as the expansion of Marxist influence.[66]

Concrete policy moves since early 1979 seem consistent with the idea of this extended South African defence perimeter. In Rhodesia Pretoria had been giving heavy backing to the Muzorewa regime. The Botha Government provided finan-cial aid, trucks, bullhorns and other logistical help during the Rhodesian elections in April 1979 and (most important) a consignment of 11 large Bell helicopters, acquired from Isreal, which strengthened the Salisbury Government's counter-insurgency campaign and boosted white morale in the crucial weeks before the election. After the election Bishop Muzorewa held in-formal talks in Cape Town with Government and Opposition leaders,[67] and in June he met Prime Minister Botha in Pretoria for secret discussions, in which the two Foreign Ministers also took part.[68] The Machel Government has charged that South African planes took part in air strikes against Mozambique.[69] Then in early December 1979 South Africa's Prime Minister publicly acknowledged that South African security forces had been operat-ing 'for some time' inside Zimbabwe-Rhodesia to protect Pretoria's 'interests' and to defend 'vital lines of communication'. At the same time it was reliably reported that one, and possibly two, SADF battalions were operating under their own command in southern Zimbabwe-Rhodesia.[70]

South Africa's leaders thus seemed convinced that Mr Smith had finally made the kind of con-cession that they (and the West) had been urging and that the Muzorewa Government temporarily

offered the best hope for stability; hence South Africa appeared ready to intervene with military and economic support, if needed. But South Africa was not committed to any one Zimbabwe leader. Her chief interest lay in a stable Rhodesia. As Mr Botha told Parliament, 'If confusion and chaos are created for Rhodesia by outside forces, I want to warn that the South African parliament will have to consider what steps we are going to take because we do not want and cannot afford confusion on our borders'.[71] Dismayed by Mugabe's election victory, which dashed all hope of including Zimbabwe in Mr Botha's regional security scheme, Pretoria again warned that upheaval in Zimbabwe – leading to a flight of refugees into South Africa or attacks from Zimbabwe – would meet the 'full force' of its might.

Clearly events in Namibia were the other major factor in the 'Fortress Southern Africa' initiative. As discussed above, the Government was distressed at the turn taken by the negotia-tions in the winter of 1978–79. Time was not on South Africa's side: the longer the talks dragged on, the greater were the chances of general political disorder and declining morale among Namibia's internal political leaders and the greater the chance for SWAPO's influence to grow. When South Africa's leaders felt that the nego-tiations had moved inexorably beyond their minimal requirements for a settlement, they re-activated the internal process.

Several significant points for consideration emerge from South Africa's actions before and since. First, South Africa – openly hostile to the idea of SWAPO's participation in any settlement and apparently with little faith in the outcome of the Western Five's negotiations – has followed a two-track policy in Namibia: negotiating for an internationally sponsored settlement, but keeping the internal option very much alive throughout. Second, there is no indication that South Africa has any intention of with-drawing militarily. In 1977 she was expanding her military bases in the north,[72] and a year later she bought land for military housing near Windhoek.[73] Two conditions on which South Africa has insisted during the talks are her administration of the police during a transition period and her right to retain a residual troop presence in Namibia after independence, if requested to do so by the new Government.

South Africa has also kept a tight hold on executive power in Namibia. Differences have emerged between Pretoria and Windhoek on this issue. In December the South African Administrator-General for the territory stated that the newly elected Namibian Constituent Assembly would decide whether or not to hold a second election under UN auspices.[74] A few days later Prime Minister Botha corrected this notion, saying that the Assembly 'had been advised to accept' such an election and that the final decision would be South Africa's, 'in consultation' with the Assembly.[75]

Pretoria's insistence on retaining executive power, while the internal process moves forward, may be based more on internal Namibian politics than on concern about reactions in the UN and the West. South Africa wants the internal administration to be strong enough to withstand future pressure from SWAPO and the UN. This means that it must represent as broad a political consensus as possible within Namibia. Therefore Pretoria is pressuring the dominant political grouping, the Democratic Turnhalle Alliance (DTA), to allow other parties a more active role in the new legislature.[76] The DTA is thus trying to accommodate the liberal Namibian National Front (NNF), which favours a negotiated settlement with the West, as well as the right-wing, all-white AKTUR party (Act for the Preservation of the Turnhalle Alliance), which opposes the efforts of the recently sacked Administrator-General to annul many of the territory's apartheid laws. AKTUR, which has long dominated the old and now vestigial legislative assembly, also vigorously objects to the legislative powers which have been granted to the DTA-controlled National Assembly.[77] In any event, the option to continue negotiations with the UN has by no means been withdrawn, and the decision about whether or not to negotiate will, for the time being at least, rest with the South African Government. In short, Pretoria is keeping tight control over the course of Namibian political developments, as well as over negotiations with the outside world.

'Fortress Southern Africa' thus appears to be an effort on the part of the Botha Administration to draw South Africa's defence perimeter around Namibia and Zimbabwe-Rhodesia; to exert major, if not decisive influence over the course of political developments in the region;

and to help each territory to achieve moderate and stable government, protected by South Africa and (if possible) recognized internationally. Beyond these objectives, the leadership in Pretoria must hope that its future suzerainty over these areas, once established and acknowledged, would enhance South Africa's status as an important regional power, thus assuring her leadership of a more sympathetic reception in its dealings with the UN and the West.

But the 'fortress' initiative is two-pronged: its internal aspect is at least as important as the external. While adopting a hard line towards the outside world and extending South Africa's defence *laager* to encompass Zimbabwe-Rhodesia and Namibia, Mr. Botha has also been moving to enlarge the domestic *laager* to take in South Africa's coloureds and Asians and, ultimately, an urban black élite. His rationale is clear: military power alone cannot guarantee the future security of South Africa's white minority; its survival requires a political solution, in which South Africa's non-whites will gain a sufficient stake in the society to ensure their support of it.

So far the programme for co-opting non-whites has included proposals for:

Constitutional reform to give coloureds and Asians a greater voice in affairs within their own communities;

The revision of influx control (pass laws), to the advantage of selected categories of black workers;

The extension of certain trade-union rights to blacks;

A review of the Land Act, which divided the land on racial and tribal lines over forty years ago;

A review of South Africa's security laws;

Free, compulsory education for blacks.

It remains to be seen, of course, how far each of these proposals will, in fact, be implemented. And if they are implemented, the net result will be to strengthen apartheid rather than to weaken it. The constitutional proposals would further institutionalize the Bantustans and would widen the political gulf between blacks and non-blacks. The new influx controls would make life easier for the 1,500,000 black workers authorized to live in areas designated white; but for the 8,000,000 workers without such permission, infractions would carry even heavier penalties than at present. According to an authoritative

71

business journal, the new labour and influx-control proposals are designed to 'build up a privileged labour aristocracy among blacks in urban areas'.[78]

The degree to which Mr Botha's plans, if carried through, might co-opt non-whites to support continued white domination cannot be reliably assessed. Polls suggest that basic economic issues are the paramount concern of the blacks; hence the amelioration of work and living conditions would prompt many to acquiesce. But a number of non-white leaders have already criticized the reforms for not get-ting to the root of the problem: apartheid. Mr Botha's plans have also met with strong opposition from his party's right wing, although whites seem prepared to follow their Government's lead in seeing progress for non-whites in a number of areas. Mr Botha may be counting on his hardline foreign policy to win sufficient support for the 'Fortress South Africa' policy to allow him to move ahead domestically. The Mugabe victory and its effect on South African blacks seems likely to intensify the split in the National Party over the course and pace of internal reform.

V. OPTIONS FOR THE EIGHTIES

South Africa's Security Strategy

The goal of the National Party's security strategy has, of course, been the survival of the Afrikaner people and culture. The ultimate threat (now, as 150 years ago) is the disappearance of the distinctive Afrikaner *volk*, or nation, engulfed by the black majority. Against this threat the National Party has erected a structure of racial separateness and white domination – apartheid. From the start of National Party rule this strategy, central to the Afrikaners' survival, has encountered strong and growing opposition, both within and outside South Africa; hence successive National Party Administrations have perceived the *immediate* security threat to be interference in the Government's race policies.

Yet while South Africa's leaders could hardly avoid acknowledging apartheid as a major source of friction in domestic and foreign relations, they have generally portrayed the policy as the excuse which South Africa's enemies have seized on in order to stir up domestic blacks and, one way or another, to bring an end to white rule. The image of the 'enemy' has changed somewhat over the years: British liberalism (and its South African counterparts), African nationalism, hostile Western governments and radical black states have all been so viewed. But the enduring element has been to portray each of these as a witting or unwitting contributor to a master Communist plan for winning South Africa and her riches from the West.

Since South Africa is a moderate-sized power and the Afrikaners are limited in number, a common element of all past security policies has been the search for acceptable allies – that is, allies who would support apartheid or who would at least not make it an issue. The first goal was to unite Afrikanerdom behind Government policy. When that had been achieved the *laager* was expanded to embrace English-speaking South Africans. The latest attempt to enlarge the domestic *laager* still further has been Mr Botha's broad initiative (described above) to give' coloureds, Asians and urban blacks a greater stake in the system.

South Africa has made strenuous efforts to find foreign allies as well. Over the course of more than twenty years the Government has made various unsuccessful attempts to gain an *entrée* into a Western defence alliance, spending millions of rand to enlarge and modernize naval communications, docking and repair facilities in the hopes of attracting allies. South Africa has also made several attempts, since the late 1960s, to persuade moderate African states to agree to a regional security arrangement and to float the idea of southern-hemisphere security among Latin American states. So far, however, South Africa has failed to find formal allies or broad diplomatic support; indeed, over the past few years governments – particularly in Africa and the industrial West – have put a greater distance between themselves and Pretoria. The leadership nevertheless continues to pursue the African and southern hemisphere options and has not abandoned hope of an eventual military link with the West.

Meanwhile, South Africa has continued to make important gains in her informal and clandestine relations abroad. In some cases sympathetic governments have turned a blind eye to illegal South African dealings with local arms manufacturers. In their relations with two or three fellow 'pariah' states (Israel in particular) South African military and commercial representatives have established close, informal working ties of invaluable importance to South Africa's security over the years.

Of the several internal constraints on security policy, the chronic shortage of skilled white manpower is almost certain to remain the most serious. Because of manpower limitations, the Minister of Defence has been unable to create the additional PF brigade which he believes would be the most effective means of strengthening the SADF's mobility and quick-striking power. His self-styled middle-of-the-road solution – essentially, the extension of the initial period of national service to two years – falls short of meeting the need for a well trained professional force-in-being. Moreover, a shortage of trained professional cadres, exacerbated by the drain of skilled technicians to the private sector, has led to a serious shortage of instructors. This in turn limits the number of trainees who can be handled each year. As suggested in chapter IV, only a sharp recovery of white immigration would relieve the white manpower crisis, and short-term prospects for such a recovery appear bleak.

South Africa's security policies also have been marked by a number of serious (and sometimes lasting) failures to analyse correctly the motives, capabilities and likely actions of other countries. She has been particularly disposed to see Communist manoeuvring behind every manifestation of social or political unrest in Africa and to believe that other governments, both European and African, share her over-riding concern with the threat of the spread of Communism across the continent. Until recently this belief has prompted South African leaders to plan defence strategy on the assumption that the Western powers would eventually accept South Africa, apartheid and all, as an ally in the struggle against Communism. Moreover, the Western states would not do anything, it was thought, which might seriously jeopardize their strategic interests (the Cape route) or their economic interests (mineral supplies and investments) in South Africa.

The Verwoerd and Vorster Administrations believed that South Africa's growing economic power could be used effectively, both as a club and as a magnet, to gain influence in Africa. Mr Botha's Administration appears to share this conviction. South African loans and technical aid have so far had only limited and temporary success in attracting friendship and support (and thereby dampening African opposition to apartheid), even among its three virtual dependencies, Botswana, Lesotho and Swaziland. The threat of economic retaliation by Pretoria undoubtedly carries weight with Presidents Kaunda and Machel, but not nearly as much as the danger of pre-emptive or punitive strikes by the SADF.

The prime example of misjudgement, of course, remains South Africa's invasion of Angola in 1975. The leadership had, for reasons which are still not entirely clear, expected its drive towards Luanda to win the support of the United States and the OAU. Bc they promised support!

Within the constraints imposed by apartheid, by limited white manpower and by a sometimes distorted view of the outside world, South African security policies have been increasingly flexible, tough and aggressive. In Rhodesia, for example, when Mr Smith's stubbornness, together with black Africa's suspicions of South Africa, threatened to destroy the chances of a peaceful settlement, Mr Vorster suddenly reversed a six-year policy by withdrawing South African armed forces from Rhodesian operations. From time to time South Africa also applied economic pressure on the Smith regime. Yet under Mr Botha's premiership she moved quickly to provide strong political and military support for the Muzorewa Government.

Similarly, South Africa has shown flexibility and a high tolerance for ambiguity in her recent relations with black Africa. When dialogue with Pretoria was rejected by the OAU as a whole, the Government quietly cultivated its bilateral relations with the handful of states still willing to establish closer economic ties. Vocal attacks on apartheid are a regular feature of black Africa's official posture towards Pretoria. Yet a few low-key official contacts have continued, and South Africa claims extensive trade with 49 African states.[1] (To protect her trading partners' identity, South Africa's trade statistics for Africa are not broken down by country.)

Pretoria's leaders have even kept open the channels of communication with that outspoken opponent of apartheid, President Kaunda.

For more than a decade South Africa has been ready to intervene actively in the affairs of other countries in the interests of her own national security. She has intervened directly in Lesotho elections and has offered political and financial support to a number of conservative African leaders over the years: her military and financial aid to anti-MPLA guerrilla groups in Angola is an example. In the past few years the leaders' growing confidence in South African military capabilities, together with their increasing alarm over the presence of Cuban troops and Soviet heavy weapons in neighbouring countries, led them to resume an active military role in Zimbabwe-Rhodesia and to launch bold pre-emptive strikes, some of them deep penetrations, inside Angola and Zambia. The timing of some of these attacks indicates a political as well as a military objective. The apparent success of these raids, and the absence to date of any effective response, has persuaded the leaders that toughness and aggressiveness achieve results, while concessions do not.

South Africa's growing flexibility and responsiveness, as well as her sometimes badly flawed foreign assessments, reveal the peculiar strengths and weaknesses of the system with respect to security matters. Until the 'Muldergate' crisis the Government's widening parliamentary majority reflected the confidence and trust placed in it by the white electorate. Generally South African whites display limited and uncritical interest in political issues, particularly non-economic issues, which they prefer to leave to their leaders. Even within the Party and the Cabinet, policy matters are discussed and decided by a small group of men.[2]

Hence the Government has enjoyed virtually a free hand in conducting its foreign and security policies, which often bear the stamp of a strongminded leader like Prime Minister Botha. It can decide on, and carry out, new initiatives quickly and without critical Parliamentary review. This in turn permits a close convergence of threat perception and response. But it has also resulted in the absence of the sort of wideranging and continuous policy consultation that goes on in the United States and Britain,

for example, where various interest groups within and outside the government bureaucracies normally have opportunities to make their views known at various stages of the policymaking process. In South Africa, where effective policy input is restricted to a small and basically like-minded group, the chance that misguided policy decisions will be implemented would seem to be much greater. Again, the Angolan intervention is a prime example of error, but it is far from being the only one.

From the standpoint of Western interests, there are dangers inherent in South Africa's position as an international outcast. As such, her decisions are taken without benefit of the day-to-day informal consultations and exchanges that make up the bulk of diplomatic cable traffic among states which have a common concern with global problems and which participate jointly in various continuing political, military and economic fora. In the case of a state which is internationally isolated, reciprocal gaps in information and understanding are more likely to lead to unexpected policy moves; in the case of South Africa, where the Government feels that its survival is threatened, such moves may well be aggressive and destabilizing.

The major internal constraints on security strategy have already been discussed. But what about external constraints? In what ways are South African security policies vulnerable to actions by other countries?

South Africa would, of course, be vulnerable to direct attack by a superior military force. But she would offer formidable opposition. At any given time she has over 60,000 servicemen on active duty and another 100,000–150,000 trained active reservists could be quickly called up. South Africa's active police force numbers some 35,000 and the Commandos (Home Guard) 90,000, Moreover, the SADF, with varied and sophisticated armaments, has been trained for several years in co-ordinated land, sea and air exercises to defend the country against conventional as well as guerrilla attack. Therefore during the ten-year time-frame of this assessment South Africa will almost certainly be able to cope effectively with any conventional attack by black African forces.

There are two situations, however, in which South Africa would be in deep trouble. First, if an external attack were to be co-ordinated with a massive internal uprising. Second, if the assault were to be backed by one or a combination of the industrial powers – the United States, Western Europe or the Soviet Union.

The recent history of violent protest in South Africa – such as the sabotage efforts of the 1960s and the attempts of armed guerrillas to infiltrate the country in the past couple of years – suggests, however, that the chances of an armed insurrection during the decade ahead are slim. White unity, the effectiveness of the security police, the disunity and geographical isolation of non-white communities and the distance of major cities from South Africa's borders are all factors which will continue to work in the Government's favour during the next ten years.

An assault on South Africa involving major powers seems a similarly remote possibility during the 1980s. The high costs and uncertain results of launching an invasion several thousands of kilometres away, where it would be necessary to make use of the inadequate roads, ports and airfields of nearby African states, would themselves be serious logistical inhibitions. For the Western powers an armed attack on South Africa (barring some outrageous provocation by Pretoria) would find so little support at home that it would be politically unthinkable. For the Soviet Union and her Communist allies – Cuba and the German Democratic Republic for example – it is a long step from arming and training guerrilla groups and the armed forces of pro-socialist states in Africa to launching a conventional attack on South Africa. No Soviet combat unit has yet participated directly in the guerrilla wars; indeed, even Cuba's direct role has been defensive. The Soviet Union is unlikely to encourage or offer support for an assault on South Africa by African states, since this might ultimately entail a far heavier military commitment and more serious risks (for example, what would she do if the attackers faced imminent defeat?) than Soviet leaders would be willing to countenance.

There are several other areas in which initiatives by other powers would hold serious dangers for South Africa. In the event of mandatory, comprehensive UN sanctions, for example, an international blockade of South Africa's coasts could lead to a serious incident between Soviet and South African naval forces. It is doubtful, however, that during the next ten years either the Western states or the Soviet Union would be eager to incur the costs of a long-term blockade of South Africa's long coastline, the success of which, in any case, would probably be limited. So far no offer has apparently been made to police the UN's mandatory arms embargo of 1977, nor has the Soviet Union expressed any interest in participating in a blockade. Moreover, the ports of Walvis Bay, Cape Town, Durban, Richards Bay, Maputo and Beira are not only important to South Africa – they are the economic lifelines of Botswana, Swaziland, Zambia, Malawi, Zimbabwe and Mozambique: so totally blockading them seems out of the question. At most there might be a random and occasional search at sea of a few of the 2,000 ships a month which pass by the Cape, and this arrangement would presumably allow South Africa enough leeway for her to refrain from belligerent acts.

More germane is the question of how international sanctions might affect South Africa's security. It is clearly outside the scope of this study to discuss the likelihood and possible impact of the wide range of measures that might fall within the definition of 'sanctions'. But a few general propositions on this issue, and its particular relevance to security, seem appropriate.

First, South Africa is a vigorous trading nation. Her economic growth depends on a high level of imports. While a total embargo on exports to South Africa would lead to extensive import substitution, and perhaps to a temporary spurt in economic growth (as in Rhodesia in the late 1960s), most observers agree that initially there would be considerable economic disruption and, in the long run, a slowing of economic growth and a rise in unemployment.

South African authorities, however, have been preparing for just such an eventuality since 1963. Preparations have included the heavy stockpiling of essential goods (especially petroleum), the development of a comprehensive design and production capability in weapons and ammunition and inducements to encourage the automotive and other industries to increase the percentage of locally manufactured components in their end-products. More recently

South Africa has converted older naval craft into minesweepers with a view to keeping her harbours open in the event of maximum sanctions. Moreover, South Africa has gold, uranium, nuclear technology and other valuable bargaining chips with which to encourage sanction breaking.

In so far as South Africa's national security is concerned, weapons, weapons technology and oil remain serious vulnerabilities. The Government's efforts over the past 15 years to achieve a high degree of self-sufficiency in arms and ammunition have been described and assessed in Chapters III and IV of this study. To summarize briefly, South Africa is to all intents and purposes self-sufficient in the manufacture of small arms and small-arms ammunition and produces a rather narrow range of military aircraft, rockets, artillery, armoured cars, small naval craft and communications equipment. But for a number of heavy and sophisticated weapons, including tanks, submarines, long-range maritime patrol aircraft, heavy artillery, radar and communications equipment and certain types of ammunition, South Africa remains dependent on imports. A number of items, (for example, certain aircraft engines) are produced locally but they are dependent on foreign supplies of major components.

The mandatory arms embargo of 1977 has already hurt, but South Africa's greater concern is for the future. If the arms ban is strictly enforced, prolonged isolation from new developments in Western military technology could force South Africa's armoury to fall behind in quality. This might not be critical, unless a hostile and aggressive nearby state were to acquire substantially more sophisticated weapons than those available to South Africa – an attack aircraft able to penetrate her radar, for example. While such a dramatic development cannot be entirely ruled out, it seems unlikely during the decade ahead. Moreover, if the recent history of South Africa's sanctions-breaking is a fair guide to the future, her acquisition of sophisticated weapons from commercial arms dealers, sometimes working closely with the defence establishment in a potential supplier country, is likely to continue. But the arms embargo and the growing media exposure of illicit arms traffic to South Africa will make such transactions more difficult and more costly than in the past.

With regard to petroleum, South Africa is believed to have stockpiled about 40 million tons, or roughly two to two and a half years' requirement at current levels of consumption. In gross terms, oil accounts for only 20 per cent of South Africa's total energy requirements and less than 10 per cent of the energy needs of commerce and industry. The transport sector alone takes two-thirds of the total.

In about three years the recently planned expansion of South Africa's oil-from-coal facility is officially expected to meet a third of the country's petrol and diesel fuel needs. Meanwhile, the stoppage of Iranian deliveries, which previously met over 90 per cent of South Africa's needs, has forced South Africa to buy on the spot market at premiums of up to 50 per cent. The oil industry does not believe that there have been difficulties over the *total* amount of available oil, but there are shortages of certain products, particularly of diesel fuel. Since priority allocations would go to South Africa's mechanized forces, which are almost completely dependent on diesel fuel, the burden of such a shortage would fall on the road haulage industry.

The future of oil supplies is gloomy at best. Pretoria's energy officials have so far shown no signs of panic. Presumably, the spot purchases and the British-authorized exchange arrangement of June 1979 mean that no crisis is imminent. Whether South Africa will be able to find a regular supplier to replace Iran is questionable. In the event of mandatory sanctions, it is doubtful whether any major international oil firm would agree to become directly involved in illicit transactions, since exposure would put at risk its facilities and sources of supply in other countries. It might still be possible, of course, for South Africa to work out a secret exchange – say, nuclear fuel and technology for oil – with a potential supplier state. But such an arrangement would be difficult to negotiate and impossible to keep secret.

South Africa's leaders acknowledge that *any* interference in trade and finance would have serious consequences for the Republic. They are anxious to escape the imposition of such measures. Nevertheless, both the leadership and the electorate seem prepared to face sanctions as long as the alternative is seen to be acceptance of the principle of black majority rule. Indeed, the Government has tried – apparently with considerable success – to convince its constituents that they face an even starker choice: to hold out against pressure from abroad or to concede the principle of one-man-one-vote.

Options

South Africa will have few real security options during the decade ahead. Her range of choices and her chance of success will be limited by forces that have been at work for a long time (those that have been analysed in this study). There is always the possibility, of course, that totally unexpected developments may radically alter the outlook: for example, the defeat of the National Party at the polls and its replacement by a liberal administration committed to multi-racial government, or a series of right-wing coups in nearby states, bringing to power regimes friendly to Pretoria and dependent on its protection. But these developments would amount to a complete reversal of the underlying trends of the past twenty-five years, and such a reversal appears to be an extremely unlikely proposition during the next decade.

Developments elsewhere in southern Africa will, of course, influence Pretoria's threat perceptions, as well as its choice of available security strategies. And since South Africa plays such an important role in the region, her policies and behaviour will themselves influence the course of events there. However, one can make a number of predictions about conditions in the region which are likely to persist during the 1980s and with which the South African leadership will have to reckon in formulating its security policies. For one thing, southern Africa will almost certainly remain an area of marked political turbulence and instability throughout most, if not all, of the decade, regardless of what South Africa does.

Zimbabwe will probably be unsettled for some time. The post-election euphoria among blacks, together with Mr Mugabe's early conciliatory gestures towards those apprehensive about his leadership should ensure a peaceful start for the new state. But fine tuning will be needed to retain the support of the Nkomo and Smith parties, either of which could precipitate civil war and outside intervention if

seriously disaffected. And in the long term the Government will face certain unrest if it fails to meet the black majority's pressing demands for land, jobs, housing and education.

In Namibia, too, South Africa will probably be faced with a prolonged period of political turmoil. Even if a joint settlement including SWAPO were to be arranged, it would almost certainly lead to a divisive and violent struggle between SWAPO and a coalition of parties opposed to the organization and fearful of domination by the Ovambo people. If South Africa does go ahead with a unilateral settlement that excludes SWAPO, the insurgency will continue. Indeed, in the absence of a settlement recognized internationally, the chances are considerably better than even that SWAPO will receive more military training and weapons to enhance its fighting capabilities in the years that lie ahead. In late 1979 South Africa's Deputy Defence Minister expressed alarm at what he called East Germany's 'Afrika Corps', the 4,000 to 6,000 troops which South Africa believed to be deployed in Angola and Mozambique and which, it was feared, might become directly involved in SWAPO operations.[3] Moreover, the Mugabe landslide raised the prospect of a SWAPO victory in any free Namibian election: an analogy that will not be lost on Pretoria.

In all probability Angola will continue to provide SWAPO with sanctuary and material aid as long as they are needed. This will expose Angola to further armed incursions by South Africa unless a settlement involving SWAPO can be agreed. Festering insurgencies within Angola's own borders are also likely to go on for the next few years, and that will be cause enough for Cuban troops to remain. The Angolan Government, even with continuing Cuban participation in counter-insurgency, seems likely to have only limited success in crushing UNITA, which enjoys broad support among the peoples of east-central Angola. It is possible, but not likely, that future Government unification efforts will persuade UNITA to give up its fight for regional autonomy. The most uncertain element is the flow of foreign arms and material on which UNITA depends. South Africa and Zaire have been major sources of past support, though others have been involved. The *rapprochment* between Angola and Zaire may have induced President Mobutu to reduce military aid to UNITA. But as long as Angola is seriously threatened by the insurgents and by the prospect of South African invasion, she will want the Cuban and East German forces to remain.

A further proposition is that the Soviet Union will continue to offer weapons and military training to guerrilla groups operating against South Africa, and to socialist-oriented states in the region, for as long as such aid is sought. If Zimbabwe is threatened with civil war, or if the Namibian conflict escalates during the next few years, Soviet influence seems almost certain to grow. The Soviet Union is likely to continue to play a cautious hand, however, to follow the lead of the Front Line leaders and to avoid direct involvement in combat.

Cuba will probably continue to make her troops available to pro-socialist governments and guerrillas, and other Communist states may play an increasing role in supplying the guerrillas with instructors and advisers.

If conditions even approximately like those outlined above prevail throughout much of the new decade, what are the implications for South Africa's security strategy? Certainly, her leaders will not see in this situation any valid grounds to relax their thirty-year vigilance against external enemies or to modify their official conviction that world Communism is at the root of the attacks on the Republic. Given this perspective, which option or options will they choose? And with what chance of success?

A Defence Alliance with the West
This undoubtedly remains South Africa's first choice. From Pretoria's vantage point the greatest attraction of such an alliance is the deterrent effect it would have on the Soveit Union and Cuba and on the long-anticipated 'ultimate Communist onslaught' against the South African homeland. It would also convey to black African countries and others the message that the survival of white rule in South Africa was underwritten by the Western powers. South African whites, who have been increasingly apprehensive about their future, would be re-assured that South Africa was no longer isolated, that she had powerful friends and that she had finally won her long-sought admission to the Western white Christian family of nations.

More practically, South Africa would then presumably have access to advanced Western arms and military technology.

Thus the South African leaders' talk of remaining neutral in any future East–West conflict must be discounted. South Africa remains eager to join in Western defence.

Moreover, South Africa would be willing to pay a high price for admission. In exchange for a binding, long-term defence pact she would almost certainly agree to UN-supervised elections in Namibia – the more so a few years hence, when Namibia's own defence capabilities are likely to be considerably stronger than at present. If the pact also provided for the supply of enriched uranium for South Africa's nuclear reactors, the Government would probably agree to sign the Non-Proliferation Treaty (NPT). South Africa's willingness to assume joint responsibility for patrolling and monitoring the Cape sea route again can be taken for granted. If pressed hard – and *only* if pressed hard – the leadership would give private undertakings to Western leaders to make limited concessions in its domestic race policies; petty or 'park bench' apartheid and black job opportunities would seem the most promising areas for concession.

Much as South Africa wants to be associated with a Western alliance, however, she would be tough and demanding in any negotiations. The hardening of Western policies in the late 1970s and the termination of various forms of co-operation with Pretoria in the fields of defence, arms supply and peaceful nuclear exchanges have made a deep impression on South African leaders. Any South African Administration would be extremely wary of relinquishing or reducing South Africa's independent defence capability and would look for firm and lasting guarantees from the West. This would be the case particularly where the leadership was under critical surveillance by Afrikanerdom's vocal right.

Moreover, prospective Western allies would almost certainly demand a higher price than South Africa would be willing to pay for a defence pact. Antipathy to apartheid is now so well established and so universal that even conservative Governments in the West would be likely to demand that some concrete steps be taken towards dismantling separate development and bringing non-whites into the central political process. Only the prospect of imminent economic collapse or massive invasion (neither of which appears likely during the next decade) could be expected to force South Africa to agree to such concessions. If South Africa were in fact faced with an all-out Soviet- and Cuban-led assault, the Western powers might take active steps to defuse the crisis, but these would be likely to fall far short of a defence pact with Pretoria. In any event, for the time being at least, South Africa appears to have written off the chances of an alliance with the West.

A Regional Security Arrangement

A formal security framework is a live objective for South Africa. Its possible scope and content, however, have yet to be defined officially. In fact, South Africa seems to have several goals in mind. The first is a small, close security grouping originally to include South Africa, Namibia, Zimbabwe-Rhodesia and, presumably, the formally independent Bantustans. This notion of a secondary *laager* emerged only after the collapse of the Western peace initiative in Namibia early in 1979 and South Africa's decision, at roughly the same time, to give full support to the Muzorewa Government in Zimbabwe-Rhodesia – a decision which apparently meant extending once again South Africa's defence perimeter to the Zambezi River.

This proposed unfolding of a South African security umbrella over Namibia and Zimbabwe-Rhodesia seemed to revive Pretoria's policy of twenty-five years ago: that of keeping the battle against Communism as far as possible from South Africa's borders. It was also the Government's reaction to feeling abandoned by the West in the Namibian negotiations. But if this policy were implemented – that is, if Pretoria were to intervene militarily to support a coup against the Zimbabwe Government, or if it committed its forces to defend a narrow internal settlement in Namibia – the over-extension of her defence lines probably would weaken rather than enhance, South African security. And such intervention would hardly bring peace to the region, since both SWAPO and the new Zimbabwe Government have the support of all the major African states.

South Africa also appears to have in mind a broader southern African 'constellation', involving extensive economic and technical co-operation with most countries in the region. South African spokesmen have been vague about any concrete plans, but they have made it clear that although South Africa's capacity to extend loans and grants is extremely limited, *technical* aid and joint projects of mutual economic benefit are what Pretoria has in mind. While the more dependent and compliant states (Namibia, Malawi and the BLS countries) would clearly be included, closer ties with Zambia and Mozambique are by no means ruled out. This option seems, at face value, an unpromising one, in view of the local states' long-standing hostility to apartheid and the role of Zambia and Mozambique in supporting Rhodesian and Namibian guerrillas. But without doubt South Africa is hoping that economic need and the key role which she could play in regional economic development will move these states towards some form of accommodation with the Republic.

As recent events have shown, there are at least some grounds for South Africa's optimism. Zambia's deepening economic crisis and the threat of domestic disorder seem to have made President Kaunda somewhat more receptive to economic overtures from Pretoria. Mozambique also shows no signs of being able to reduce her economic and technical dependence on South Africa. In spite of renewed efforts by all these states to loosen their ties with Pretoria, the long-standing economic realities of the region mean that breaking away will be a long process, even in the most optimistic conditions. Botswana, Lesotho and Swaziland will find it particularly difficult to diminish their need for close economic links with South Africa. Sanctions against Pretoria would increase this dependence since virtually all imports come through South Africa, and exports are marketed along with the Republic's. A strong Zimbabwe, however, might help to reduce the region's dependence on South Africa.

In sum, the economic vulnerability of the southern African countries will continue to provide South Africa with leverage in the region during the 1980s, opening up possibilities for unpublicized bilateral deals and (perhaps) some moves towards detente. This does not imply diplomatic recognition or a softening of attitudes towards apartheid. At most, mutually advantageous economic and technical agreements might be expanded; tacit limits for aid to guerrillas could be established; and more co-operation on regional issues might be forth-coming. But the chances of a formal or lasting *rapprochement* between South Africa and the rest of Africa during the decade ahead are slim. Indeed, in view of the failure of South Africa to move towards fundamental change in her domestic race policies – the one issue about which black Africa agreed to engage in a dia-logue with Pretoria – the chances of *rapproche-ment* are slighter now than they were a few years ago. South African intransigence on this issue has left even the most conservative African leaders without a plausible basis for seeking closer relations with the white leadership in Pretoria.

A 'go-it-alone' posture

Clearly, such a stand has sometimes been adopt-ed by the South African leadership, but only when hopes of establishing global or regional defence ties have been seen temporarily to fade. In spite of the Afrikaner's traditionally ambiva-lent attitude towards standing alone but righteous in a hostile world, this is not his preferred position. It is one he feels forced to assume only when outside pressures seem to have removed other options. The need for allies still remains. Thus a prolonged 'go-it-alone' stance would probably be accompanied by even greater efforts to extend the *laager* by cementing strong military, economic and political links with nearby dependencies (Namibia, the Bantu-stans and the BLS states) and by continuing moves designed to give South Africa's non-whites, particularly coloureds and Asians, a greater stake in the survival of white rule. The winning of non-white support inside South Africa would be especially important in view of the need to recruit large numbers of coloureds and Asians into the armed forces if white immigration continues to fall.

But as a long-term security posture for South Africa in the 1980s, this defiant strategy is a last resort, even assuming Pretoria's success in extending the *laager*. The greater the ex-ternal threat, the greater South Africa's need for sophisticated weapons. If direct access to Western arms is denied, the role of other tech-nologically advanced 'pariah' states, like Taiwan and (particularly) Israel, could become critical.

The need to maintain the mobility and quick-strike capability which are the hallmarks of the SADF will be another reason for South Africa to seek assured sources of oil for the decade ahead.

As Defence Minister, Mr P. W. Botha occasionally cited Israel's defence policy as the appropriate model for South Africa to adopt. Like Israel, white South Africa is essentially a small, wealthy, productive, modern society surrounded by hostile territories which are poorer and short of both technology and skilled manpower. In the interests of survival, each maintains a high state of military pre-paredness and spends a high proportion of its budget on defence. But on one crucial point the analogy breaks down: the Western demo-cracies, the United States in particular, are com-mitted to Israel's survival. This raises another question about Mr Botha's analogy: will South Africa, like Israel, go for a nuclear option?

The Nuclear Option

Acquiring a nuclear weapons capability would be consistent with the South African leaders' shifting threat perception after 1975, when they began to prepare for an all-out conventional attack on South Africa. (Prior to 1975 the only external threat had been the guerrillas; a nuclear capability would have been difficult to justify, at least on strictly military grounds.) The acquisition of a nuclear weapon would also be consistent with South Africa's current defiant stance towards the West. It would offer a viable, though less desirable, alternative to the Western nuclear umbrella which a few years ago South Africa's Chief of Staff said was essential to South African security.

Indeed, in the absence of a military alliance with the West, possession of a nuclear weapon would seem the only way to make the 'go-it-alone' option credible. In addition to its dampening effect on any aggressive urges on the part of nearby states, it might be viewed as the best long-term assurance of Afrikanerdom's survival. The leadership might also see it as a means of forcing the major powers to acknowledge South Africa's claim to be treated seriously as a military power. Thus the decision of whether or not to develop a weapon (which depends on the perceived need for it) may be determined on purely political grounds.

But of what direct *military* value would a nuclear capability be to South Africa? Against what possible targets might it be used? Presumably, South Africa would not use it against guerrillas, where standard counter-insurgency tactics, aided by electronic surveillance and similar devices, seem likely to be the most effective counters. The threat of a nuclear weapon would be unlikely, in any case, to deter guerrillas, and its use would not constitute a sufficiently telling addition to South Africa's anti-insurgency arsenal to warrant the heavy political costs involved. Nor, for much the same reasons, would it make sense to threaten Luanda, Maputo or Lusaka with nuclear destruction. The only plausible use of a nuclear deterrent by South Africa would be against the threat of conventional attack, which, the leadership appears to believe, would be most likely to originate in Angola. The threat to use tactical nuclear weapons against a conventional cross-border assault from Angola would certainly present a formidable new deterrent.

Yet there would be grave risks. A declared or demonstrated nuclear capability would isolate South Africa further from the Western democracies and from the rest of Africa. It would also mean the loss of a major South African bargaining counter in future negotiations with the West, particularly (but not solely) in the important area of commercial nuclear exchanges. The chances of achieving general and gradual detente in southern Africa through Pretoria's initiative would be all but finally foreclosed. Further polarization of the region would probably follow. A few of the smaller and more dependent states might draw closer to the South African security system, but countries like Angola and Mozambique (and perhaps Zambia) might then seek binding security guarantees from other nuclear powers (perhaps from the Soviet Union), thereby giving the USSR the opportunity to acquire a cluster of military dependencies in southern Africa. At the UN the pressure for complete and comprehensive sanctions against South Africa would be virtually universal.

What hard evidence is there, then, of South Africa's nuclear capabilities and intentions? According to a growing body of scientific and technical expertise, South Africa has, or very soon will have, the knowledge and material to produce a weapon. In 1977 a 'well informed' American Government official was quoted as saying that South Africa was within two to four years of producing a bomb.[4] Similarly, a Stockholm-based arms expert[5] believes that South Africa has the technical ability, and 'probably the fissile material, to produce sophisticated nuclear weapons quickly and can, to all intents and purposes, be counted as a nuclear power. South Africa's nuclear chief has said that her programme would be peacefully implemented until the Government 'might decide otherwise'.[6] Former Prime Minister Vorster acknowledged in 1976 that South Africa could enrich uranium and had the capability to mount a nuclear defence.[7] Thus South Africa, while consistently denying her intention of acquiring a weapon, has done nothing to discourage other countries from believing that she has the capacity to do so.

The question of Pretoria's intentions suddenly became prominent in August 1977, when Soviet leaders informed the White House that their intelligence indicated South African preparations for an atomic explosion in the Kalahari Desert.[8] The Soviet Union asked the help of the United States – and, in the next few days, that of Britain, France and West Germany – to stop the test. A reconnaissance satellite sent up by the United States showed a 'cluster of sheds and other buildings around a prominent tower', which American officials seemed reasonably certain was a test site. The American and West European Governments warned Pretoria of the serious consequences of a test. The United States drafted a statement of the assurances she sought from South Africa, and on 23 August President Carter announced that Mr Vorster had assured him that South Africa had no intention of developing nuclear devices, that the Kalahari site was not for nuclear testing and that South Africa would not test any nuclear explosive.

The site and its intended use have nevertheless remained a mystery. Had South Africa planned to test a weapon, and if so, why? President Carter's continuing suspicions of South African intentions were revealed by his statement (made *after* receiving Pretoria's assurances) that the United States would 'of course, continue to monitor the situation very closely'. Two years later, in September 1979, the issue came very

81

much alive when a *Vela* reconnaissance satellite detected the tell-tale double flash of a nuclear explosion in the vicinity of South Africa. South African spokesmen denied any knowledge of such a test.

The answer to the question of South Africa's intentions may lie in part in her need to resume commercial nuclear exchanges with the West. In responding to the Carter *démarche*, Prime Minister Vorster said that South Africa would consider signing the NPT, as urged by the United States, but that he tied his country's accession to the NPT directly to South Africa's need for guarantees of American deliveries of nuclear fuel, which the United States had been holding back since 1975.[9] In June 1978, when the United States sent a senior diplomat to Pretoria to find out the exact price of getting South Africa to sign the NPT, South African demands were revealed to be substantial. They were:

the resumption of US deliveries of highly enriched uranium (HEU) for South Africa's research reactor;

the supply of low-enriched uranium (LEU) for two nuclear power stations under construction;

an assurance of American export permits for non-sensitive technology for South Africa's uranium-enrichment plant;

American help in reinstating South Africa in her seat on the Board of Governors of the International Atomic Energy Agency (IAEA), the 'watchdog' on proliferation.[10]

All these issues are important to South Africa. For one thing, South Africa faced a major investment decision in 1977: how large a commercial nuclear-enrichment plant to build at Valindaba.[11] A large plant would be able to supply the low-grade fuel needed for South Africa's two nuclear power stations, as well as supplying a potentially lucrative export market, estimated to be as high as 250 million rand per annum. But a large plant would not be completed before 1984 – too late to fuel the power stations, which were scheduled for completion in 1982 and 1983. In the meantime the power stations would be dependent on imports of LEU. A small enrichment plant could be built more quickly but would be too small to supply an export market. Thus the availability of imported LEU was critical to Pretoria's decision. Similarly, resumption of the supply of American HEU for South Africa's research reactor is a critical issue for several planned programmes, including the production of medical isotopes, neutron activation analysis (for uranium prospecting, among other uses) and fundamental research in materials testing.[12]

In February 1978 South Africa announced that she had opted for the smaller enrichment plant, which was capable of supplying LEU for domestic needs only.[13] Although the Minister linked the decision with uncertainty over future access to LEU imports, economic factors (rising construction costs and less promising future export prospects) are also thought to have played a part. In November 1978 the United States cancelled her frozen contract to deliver HEU for the research reactor.[14]

So far the several low-key American–South African discussions which have taken place on this issue have failed to resolve outstanding differences. Thus if the Kalahari episode was intended, in whole or in part, to jolt the proliferation-sensitive Carter Administration into making substantial concessions in the area of nuclear exchanges, it has yet to pay off. Meanwhile, South Africa has threatened to start producing her own HEU (from which weapons can be made) in a couple of years.[15]

How is South Africa likely to weigh these advantages and risks? What would be her most likely nuclear strategy? Her long-standing programme of peaceful nuclear development neither rules out, nor is incompatible with, movement towards a weapons capability. In view of South Africa's long-term threat assessment and her growing international isolation, it is highly unlikely that her leaders would at any point have rejected the opportunity to develop such a capability. Rather, they would have elected to keep this option open. Technical experts generally agree that it is entirely possible for a country to develop a reliable capability – meaning, in rough terms, the ability to assemble, deliver and detonate a credible weapon at short notice – without pre-testing the weapon. In view of the political costs of conducting a test mentioned above, the most rational course for South Africa to follow would indeed seem to be to emulate the so-called 'Israeli model': to have a weapons capability and to encourage the world to believe that the weapon is there, without confirming its existence by detonating a device.

82

South Africa's leaders, however, may be marching to a different set of priorities. If, as American experts believe,[16] the Kalahari location was a planned test site, this would mean either that the South African leaders were prepared to defy the world in an extremely blatant and provocative way, or that they believed a test would go undetected. In either case the incentive to test a weapon would have persisted, and the test postponement may have been only a temporary expedient to see what concessions might be wrung from the West following the discovery of the site. Thus the suspected South African test in September 1979 signified perhaps that Pretoria had decided that the chances of Western nuclear co-operation were slim and that South Africa should proceed to test – though still hoping to be able to make a plausible denial. In view of the risks and limitations associated with each of the alternative strategies discussed, what course is South Africa likely to follow? And what will her basic security strategy look like in the 1980s?

All such projections are hazardous. South Africa's leaders, like those of other states, will try to be flexible and responsive in the face of changing security conditions within and outside the country during the decade. Yet, as has been argued above, their range of choices, both perceived and actual, will be restricted by a number of conditions peculiar to South Africa. These include: world views of South Africa's leaders and their domestic political imperatives; her social and political structure; her geographical position; her history of racial struggle; and her international status as an outcast.

These factors will exert strong pressure for continuity in security policies during the next decade. Hence it is probable that, in the face of increasing outside hostility towards white minority rule, any likely government in Pretoria will continue to pursue something like the current two-pronged national strategy: the strengthening of the military power of the 'fortress' (however broadly or narrowly 'fortress' is defined) to discourage, or if necessary, repel external attack and internal rebellion; and the adoption of internal programmes to win the support of South Africa's non-whites. That the internal reforms will fall short of meeting the demands of apartheid's *opponents* seems a virtual certainty. But this will be of less concern to the leaders than their success or failure to gain widespread acquiescence among domestic non-whites and to quell internal unrest.

A second general proposition is that any South African Administration must give the appearance of toughness and of being in control if it is to retain the confidence and support of the beleaguered white community – particularly of the Afrikaans-speakers, who make up the majority of whites. Hence any significant concessions to South Africa's non-whites will be accompanied by harsh measures against internal dissidents and a belligerent posture toward external opponents. Similarly, a sharp South African military initiative is likely to follow any substantial concessions by Pretoria in the negotiations over Namibia. Moreover, the leadership's perception of its negotiations with the West over the past few years has reinforced the Afrikaner leaders' built-in historical sense that concessions to opponents are both futile and dangerous.

There will be other continuities, of course: the unceasing (though sometimes half-hearted) search for Western allies and links with other 'pariah' states; the probing for weak links in foreign political groupings (such as the OAU and the British Conservative Party) that are opposed to apartheid; the drive to obtain oil and modern weapons. But South African security strategy in the coming decade will also be affected by a number of factors which are new, or which have only recently begun to have a significant influence on strategy.

The first of these is South Africa's fear of a large-scale conventional military attack across her northern borders – a fear that has become acute since the arrival in Angola and Mozambique of Cuban forces and, more recently, East German military advisers and technicians. If the post-Neto Government in Angola moves towards still closer ties with the Soviet Union, Pretoria's apprehension will grow. A second new cause for South African concern is the accession of Mr Mugabe to power in Zimbabwe. This development demolished Mr Botha's hopes for a conservative security alignment in the region, although by no means ruling out peace and growing economic ties between the two countries. Another new factor will be a gradual rise in terrorism, fed and stimulated by neighbouring territories, within South Africa proper. Most critical is the probability that South Africa already has a nuclear weapon or will have one within the next couple of years. When taken together, these three factors suggest the strong possibility that South Africa might, at some point, detonate a nuclear device if she has not already done so, and might subsequently threaten to deploy nuclear weapons against nearby states.

This study of South Africa's security strategy offers no policy prescriptions for the West, but it does point to some problems as well as opportunities which South Africa may present during the coming decade. This is the more important since South Africa will be a major actor in the tragic drama now unfolding in southern Africa.

South Africa's bid to assume a guiding role in the fragile situation in Namibia and in the Rhodesian crisis came at a time when her leaders were internationally more isolated than ever before, as well as being constrained by domestic politics to adopt a defiant, uncompromising posture towards the West. The Government's strong backing of the conservative internal parties in both territories made it difficult for the Western powers to influence such groups or to regain the initiative in the search for a peaceful settlement. South African support for a well-organized coup attempt in Zimbabwe cannot be ruled out; nor is it likely that her leaders will refrain from punitive armed attacks against Angola or Zambia as a means to dampen SWAPO aggression. In the fragile and volatile southern African environment, a misguided or unexpected act of aggression by Pretoria could have serious consequences for the West, for clearly the Soviet Union and Cuba, in order to maintain credibility among the national liberation groups and their African sponsors, would have to respond convincingly to a South African military challenge.

For the West, then, South Africa will almost certainly pose serious and growing problems in the next ten years. The realities of domestic politics and bureaucratic inertia in South Africa will continue to inhibit the Government from moving far enough or fast enough on race policy to put a stop to the rising tide of global hostility and belligerence directed at the white minority. Other states will therefore find it more difficult, in terms of both their own domestic and foreign politics, to conduct official relations of any sort with South Africa. Since neither the West nor Pretoria can risk making the sort of concession needed to bring the other to change its basic policies, the West is likely to lose what little influence it had in the past over South Africa's leaders. In its relations with Pretoria the West will face the problem of dealing with a cornered wild-cat – small but potentially lethal, unpredictable, dangerous to approach and difficult to control.

NOTES

INTRODUCTION

[1] D. F. Malan, cited in T. D. Moodie, *The Rise of Afrikanerdom* (Berkeley: University of California Press, 1975), p. 248.

[2] Unless otherwise stated, 'South Africa', 'South Africa's leaders' and similar terms are used in the limited sense of the white-elected central government.

[3] All but two of South Africa's Prime Ministers have been graduates of Stellenbosch University. The *Broederbond*, whose membership is supposedly secret, was recently reported to number among its members 171 professors, 468 headmasters, 22 newspaper editors, 16 judges and 59 Secretaries of State Departments. See F. van Zyl Slabbert, in L. Thompson and J. Butler, *Change in Contemporary South Africa* (Berkeley: University of California Press, 1975) p. 9.

[4] *Ibid.*

[5] 'Strategy', as used in this paper, thus goes beyond the narrow military sense of the term and means the comprehensive direction of power to control situations in order to achieve broad objectives. See H. E. Eccles, *Military Concepts and Philosophy* (New Brunswick: Rutgers University Press, 1965), pp. 47–9.

I. THE CORE STRATEGY

[1] Andre duToit, 'Ideological Change, Afrikaner Nationalism and Racial Domination in South Africa', in Thompson and Butler, *op. cit.* in Introd, n. 3, pp. 37–44. 'Apartheid' and 'separate development' are used interchangeably in this Paper to describe the entire package of government policy measures based on race.
[2] De Wet Nels, cited in Moodie, *op. cit.* in Introd, n. 1 p. 265.
[3] For example, see D. Hobart Houghton, *The South African Economy* (Cape Town: Oxford University Press, 4th edn, 1976), pp. 153–7.

[4] For a discussion of this ambivalence in apartheid, see Moodie, *op. cit.* in Introd, n. 1, chs 12, 13. For a more cynical view, see duToit *op. cit.* in n. 1.
[5] Quoted in Moodie, *op. cit.* in Introd, n. 1, p. 249.
[6] Arnold-Bergstrasser Institute, *Sud Afrika: Friedlicher Wandel?* cited in *The Financial Times*, 22 June 1978. There is, however, some recent evidence that the white community is now prepared to see some modifications in apartheid if the leadership promotes them.

II. THE FIRST DECADE: THE SEARCH FOR SECURITY

[1] Eric Walker, *A History of South Africa* (London: Longmans Green, 1957), pp. 778–9.
[2] E. S. Munger, *Notes on the Formation of South African Foreign Policy* (Pasadena, California: Castle Press, 1965), p. 46.
[3] Walker, *op. cit.* p. 807.
[4] Newell Stultz, 'The Politics of Security: South Africa Under Verwoerd, 1961–66', in *Journal of Modern African Studies*, vol. 7, no. 1, 1969.
[5] Unless otherwise indicated, factual material on internal disorders is taken from Margaret Ballinger, *From Union to Apartheid*, (Tiptree, Essex: Anchor Press, 1969).
[6] Moodie, *op. cit.*, in Introd., n. 1, pp. 168–9.
[7] Later codified as *Internal Security Act No. 44 of 1950*.
[8] Hansard, 24 March 1961, cols. 3620–1; 20 February 1961, cols. 1563–8; *Argus*, 10 December 1960.
[9] Walker, *op. cit.*, p. 793.
[10] In 1951 the Afrikaner Party merged with the National Party, giving the latter a clear parliamentary majority. By 1954 this majority had increased to 29 seats.
[11] In 1952 South Africa's Foreign Minister warned a Commonwealth Conference of India's 'aim to secure *lebensraum* for her wretched starving millions'. Similarly Chinese construction of the Tazara railroad was seen as a pretext for Chinese colonization of East Africa. See Hansard, 18 February 1972, col. 1398.
[12] James Barber, *South Africa's Foreign Policy, 1945–1970* (London: Oxford University Press, 1973), ch. 7. In the face of a generally apathetic Commonwealth response, Britain later gave up the idea of MEDO.
[13] *Ibid.*, p. 82.
[14] Hansard, 11 May 1949, col. 5662.

[15] Sam C. Nolutshungu, *South Africa in Africa: A Study of Ideology and Foreign Policy* (Manchester: Manchester University Press, 1975), p. 46.
[16] *Ibid.*, p. 49.
[17] Barber, *op. cit.*, pp. 105–6.
[18] K. W. Grundy, in T. M. Shaw and K. A. Heard, *Cooperation and Conflict in Southern Africa* (Washington: University Press of America, 1977), p. 356.
[19] K. W. Grundy, *Confrontation and Accommodation in Southern Africa: The Limits of Independence* (Berkeley: University of California Press, 1973), p. 233.
[20] B. M. Schoeman, *Van Malan tot Verwoerd* (Cape Town: Dagbreekpers, 1973), ch. 9.
[21] Hansard, 1 September 1948, cols. 1323–4.
[22] J. E. Spence, *Republic Under Pressure* (London: Oxford University Press, 1965), p. 70.
[23] *Ibid.*, p. 74.
[24] For a fuller treatment of this issue, see Barber, *op. cit.*, ch. 8.
[25] Walker, *op. cit.* in n. 1, p. 804.
[26] *Ibid.*, p. 912.
[27] Gail Cockram, *Vorster's Foreign Policy* (Pretoria: Academia, 1970), ch. 8.
[28] Verwoerd, quoted in Hansard, 21 January 1964, cols. 59–60.
[29] Cockram, *op. cit.* p. 122.
[30] *Review of Defence and Armaments Production, 1960–70* (hereafter cited as *Review*) (Pretoria: Defence Headquarters, April 1971), p. 5.
[31] *Ibid.* p. 5.

III. FROM SHARPEVILLE TO LISBON

[1] Except where otherwise noted, factual material in this subsection is taken from Edward Feit, *Urban Revolt in South Africa, 1960–64* (Chicago: Northwestern University Press, 1971).
[2] Ballinger, *op. cit.*, in ch. II, n. 5, p. 425.
[3] Feit reports a police statement to a black newspaper that 'a man with attentive ears' could earn 250 rand a month.
[4] *Review*, *op. cit.*, in ch. II, n. 30, pp. 5–6.
[5] *Ibid.*
[6] Hansard, 8 June 1961, col. 7399.

[7] When South Africa planned to become a republic, she had to re-apply for admission. African members reserved the right to oust the Republic at any time over her race policies; hence negotiations broke down, and Verwoerd withdrew the application.
[8] Hansard, 6 June 1961, col. 7394.
[9] Hansard, 29 March 1962, cols. 3444–57.
[10] *Ibid.*, cols. 3409–11.
[11] Michael Morris, *Armed Conflict in Southern Africa* (Cape Town: Jeremy Spence, 1974), p. 290.
[12] Barber, *op. cit.*, in ch. II, n. 12, p. 197.

[13] Hansard, 9 February 1971, cols. 541–4.
[14] Patrick Wall, (ed.), *The Southern Oceans and the Security of the Free World* (London: Stacey International, 1977).
[15] The SADF consists of four main groups. The *Permanent Force* (PF) is the long-term career component. The *Active Citizens Force* (ACF) is composed of volunteers and national servicemen on compulsory active duty. The Commandos form a Home Guard on active duty along the borders and at security installations. There is also a large Citizens' Force reserve subject to call-up. The police are a separate organization entirely. Currently the PF makes up something less than 10 per cent of the total SADF.
[16] *Defence White Paper, 1964–65* (Pretoria: Government Printer, 1965), hereafter cited as *WP 64/65*; and *Review, op. cit.*, in ch. II, n. 30. In the absence of a consistent series on SADF strength, all data are approximate.
[17] *Ibid.*
[18] *White Paper on Defence and Armaments Production, April 1969* (Pretoria: Government Printer, 1969), hereafter cited as *WP 69*.
[19] *White Paper on Defence and Armaments Production, 1973*, (Pretoria: Government Printer, 1973), hereafter cited as *WP 73*.
[20] Hansard, 26 April 1972, cols. 5859–60.
[21] *Ibid.*, 7 February 1974, cols. 304–5.
[22] *WP 69, op. cit.*, n. 18, p. 2.
[23] *Review, op. cit.*, in ch. II, n. 30, p. 7.
[24] Geoffrey Kemp, 'South Africa's Defence Program', in *Survival*, July/August 1972.
[25] Hansard, 15 June 1964, cols. 8509–14.
[26] *White Paper on Defence* (Pretoria: Government Printer, 1967); hereafter cited as *WP 67* p. 8.
[27] Hansard, 5 May 1971, cols. 6006ff.
[28] Norman L. Dodd, 'The South African Defence Force', in *Defence Studies Journal*, December 1974, p. 37.
[29] *WP 73, op. cit.*, p. 17.
[30] Anthony Sampson, 'The Long Reach of the Arms Men', in *The Observer*, 4 February 1979. Presumably he means the 'weakest link' in terms of government oversight and enforcement of the UN arms embargo.
[31] *Ibid.* BBC *Panorama* investigators, however, concluded that the craft went directly from Israel to Durban, then to Rhodesia through several shipping and forwarding agents.

[33] Hansard, 11 February 1963, col. 1067.
[33] *White Paper on Defence, 1977*, (Simonstown: Navy Printers, March 1977); hereafter cited as *WP 77*.
[34] *Ibid.*
[35] In current prices. See Houghton, *op. cit.*, in ch. I, n. 3, ch. 10.
[36] Cockram, *op. cit.*, in ch. II, n. 28, p. 126.
[37] *Rand Daily Mail*, 1 June 1967.
[38] Barber, *op. cit.*, in ch. II, n. 12, p. 227.
[39] *Ibid.*, p. 251.
[40] *Die Transvaaler*, 18 June 1968.
[41] Grundy, *op. cit.*, in ch. II, n. 20, p. 247.
[42] *Ibid.*, Appendix 2. Signatories included the (then) Congo Kinshasa, Ethiopia, Kenya, Sudan, Tanzania, Zambia and seven less important states.
[43] Nolutshungu *op. cit.*, in ch. II, n. 15, pp. 268–76. The 6 'nays' were Malawi, Lesotho and 4 Francophone states.
[44] *Ibid.*, pp. 282–3.
[45] Hansard, 6 February 1974, col. 212.
[46] Grundy, *op. cit.*, in ch. II, n. 20, pp. 260–1.
[47] S. Cleary, in *International Affairs Bulletin*, SAIIA, No. 3, 1978. He writes of an aborted television set plant. A European chemical salesman told the author of a similarly blocked fertilizer factory. Neither charge has been confirmed.
[48] John Sprack, *Rhodesia: South Africa's Sixth Province* (London: International Defence Aid Fund, 1974), citing major British newspapers of the time.
[49] *The Economist*, 6 March 1969.
[50] John Marcum, *The Angolan Revolution*, (Cambridge, Mass.: MIT Press, 1978), vol. II.
[51] Nolutshungu, *op. cit.*, in ch. II, n. 15, p. 203n.
[52] Spence, *op. cit.*, in ch. II, n. 23, p. 80.
[53] Grundy, *op. cit.*, in ch. II, n. 20, p. 249.
[54] Hansard, 10 September 1974, col. 2629.
[55] R. Stevens and M. Abdelwahab, *Israel and South Africa: the Progression of a Relationship* (New Jersey: New World Press, 1976), pp. 80–81.
[56] Hansard, 26 April 1972, cols. 5783–6.
[57] *Ibid.*, 6 May 1971, col. 6158.
[58] Norman L. Dodd, 'The South African Navy, Guardian of the Ocean Crossroads', in *US Naval Institute Proceedings*, September 1976.
[59] Schoeman, *op. cit.*, in ch. II, n. 21, ch. 15.
[60] Thompson and Butler, *op. cit.*, in Introd, n. 3, p. 41.
[61] Schoeman, *op. cit.*, in ch. II, n. 21, ch. 15.

IV. TOWARDS 'FORTRESS SOUTHERN AFRICA'

[1] Since the IMF abolished an official price for gold, remittances have been paid in cash. Moreover, the number of Mozambican migrants employed in South African mines has fallen, from 60,000 a few years ago to 34,000 in 1978. Mozambique's earnings from this source fell from a one-time high of 120 million rand to less than 25 million in 1977. See 'Mining Survey' *Financial Mail*, 28 July 1978, and *Wall Street Journal*, 20 April 1977.
[2] *Guardian*, 8 August 1979.
[3] Data for this sub-section taken from Colin Legum, *Vorster's Gamble for Africa* (London: Rex Collings, 1976), and J. Spence, 'Detente in Southern Africa: An Interim Judgement', in *International Affairs*, January 1977.

[4] *Guardian*, 8 August 1979.
[5] *Ibid.*, 11 June 1979.
[6] Tony Hodges, 'The Struggle for Angola', in *The Round Table*, London, April 1976.
[7] *Ibid.*
[8] S. J. Baynham, 'International Politics and the Angolan Civil War', in *The Army Quarterly*, January 1977, vol. 107, no. 1.
[9] Nathaniel Davis, 'The Angolan Decision of 1975: A Personal Memoir', in *Foreign Affairs*, Fall 1978.
[10] Hansard, 26 January 1976, col. 50.
[11] *Paratus*, Journal of the SADF, March 1977. Unless otherwise indicated, data on the South African advances are from the detailed account given in *Paratus*.

[12] *Rand Daily Mail*, 25 December 1975.
[13] Hansard, 3 February 1976, col. 851–3.
[14] *Ibid.*, 30 January 1976, col. 369.
[15] Lawrence Schlemmer, 'Political Adaptation and Reaction Among Urban Africans in South Africa', in *Social Dynamics*, Cape Town, No. 1, 1976.
[16] *Annual Report of the Commissioner of South African Police* (Pretoria: Government Printer, 1977, 1978).
[17] *Survey of Race Relations in South Africa 1977* (Johannesburg: South African Institute of Race Relations, February 1978), p. 130.
[18] *Ibid.*
[19] *Rand Daily Mail*, 2 June 1978.
[20] *Ibid.*
[21] *Pretoria News*, 27 January 1979.
[22] *Strategic Survey 1978* (London: IISS, 1979), p. 82.
[23] *The Star*, (Johannesburg), 12 May 1979.
[24] *The Weekly Star*, (Johannesburg), 5 May 1979.
[25] *Die Transvaaler*, 26 August 1977.
[26] *White Paper on Defence, 1975*, (Pretoria: Government Printer, 1975); hereafter cited as *WP 75*. Italics added.
[27] *Ibid.*
[28] Hansard, 22 April 1975, col. 4551.
[29] *The Military Balance, 1975–1976* (London: IISS, 1975), p. 92.
[30] Hansard, 2 February 1976.
[31] *Ibid.*, 6 May 1976, col. 6218.
[32] *WP77, op. cit.*, in ch. III, n. 33, p. 22.
[33] *Ibid.*, p. 5.
[34] Hansard, 3 February 1977, cols. 851–3.
[35] *Ibid.*, 18 April 1978, col. 4817.
[36] *Rand Daily Mail*, 1 June 1978.
[37] *White Paper on Defence 1979*, (Pretoria: Government Printer, 1979); hereafter cited as *WP 79*.
[38] *Financial Mail*, 23 June 1978.
[39] *WP 79, op. cit.*, in ch. IV, n. 37, pp. 8–11.
[40] *Financial Mail*, 23 June 1978.
[41] *Paratus*, November 1978.
[42] *Strategic Survey 1978, op. cit.*, in n. 22, p. 88.
[43] *Guardian*, 4 September 1979.

[44] John Seiler, 'South African Response to External Pressure', in *International Affairs Bulletin*, SAIIA, vol. 3, no. 1, 1979.
[45] *Financial Mail*, 27 April 1977.
[46] *WP 77, op. cit.*, in ch. III, n. 33, p. 15.
[47] *Ibid.*, p. 18.
[48] *Strategic Survey 1978, op. cit.*, in n. 22, p. 84.
[49] *South African Digest*, 23 February 1979.
[50] Hansard, 28 March 1978, col. 3316.
[51] *Ibid.*, 21 April 1977, col. 5770.
[52] *WP 75, op. cit.*, in note 26, p. 15.
[53] *WP 79, op. cit.*, in note 37, p. 5.
[54] Hansard, 22 April 1977, col. 5903.
[55] *Ibid.*, 30 April 1975, col. 852–3.
[56] *International Herald Tribune*, 25 April 1979.
[57] *Paratus*, February 1977.
[58] *WP 73, op. cit.*, in ch. III, n. 19. pp. 9, 10, 21.
[59] *Rand Daily Mail*, 2 January 1977.
[60] *Address by the Hon. R. F. Botha . . .* 7 March 1979, South African Embassy, Berne, Bulletin 5/1979, 16 March 1979.
[61] *The Star*, (Johannesburg), 12 April 1979.
[62] *Guardian*, 21 May 1979, citing 'US diplomats'.
[63] *Financial Mail*, 4 May 1979.
[64] *The Star*, (Johannesburg), 7 July 1979.
[65] *The Weekly Star*, (Johannesburg), 25 November 1978.
[66] *WP 79, op. cit.*, in note 37, pp. iii, 1.
[67] Private eye-witness source.
[68] *Guardian*, 21 June 1979.
[69] Cited by Basil Davidson in the *Guardian*, 25 June 1979.
[70] *Washington Post*, 1 December 1979.
[71] *Washington Post*, 29 September 1979.
[72] *Paratus*, February 1977.
[73] *Strategic Survey 1978, op. cit.*, in n. 22, p. 86.
[74] *Informations*, Afrikaans-Deutsche Kulturgemeinschaft (SWA), Windhoek, December 1978.
[75] *The Star*, (Johannesburg), 23 December 1978.
[76] *Financial Mail*, 4 May 1979.
[77] *Ibid.*, 11 May 1979.
[78] *Ibid.*

V. OPTIONS FOR THE EIGHTIES

[1] *Ibid.*, 9 March 1979.
[2] Planned policy changes of a major sort are explained down the line to leaders of the Afrikaans community and vetted in at least a general way at NP regional caucuses. See the Introduction to this Paper.
[3] *The Daily Telegraph*, 28 August 1979.
[4] *Washington Post*, 16 February 1977.
[5] Dr Frank Barnaby in *New Scientist*, 19 October 1978.
[6] *Financial Mail*, 10 November 1978.
[7] *Washington Post*, 16 February 1977.
[8] M. Marder and D. Oberdorfer, 'How West, Soviets Acted to Defuse S. African A-Test' in *Washington Post*, 28 August 1977. Except where otherwise noted, this source is the basis of data on this matter.
[9] *Financial Mail*, 17 February 1978.
[10] *The Financial Times*, 27 and 29 June 1978.
[11] *Financial Mail*, 17 February 1978.
[12] *The Financial Times*, 5 July 1979.
[13] *Financial Mail*, 17 February 1978.
[14] *Ibid.*, 3 November 1978.
[15] *The Weekly Star*, (Johannesburg), 14 July 1979.
[16] Marder and Oberdorfer, *op. cit.*, in n. 8.

3 A Regional Security Role for Africa's Front-Line States

ROBERT JASTER

FOREWORD

A major and unique source of information for this study is a series of more than three dozen private interviews conducted by the Author over a two-year period (up to and including June 1982) with senior officials from the Front-Line States, the Commonwealth, South Africa, and the UN, and with Western diplomats involved in southern African peace negotiations. The Author is indebted to these officials for their time and assistance, and for their candour in recounting events as they witnessed them, even where the recounting did not always show their side in a favourable light. For obvious reasons, attribution cannot always be given. The Author is particularly indebted to the International Institute for Strategic Studies and a grant from the Rockefeller Foundation for making possible this study and a six-week visit to southern African capitals to interview senior officials, past and present, who have been involved in Front-Line affairs.

INTRODUCTION

The past few years have seen the emergence of a new sub-grouping in Africa, the so-called Front-Line States. As a loose coalition of southern African countries (Angola, Botswana, Mozambique, Tanzania and Zambia), the group was first recognized as such in 1976, when its efforts to bring unity to the faction-ridden national liberation movement in Rhodesia were given informal endorsement by the Organization of African Unity (OAU). As the war in Rhodesia intensified and successive Western peace initiatives were launched, the Front-Line leaders became more deeply involved both with the two guerrilla groups, during the course of the insurgencies and with the Anglo-American peace efforts to solve it. They played a major supporting role in getting the Lancaster House Peace Talks started in September 1979. Their mediation during the Conference itself was crucial to its ultimate success.

Since then the Front-Line States, enlarged to six with the addition of Zimbabwe, have become more actively engaged as a group in other regional security issues. They have acted as broker in a possible Namibian settlement with the South-West African People's Organization (SWAPO) – the Namibian insurgent organization – thereby removing a number of obstacles to agreement. They have also effectively enlisted Western interest and financial support behind a comprehensive plan for regional economic development, a plan which contains an explicit security aspect.

This diverse group called the Front-Line States has been effectively playing the role of a regional power in a number of important issues; yet it lacks some of the important attributes of such. For one thing its very diversity could thwart its capacity to act in a crisis. Moreover, these states, both individually and as a group, are economically weak, and several have serious internal political dissidence to contend with. By far the most serious limitation on their actions is the continuing tension with their powerful neighbour, South Africa, whose superior military and economic power dwarfs that of the rest of combined southern Africa.

But South Africa, because of her egregious apartheid system and her continued hold on Namibia, stands condemned by almost every country in the world, and particularly by other African states. Therefore she has been unable to translate her power into anything like the degree of regional influence which she would otherwise exert. Moreover, one or both of these issues in all probability will continue for a long time to deny her the regional leadership role she has long been seeking.

But what are the factors that have so far enabled the Front-Line States to jointly assume the role of a regional power? How do Front-Line strengths and weaknesses relate to a future guiding role in regional affairs? In particular, to what degree and in what ways can the Front-Line States bring about and maintain regional security, defined here simply as solving, avoiding or limiting conflict in the area? What are the policy implications for the West? And finally, is the Front-Line experience a useful model for other Third-world states trying to promote regional security in zones of local conflict? It is these questions that the Paper sets out to address.

In this Paper the activities of the Front Line in regional affairs are analysed and assessed, mainly with a view to setting forth the major factors likely to expand or limit its future role in the security of the region. The origins of Front-Line interest in regional security matters are briefly outlined. The major focus of the analysis is the important and hitherto unpublicized role of the Front-Line States during the final stages of the Rhodesian conflict, including the events leading to the Lancaster House Peace Conference and the Zimbabwe elections. This regional crisis, more than any other so far, engaged the Front-Line States as a group acting in concert; hence it offers the most insights into Front-Line strengths, weaknesses and *modus operandi*.

The region's most serious current security issues – Namibia and the confrontation with South Africa – are also examined, and an attempt is made to identify the major forces working to intensify or to dampen these conflicts. The role of economic co-operation *as a move toward assuring regional security* is also discussed. The concluding sections draw together the implications of the analysis, both for the Front-Line States' likely regional initiatives in the future, and for Western policy interests. A brief final note addresses the issue of the Front-Line experience as a relevant model for the resolution of other Third-world conflicts.

I. THE GENESIS OF FRONT-LINE COLLABORATION

Early Struggle Against White Minority Rule
In the mid-1960s the winds of change which had been blowing through Africa for a decade suddenly dropped at the banks of the Zambesi. The new black-ruled states had just emerged from colonialism and white minority rule; yet these same forces remained entrenched in South Africa, South-west Africa (later known as Namibia), Rhodesia, Angola and Mozambique.

Anti-colonialism and anti-(white) racism were deeply ingrained attitudes among the leaders of Africa's new states. Facing a staggering array of intractable problems at home, and seeking a transcendant issue which might bind their diverse states closer, they found a ready-made cause in their common antipathy towards white minority rule. Hence a commit-

ment to independence and majority rule for the remaining white-dominated territories quickly became the single great unifying force in black Africa, and the closest thing the new national leaders had to a common ideology. For some, particularly for President Nyerere of Tanzania, the moral or ideological side of the issue was paramount. For others, an end to white minority rule was seen as critical to national security.

This was particularly true for Zambian leaders. They feared that Zambia's 75,000 whites, most of whom supported the breakaway Smith regime in neighbouring Rhodesia, were a Fifth Column which would seek Rhodesian help to topple Zambia's new government and re-institute white rule. Numerous acts of sabotage following independence in 1964, and the discovery of an alleged Rhodesian spy network in 1967, fuelled Zambian suspicions. President Kaunda of Zambia also feared a secessionist plot by the Portuguese, who had indeed offered help to tribal separatists in Zambia and were training Zambian dissidents. This fear, too, was underlined by such efforts as the invasion of Guinea by Portuguese-supported mercenaries from neighbouring Portuguese Guinea, and by the threatened withdrawal of Katanga from the Congo in the late 1960s.[1] Moreover, at independence Zambia relied on Rhodesia for all of her oil and electric power and for the, coke needed in her vital copper refining industry. The great bulk of Zambian trade was carried on Rhodesian railways and Zambia was therefore highly vulnerable to Rhodesian economic pressure. Taking account of all this, President Kaunda was convinced that Zambia's independence would be secure only when white rule had ended in the countries to the south.

Zambia's national weakness was a trait she shared with other new African states. As they struggled to master the skills of running a government and bringing their often disparate peoples together as a nation, they found that their own independence was something less than real. Their economies were weak, the modern sector dominated by foreign-owned enterprises and run by expatriate managers and technicians. Foreign exchange earnings depended in most cases on the export of one or a few commodities to the leading industrial states. Wealthier outside countries, often the former metropolitan powers, helped to stave off economic collapse with credits, technical aid and emergency food supplies. Foreign assistance was also required to build fledgling armed forces, which were designed to maintain internal order rather than to fight conventional wars.

Black Africa's weakness was the more pronounced because of the contrasting strength of the white redoubt in the south. South Africa dominated the regional economy, while her military might was far greater than that of the rest of the region combined. Furthermore, South Africa's economic and military support of the other white-ruled territories strengthened Portugal's hold on

Angola and Mozambique, and enabled the beleaguered Smith Regime to hold out for almost fifteen years.

Since they were too weak and divided to take on the white redoubt directly, the independent black states tried to weaken it diplomatically, through the OAU and the UN, and particularly by trying to persuade the Western democracies to apply the leverage which they themselves could not. President Kaunda of Zambia and President Nyerere of Tanzania played leading roles in this. The two had worked together in pre-independence politics, and their shared view on the urgency of African liberation was reinforced by close personal ties. Following Ian Smith's unilateral declaration of independence (UDI) in 1965, President Kaunda offered Britain Zambian bases from which to prepare for an invasion of Rhodesia. Nyerere and Kaunda drafted the 1969 Lusaka Manifesto of Southern Africa which was signed by a dozen states taking part in a conference of Central and East African countries. The Manifesto set forth the rationale for an escalation of guerrilla warfare against Africa's white minority states: since independence could not be achieved by peaceful means under present circumstances, the subject peoples had no choice but to fight for it. The Manifesto was endorsed by the OAU Summit Meeting and the UN General Assembly. Nyerere's hand was apparent, too, in the Mogadishu Declaration of 1971, in which the signatory states pledged to give their 'fullest support' to the armed struggle in the south. This was also adopted as official OAU policy. Kaunda and Nyerere were thus remarkably successful in gaining broad acceptance of the principle that the continued existence of white minority domination was, in itself, a threat to peace, justifying international coercive action.

Several African states (Zambia, Tanzania and Algeria, in particular) went far beyond diplomatic manoeuvering, and took active steps to help launch armed warfare against the white-ruled south. They did this indirectly, by nurturing, guiding and supplying various national liberation movements in each of the white-controlled territories. In this way they sought to weaken white rule while avoiding direct intervention in the

90

fighting and, in some cases, maintaining vital economic links with white-run states.

Both Zambia and Tanzania have been leading members of the OAU's African Liberation Committee (ALC), whose co-ordinating staff was permanently based in Dar-es Salaam. The various liberation movements were permitted to open administrative headquarters in both Dar-es Salaam and Lusaka. The latter has played host at various times to such diverse groups as *Frente de Libertação de Moçambique* (FRELIMO), *União Nacional para a Independencia Total de Angola* (UNITA), the UPA (Angola), the Caprivi African National Union (Namibia), the Zimbabwe African People's Union (ZAPU) and the Zimbabwe African National Union (ZANU). Because of Zambia's vulnerability to cross-border reprisal raids by the Portuguese and Rhodesians, Kaunda tried to keep a close rein on the guerrillas using Zambian sanctuary; indeed, he closed down two groups who blatantly flouted his formal insistence that only transit camps be maintained on Zambian soil. Tanzania, less subject to attack from white-ruled states, offered training facilities and more direct logistical support to guerrilla groups, particularly FRELIMO. The growing recognition of the special Zambian and Tanzanian relationship with the liberation movements was shown as early as 1972, when the OAU authorized Nyerere and Kaunda, together with President Mobutu of Zaire and President Ngouabi of the Congo to try to unify the several Angolan nationalist movements.

But by the early 1970s, the efforts of the black-ruled states to weaken the white redoubt had achieved few concrete results. The Western powers had subordinated the interests of African independence to higher priority concerns, as a result of which Western economic and military links to the white-ruled territories had been reinforced, not weakened. Although the guerrilla movements were tying down a hundred thousand Portuguese troops by the early 1970s and counter-insurgency costs were taking an ever-larger share of Rhodesia's budget, the Portuguese and Rhodesian responses had been to stiffen their resistance to change, a stance facilitated by South Africa's growing support to their counter-insurgencies. In Namibia occasional raids by small guerrilla bands, together with numerous UN Resolutions demanding South African withdrawal, had only accelerated South African moves to strengthen her hold on that territory. Thus, after almost a decade of struggle, the black-ruled states of Africa had failed to dislodge any of the five white minority regimes, some of which were even stronger than before.

Guiding the Rhodesian Insurgency: the Emergence of the Front-Line Coalition

It was a revolution in Portugal which led to the decolonization of Angola and Mozambique and to the first break in the white redoubt in 1974. That revolution, though triggered by domestic opposition in Portugal to the colonial wars in Africa, had its roots not in the African issue, but in growing social and economic dislocations in Portugal. The impact on southern Africa was nonetheless stunning. The accession of guerrilla leaders to power in Angola and Mozambique meant that Zambia had black-ruled states to her east and west, while Rhodesia's long border with Mozambique would soon become a new front for guerrilla attacks against the Smith regime. South Africa's failure to keep the Cuban- and Soviet-supported *Movimento Popular para a Libertação de Angola* (MPLA) from seizing power in Angola meant that South Africa, like Rhodesia, faced a hostile neighbour which would offer sanctuary and passage for guerrillas operating against South Africa and Namibia.

One important result of this sudden shift in the regional power balance was the impetus it gave to the local black-ruled states, augmented by two new members, to assume a more direct role in guiding Rhodesian national liberation groups and helping them organize a more effective insurgency. The leaders of Zambia, Tanzania and Botswana, joined by those of Mozambique and (in 1975) by Angola, felt for the first time that their combined efforts could be a decisive force in regional affairs. This is not to say they could ignore South Africa's awesome power, nor could they hope to bring about majority rule in Rhodesia without the intervention of Western powers and (indirectly) the East. But the scales had tipped far enough in their direction to allow them to mount a credible challenge to the Smith regime.

Yet the events of 1974 also had a sobering effect, particularly on Zambia and Botswana, which were concerned at the prospect of Soviet-supported, self-declared Marxist governments coming to power in the region. Moreover, all the local states were alarmed by the growing spectre of an East–West confrontation in southern Africa. These concerns led some of the Front-Line governments to re-assess their attitudes towards the insurgencies, and to favour stronger initiatives to search for peaceful ways of bringing majority rule to Rhodesia.

This attitude resonated with that of the South African government. Alarmed at the developments in Angola and Mozambique, the South African Prime Minister, Mr Vorster, initiated in mid-1974 a policy of detente towards the region's black-ruled states, with whom he sought to work for a peaceful resolution of the Rhodesian conflict. Detente found a ready response from President Kaunda; indeed, for a couple of months Zambia and South African officials met in secret and worked out a proposed 'detente scenario' for resolving the conflicts in both Rhodesia and Namibia.[2] In the Autumn of 1974 Kaunda informed Presidents Nyerere, Khama of Botswana and Machel of Mozambique of these discussions. Since all four were suspicious of South African intentions, they made clear their position that independence under majority rule, preceded by the release of political detainees from Rhodesian gaols, would be the true test of detente.

In November 1974, Ian Smith, under pressure from Vorster, met their demands for the release of Rhodesian nationalist leaders from detention. The four Presidents then began what was to become a five-year, uphill struggle to unify the Rhodesian national liberation movements, so that together they could be an effective force in bringing majority rule to Rhodesia, whether through negotiation or war. In 1974 the Rhodesian nationalists were split into four major groups, and some of these groups into rival factions, each claiming to represent the majority of the membership. Frustrated and angered by the Byzantine scheming, shifting personal loyalties and mutual hostility between and within these groups, the four Presidents scored at least a temporary success in December 1974, when they bludgeoned the four leading groups (ZAPU, ZANU, the UANC (United African National Council), and FROLIZI (Front for the Liberation of Zimbabwe)) into coming together in an umbrella organization under the African National Council (ANC).[3]

During the next eighteen months, the four Presidents became deeply and personally involved in mediating among the nationalists and the guerrilla commanders. And even though they had been given no mandate by the OAU to assume a crisis-management role on its behalf, the Presidents were soon playing an independent and leading role with only nominal OAU approval. Kaunda, in consultation with the other three Presidents, worked with South Africa to arrange talks between Smith and the ANC. This led to the well-known August 1975 meeting in a railway carriage at Victoria Falls, attended by Smith's delegation on one side and an ANC delegation, headed by Bishop Muzorewa, on the other, with Vorster and Kaunda in the background. Dissension within the ANC group allowed Smith to resist making any concessions at all, and the conference collapsed after two days. Following one more abortive attempt at arranging a peaceful settlement between Smith and the nationalists, the four Presidents met during February 1976 in Quelimane, Mozambique, where they reached the unanimous conclusion that further talks were useless, and that the armed struggle must be intensified.

In the Spring of 1976, as guerrillas opened a new front in north-eastern Rhodesia, the American Secretary of State, Henry Kissinger, went to southern Africa to launch a Rhodesian peace initiative. Kissinger tacitly acknowledged the leading role of the four Presidents by choosing Lusaka from which to announce the new US proposals, and later by telling Smith that any constitutional proposals would have to be vetted by the Front-Line leaders.[4] By mid-Summer, the four – not the OAU – were being consulted by American and British officials on an Anglo-US settlement plan to dump Smith and establish a caretaker government to negotiate a peace settlement with the nationalists.

By then the designation 'Front-Line States' had replaced the appellation 'four Presidents'. Moreover, they had received an indirect OAU endorsement – the strongest endorsement they would get from the OAU – for their activities. In June 1976, a meeting of the ALC had called on the Front-Line States of Botswana, Mozambique, Tanzania and Zambia, who were closely involved in the Rhodesian liberation struggle, to continue trying to bring the ANC leaders together. The July 1976 OAU Summit Meeting endorsed attempts by the 'so-called Front Line' and the ANC to negotiate a settlement.[5] A couple of months later, however, the Front-Line Presidents decided on their own to abandon the faction-ridden ANC and throw full support to the Zimbabwe People's Army (ZIPA), the new guerrilla command, made up mostly of young ZANU members, which was successfully carrying the war deep into Rhodesia.

This *de facto* delegation of OAU authority to the Front-Line States was due only in part to the obvious fact that the latter were closer to the scene of action and in better touch with the nationalists from day to day. A major factor was the dissension within the OAU, chiefly but not exclusively along radical-conservative lines, over a number of issues, including southern Africa. The Front-Line Presidents had boycotted the 1975 OAU Summit in Kampala, for example, following Idi Amin's call for their overthrow for seeking a peaceful solution in Rhodesia. Conservative member-states wanted to prevent some of the more radical and bellicose OAU members from becoming directly involved in the Rhodesian insurgency, which they feared might lead to the enlargement and radicalization of the conflict. In the event, the conservative majority found it possible to avoid a confrontation on the Rhodesian issue by winning general support for a Front-Line leading role, a move made easier by the wide acceptance of Nyerere as a champion of national liberation.

In September 1976, following Zambia's nine-month delay in recognizing the MPLA government in Angola, President Neto of Angola became the fifth Front-Line President, in time to join a Front-Line summit discussion of the Kissinger peace proposals. The Front-Line leaders hailed Smith's acceptance of majority rule within two years but were decidedly cool towards the Kissinger–Smith package, since it would have ensured that the existing power structure remained very much intact. An interim two-tier government would have left the Defence and Law and Order portfolios, as well as military command, in white hands. But, clearly recognizing that intervention by an outside power would be needed to bring about a negotiated peace, they called on Britain as the responsible colonial power to organize a conference *without* any preconditions. The Front-Line States did nothing, however, to block the convening of the Geneva Conference, which was to discuss the accord reached bilaterally by Smith and Kissinger. In preparation for Geneva, the Front-Line Presidents pressured ZAPU and ZANU into a nominal merger, known as the Patriotic Front (PF).

ZANU and ZAPU went to Geneva to negotiate on the basis of the Kissinger/Smith accord. Smith went only to join them in signing the accord, unchanged. Not surprisingly, therefore, the Geneva Conference sputtered to an end in January 1977 after two months of inconclusive wrangling.

The collapse of the Kissinger initiative was followed in a few months by a joint Anglo–US plan put forward by David Owen, Britain's new Foreign Secretary, and Cyrus Vance, the new US Secretary of State. The Anglo–American proposals, which essentially called for a British Resident Commissioner to run a transitional government for six months leading to elections and independence, and a UN force to monitor a ceasefire, found the Front-Line leaders unable to resolve serious differences among themselves on the timing of the elections and other issues. They finally agreed to support 'positive aspects' of the plan, and to leave the contentious elections issue up to the PF. The issue became moot after the PF rejected the plan at an exploratory meeting with British, American and UN officials in January 1978. Two months later Smith announced that he and several black nationalist leaders inside

Rhodesia had agreed on the terms of an internal settlement.

The limits of Front-Line influence over the PF at that time were demonstrated when Secretaries Vance and Owen themselves went to Maputo in April 1978 to negotiate with the two PF leaders. They went only after being assured by the Front-Line leaders that Nkomo and Mugabe were ready to accept the Anglo–US proposals. In Maputo, however, it quickly became apparent that the two PF leaders remained adamantly opposed to key parts of the proposals, including broad powers for a British Resident Commissioner and an effective monitoring role for the UN.

Meanwhile, as the fighting intensified, a number of sharp disagreements had arisen among the Front-Line leaders. Nyerere was 'furious' on learning in late 1977 that Neto and Kaunda had been secretly training Nkomo's guerrillas, in breach of a Front-Line agreement that both ZANU and ZAPU fighters would be trained jointly at Tanzania's Nachingwea base.[6] Nyerere also sharply challenged a proposal by Kaunda to drop the idea of elections in favour of a government of national unity.

The most serious rupture occurred in early 1978 when Zambia announced the re-opening of her southern rail route to Rhodesia which she had closed in 1973. This episode illustrates both the fragility and resilience of the Front-Line coalition. Before the announcement Zambia had sent emissaries to all Front-Line capitals to explain the urgency of re-opening the line, which was the only route by which Zambia could obtain delivery of 90,000 tons of fertilizer in time for the planting season. Kaunda himself flew to Dar es-Salaam to explain this to Nyerere. Initially all the leaders expressed their understanding. At the last minute, however, Nyerere and Machel appear to have had second thoughts, and argued vigorously against the re-opening of the line, claiming they had been told that only the road would be re-opened. Kaunda stood fast, noting that the road had remained open all along. Machel, whose economy (like

that of Zambia) was suffering from the closure of her own important rail links to Rhodesia, was so angry that he condemned Kaunda's move in the press. He also refused to attend the next Front-Line summit at Dar es-Salaam, called by Kaunda to express displeasure at his fellow Presidents' criticism. At Dar es-Salaam the rancour in the air was such that no real dialogue took place, but, by the next summit in March 1979, the incident had been buried and no hard feelings were apparent.[7]

Frictions such as this were but one feature of Front-Line collaboration in its initial period. They should be seen in the broad perspective of a group of new, politically diverse and economically weak states jointly pursuing a difficult foreign policy objective under a growing threat to their countries' political and economic stability. Moreover, much of the friction reflected differences in personality and style, and differing degrees of militancy among the Front-Line Presidents. In a process particularly marked by *ad hoc* summitry, the interplay among the leaders' personalities had a decisive impact on their state-to-state relations. No attempts were made to discourage an individual Front-Line President from undertaking unilateral, often personal, initiatives which he felt might help the agreed common goal. Summitry, rather than reliance on permanent secretariats or staffs, was sometimes afflicted by uncoordinated initiatives and a lack of follow-through on agreed policy. A serious disagreement was sometimes simply left unresolved rather than forced to a potentially divisive show-down. Yet it is questionable whether any other *modus operandi* would have worked as well, particularly in this early period of Front-Line collaboration. Summitry allowed the leaders to run their own foreign policy, and to deal jointly and immediately with a fractious nationalist leader or a new Western peace proposal. This gave the leaders a flexibility that a permanent Front-Line bureaucracy would have undermined.

II. THE FRONT-LINE STATES AND THE RHODESIAN PEACE SETTLEMENT

Growing Pressures on the Front-Line States

By the last half of 1978, the costs of the war to Zambia, Mozambique and Botswana were rising rapidly and soon were approaching the limits of tolerance. In September and October of that year Rhodesian forces launched heavy ground and air attacks against guerrilla bases and refugee camps deep inside the Zambian and Mozambican sanctuaries, where they remained several days. One of the camps attacked was situated only a dozen miles outside Lusaka.

These raids, which resulted in some 2,000 guerrilla casualties and the capture or destruction of large quantities of weapons and other stores, placed a considerable burden on the host countries' already-strained medical, food and logistical capabilities. They also revealed the glaring inability of the Front-Line States to defend their air-space and territory against attack: an embarrassing weakness which led Kaunda immediately to seek military aid from Britain and the USSR. Botswana, which had already experienced numerous Rhodesian incursions on a small scale, had reason to fear heavier raids in the future; indeed Rhodesian military spokesmen pointedly charged that Nkomo's ZIPRA guerrillas, (Zimbabwe People's Revolutionary Army, the military element of ZAPU), were crossing through Botswanan territory at the rate of 1,200 a month to attack targets inside Rhodesia.

The guerrilla presence in the region was also causing other problems for the Front-Line States. In Zambia armed guerrillas were commandeering automobiles and seizing grain and other supplies at gunpoint. The easy availability of weapons and the lack of discipline among ZIPRA followers led to an alarming wave of thuggery and violent crime which reached Lusaka itself. Moreover, by 1978 ZIPRA's 12,000–15,000 Soviet- and Cuban-trained forces outnumbered and out-gunned Zambia's 8,000-man national army. The potential threat which this posed for Zambian national security was not lost on Kaunda, whose ultimate control over the activities of ZIPRA forces inside Zambia was little more than nominal. Kaunda's close personal ties to Nkomo by no means translated into control over Nkomo's more radical guerrilla commanders. Even when transport bottlenecks threatened Zambia with famine early in 1979, Kaunda postponed re-opening a key lorry route to Rhodesia for fear that such a move would antagonize the guerrillas.[8]

Mozambique's leaders were apprehensive over the growing need for a joint ZIPRA-ZANLA military operation based in Mozambique. Militarily such an operation made sense. Nkomo's well-trained and well-equipped ZIPRA forces operating out of Zambia found the Zambesi gorge to be an insuperable obstacle to large-scale border crossings into Rhodesia. Thus, to the increasing distress of Nyerere and Kaunda, Nkomo's large force remained for the most part bottled up in Zambia and confined to making small-scale and isolated attacks. Rhodesia's eastern frontier with Mozambique was far more porous to military penetration, as the success of Mugabe's ZANLA forces had shown. But Mozambique's leaders were afraid that, in the absence of a genuine unity of the two guerrilla armies, the transfer of Nkomo's forces to Mozambique would lead to renewed outbreaks of conflict between ZIPRA's essentially Ndebele-speaking guerrillas and the Shona-speaking ZANLA forces. It was feared that this might in turn lead to outbreaks of tribal conflict between Mozambique's own Shona and Ndebele peoples. Hence Mozambique pressed hard, but without success, for a total merger of ZIPRA and ZANLA forces.

Meanwhile Soviet and Cuban military support to the Rhodesian guerrillas was growing. While Nyerere and Machel were trying without success to persuade the USSR to provide arms for Mugabe's forces as well as Nkomo's, Cuba was showing a keen interest in raising her support to Nkomo and developing links with ZANLA as well. In June 1978 Nkomo announced that 75 Cuban military advisers were helping to train his army. It was also reported that Soviet military advisers were urging Nkomo to step up the scale of ZIPRA attacks against Rhodesia.[9] These developments brought home to Presidents Khama and Kaunda the danger that the Rhodesian

95

conflict could easily erupt into a larger war involving the introduction of foreign troops which would almost certainly embroil their own countries in the fighting. Khama was particularly outspoken in calling for the removal of Cuban troops from Africa – a theme which was taken up by a number of African leaders at the OAU meetings in Khartoum in July 1978.[10]

But military and security considerations were not the only concerns driving the Front-Line leaders towards seeking a settlement of the Rhodesian war. The economic cost of the war for Zambia, Mozambique and Botswana had assumed staggering proportions. By 1977 the cost to Zambia of her economic sanctions against Rhodesia were alone estimated to have reached a cumulative total of almost $750 million – equal to roughly a third of her annual GDP.[11] Sanctions were costing Mozambique in the order of $100 million a year.

Zambia's boycott of Rhodesian railways had led to massive transport bottlenecks as Zambian freight overwhelmed the ailing Tazara rail outlet through Dar es-Salaam. Towards the middle of 1978 a backlog of 100,000 tons of copper – the product on which Zambia depends for over 90% of her foreign exchange earnings – awaited shipment to Dar es-Salaam, while 90,000 tons of Zambian imports were stacked up on the docks waiting to be carried inland. In spite of Kaunda's agonized decision in the Autumn of 1978 to re-open Zambia's major Rhodesian rail link in order to bring in critically-needed fertilizer, transport bottlenecks continued to plague Zambia into the Summer of 1979, when a backlog of 75,000 tons of imported grain piled up in South African warehouses. Rhodesia raised the pressure on Kaunda further by destroying a highway-and-rail bridge near Moatize on the Zambia–Mozambique border, thereby denying Zambia the use of her only direct commercial link to the Mozambican port of Beira.

Other economic costs, only a portion of which were offset by financial and other aid from international organizations and from bilateral sources, included housing and feeding Rhodesian refugees, more than 10,000 of whom swelled Botswana's small indigenous population (800,000), while some 40,000 had sought refuge in Mozambique. Mozambique also claimed that Rhodesian raids had killed 1,800 nationals and left 50,000 uprooted from their homes and villages.

Political pressures, too, began to accelerate in 1978. In March the Smith Government announced that agreement had been reached with internal black political leaders on a transition to black majority rule. A multi-racial transitional government was established to bring about a cease-fire, draft a new constitution, and arrange for general elections. Although the Western reaction was one of grave doubt – that Smith would in fact permit majority rule to be established and that any settlement which excluded the guerrillas would actually bring an end to the fighting – there was also recognition that Rhodesia had, in the careful words of British Foreign Secretary David Owen, taken a significant step towards majority rule. The South African Government, as well as conservative political and business groups in the West, openly applauded the internal settlement, and called for Western recognition and an end to sanctions. Their argument – that it was in the interests of the West to support a moderate and responsible multiracial government with all its imperfections, rather than see the country fall into the hands of Marxist guerrillas – soon began to draw significant public and legislative support, particularly in Britain and America.

Front-Line leaders' fears that the Western powers would abandon the search for a settlement involving *all* the parties to the conflict, including the guerrillas, and would instead support Smith's internal settlement, were reinforced by events in the first half of 1979. In March, Rhodesia's internal elections took place with little disruption and, in spite of guerrilla threats and harrassment, 65% of the eligible voters took part. The party of Bishop Abel Muzorewa won two-thirds of the votes cast. In May, Britain's newly-elected Prime Minister, Margaret Thatcher, set the new Conservative policy in an interview with *Time* magazine on 14 May 1979, in which she effectively buried the already-moribund Anglo–US peace plan, stating that 'we must go from where we are now: there *is* an internal settlement'. The same month saw the US Senate vote 75–19 to call on President Carter to end sanctions within ten days of Muzorewa's swearing-in as Zimbabwe–Rhodesia's Prime Minister.

On 18 May, a few days after the Thatcher statement, the Front-Line Commonwealth members – Botswana, Zambia and Tanzania – called an emergency meeting of the Commonwealth High Commissioners to discuss Rhodesia. The meeting ended with a warning to Britain that there would be serious repercussions among the Commonwealth countries if the Thatcher Government recognized the Muzorewa Regime or lifted sanctions. Britain dispatched Lord Harlech to Africa to reassure Africa's Commonwealth leaders that Britain would not act hastily, and to explore with them ways to bring the guerrillas into the settlement. But to the Front-Line States this looked like a smoke-screen to cover what one official called 'creeping *de facto* recognition of Muzorewa', a tactic to avoid antagonizing the Commonwealth countries before the annual Commonwealth Summit Conference in August.

In July the Front-Line States received another setback when the OAU failed to give Nkomo and Mugabe's PF the overwhelming endorsement it expected. Influenced by several conservative African leaders who were sympathetic to the Muzorewa Government, the OAU Resolution called for all-party talks.

Thus, despite the failure of the Muzorewa Administration to end the war or split the uneasy Nkomo–Mugabe 'alliance', the Front-Line leaders faced the bleak prospects of growing support for the internal settlement, and an end to sanctions by the Autumn. If sanctions were lifted, Zimbabwe-Rhodesia might hold out indefinitely against the guerrillas, and the war could go on for a long time, with increasing spill-over into neighbouring Front-Line countries.

One of the war's most bizarre episodes, which only recently came to light, occurred in June 1979, when a high-level Cuban emissary, Raul Vivo, arrived in Maputo with a novel proposal.[12] To forestall world recognition of the Muzorewa Government, Cuba proposed that Nkomo and Mugabe should announce the formation of an independent Zimbabwe government in one of the guerrilla-controlled areas of Rhodesia near the Mozambique border and that this should be done at an elaborate ceremony, with foreign journalists and both ZIPRA and ZANLA troop units in attendance. To guard against Rhodesian or South African attempts to disrupt the ceremony, Mozambique's armed forces were to be fully mobilized, and a mechanized Mozambican battalion, complete with artillery and anti-aircraft weapons, would enter Rhodesia at the time of the investiture. Vivo claimed that the entire Communist camp had been consulted about the plan, and would immediately recognize the ₁newly-created government.

The most astonishing element of this episode is the apparent acquiescence in it of three Front-Line leaders: Machel, Kaunda and Neto. Had Mugabe and Nkomo not vetoed the plan, it might have won full Front-Line support, thereby leading inevitably to an extension and prolongation of the war, probably with the entry of South African combat troops. The Lancaster House initiative, counting as it did on the (at least tacit) consent of the Tory Centre and Right in Britain, would have been still-born. Front-Line leaders have not discussed the reasons behind their acquiescence in the Vivo plan, but it was apparently due to a temporary lapse; a sense of desperation when the internal settlement appeared about to be recognized and sanctions ended. Nkomo and Mugabe, each for different reasons, vetoed the plan. Nkomo was apparently reluctant to move his troops and headquarters from his Zambian base to Mugabe's area of operations in Mozambique. Mugabe was unwilling to accept second place in the proposed government. He also feared that the plan would result in an escalation of the war, with growing attacks on Mozambique leading to the introduction of Warsaw Pact combat troops into the area, and a rapid internationalization of the fighting. Following that episode, the Front-Line leaders concluded that a new and vigorous effort must be made to reach a settlement which would include the PF; and that the time for doing so was fast running out.

Prelude: Lusaka and Havana

The Front-Line States saw the Commonwealth Summit Conference, to be held in Lusaka in the first week of August 1979, as the best opportunity to put their case to the Thatcher Government. During July they initiated intensive behind-the-scenes consultations with Commonwealth leaders. Although Front-Line officials say that no formal caucuses or meetings to concert strategy were held prior to Lusaka, their efforts to bring pressure on Mrs Thatcher to withhold recognition of the Muzorewa Government and to try again for an all-parties settlement showed signs of at least some prior co-ordination. They made use of the Commonwealth Secretariat in London to keep in continuous touch with all interested parties. On 31 July – the day before the Conference opened – Nigeria announced the nationalization of British Petroleum's 20% share in BP–Shell Nigeria. While this move is said to have been taken on Nigeria's own initiative, the Front-Line States had frequently told Nigeria that she was the only African state which could put economic pressure on Britain. Other pre-Lusaka initiatives included a personal message from Botswana's President Khama to President Carter urging the US not to recognize Muzorewa, and a decision by President Machel of Mozambique (not a Commonwealth member) to send two official observers to the Lusaka Summit.

Meanwhile, a number of senior British Foreign Office officials had become deeply concerned over the direction of the Thatcher Government's Rhodesia policy. Fearing that the recognition of the Muzorewa Government and the removal of sanctions would have serious repercussions on the Commonwealth and on Britain's relations with black Africa, and that Britain might find herself forced to defend Muzorewa in a widening war, these officials began, with Lord Carrington, the new Foreign Secretary, to promote another attempt at an all-parties settlement. Their proposal had most of the features of the earlier Anglo–US plan: an all-parties constitutional conference under British auspices; the reversion to British colonial rule during a transition period; and elections to be held under British authority and with Commonwealth observers. It differed from the previous plan in that it was to be a wholly British initiative, rather than a joint Anglo–US endeavour, and the Commonwealth would play the role previously foreseen for the UN. Most important, it would be understood that failure of the proposed conference would lead to British recognition of Muzorewa and the lifting of sanctions.

It is difficult to judge how successful this group of senior officials of the Foreign Office was in changing Mrs Thatcher's position *prior* to Lusaka, and how much her reversal came during the Conference itself. She had,, at the very least, modified her initially pro-Muzorewa statements, and clearly favoured postponing the question of recognition. It is also clear that Nigeria's nationalization of BP, together with warnings from the British overseas business community, had reinforced the Foreign Office arguments and made her less receptive to the position of the pro-white Rhodesia lobby.

Yet, as the African Commonwealth leaders came to Lusaka, they felt, in the words of one participant, that 'anything can happen'. Whether or not they were aware of the Foreign Office internal effort, they found Mrs Thatcher ready to listen. Some Front-Line officials remain convinced that she came to Lusaka set on recognizing Muzorewa. In any event, the Commonwealth Front-Line Heads of State, together with a number of non-African Commonwealth leaders – notably Prime Minister Malcolm Fraser of Australia – put strong arguments to Mrs Thatcher, and it is evident from their later reactions that they were surprised at their own success. They found that, to quote one participant, 'almost over-night, she turned around'; and that, once turned, she became a forceful advocate of the new policy. British participants credit Kaunda and Nyerere with playing an important role in persuading her to hold a constitutional conference.

In the end, the Heads of State of Britain, Tanzania, Zambia, Nigeria, Australia and Jamaica, together with the Commonwealth Secretary-General, Shridath Ramphal, met in closed session to hammer out the basis for a settlement. The result was a nine-point set of principles for achieving peace in Rhodesia (see Appendix). These principles, which were largely taken from a draft proposal tabled in advance by Nyerere, were then endorsed by the 41 Commonwealth leaders as a group. Britain then announced that a constitutional conference would begin on 10 September 1979 at Lancaster House, London, and that delegations must have full powers of negotiation and commitment.

The real test of the Front-Line States' joint commitment to the peace process was about to start. The Patriotic Front, particularly ZANU's Robert Mugabe, was incensed that Nyerere and Kaunda had endorsed an all-parties' conference, thus formally dissociating themselves from the PF's standing demand that power be handed to the PF prior to elections. The PF leaders felt further betrayed by the Front-Line's agreement that Britain, which the PF did not trust to be a disinterested party, should resume colonial authority during the transition.

The extent of PF disquiet became evident at the Havana Summit Conference of non-aligned states in early September. According to participants, the PF tried to get support from the more radical non-aligned leaders for a resolution disavowing the Lusaka Commonwealth accord. When this effort became known to Front-Line leaders, there was an angry confrontation with the PF. Mugabe argued that, since the OAU had already designated the PF as 'sole and legitimate representative' of the Rhodesian people, the question was simply one of arranging a transfer of power. The Front-Line leaders, strongly supported by Nigeria, rudely disabused the PF of this notion. Mugabe was told that the PF was named 'sole and legitimate representative' for tactical reasons only: i.e., to keep other states from recognizing Muzorewa. Nyerere informed him that he was not considered to represent all the people of Rhodesia, and in fact not every Front-Line State had favoured bestowing that designation on the PF in the first place.

The Front-Line States, in the persons of Nyerere and Machel, then delivered a stern ultimatum: if the PF refused to take part in the Lancaster House negotiations, the Front-Line States would withdraw their support of the PF and close down the war. At the same time, the PF was reassured that, if the Conference failed because of Britain or Muzorewa, the Front-Line States would support fully a renewal of the armed conflict; moreover, the guerrillas could continue the war during the Conference, until a cease-fire should take effect. Following this confrontation, which Mugabe, with typical understatement, later described as 'forthright', the PF agreed (albeit with deep reservations) to attend the Lancaster House Conference.

The Front-Line Role at Lancaster House
The Stakes
On 10 September 1979, roughly a month after the dramatic Commonwealth Summit – or 'Lu-bloody-saka' as Lord Carrington chose to remember it – the Constitutional Conference on Southern Rhodesia opened at Lancaster House in London. It was to be a British show. Apart from the high-level British delegation, only those representing the Muzorewa Government and the Patriotic Front participated directly. Important and sometimes critical interventions by the Front-Line States, the Commonwealth Secretariat, South Africa and the US took place in the wings.

The prospects for success looked anything but bright. Lord Carrington, who was to prove a tough, even at times hectoring, chairman, was prepared, and apparently expected, to see the Conference fail. If it were scuttled by Muzorewa, then sanctions would be renewed; if scuttled by the PF, then Britain would opt for its 'second-class solution' which entailed the ending of sanctions and recognition of the Muzorewa Government. In either event the war would, in all probability, accelerate and become more unpleasant diplomatically for Britain and the West.

The PF came to Lancaster House only because it was forced to do so by the Front-Line States. Its delegation was sullen, angry and suspicious. They mistrusted the British, and felt that the Front-Line States had betrayed PF interests at Lusaka. However, Nkomo and Mugabe knew that, if they caused the Conference to collapse, Machel and Kaunda would withdraw their support from the insurgency. On the other hand, if it collapsed because of Muzorewa, the Front-Line States were pledged to support an intensified insurgency.

99

In spite of this stick-and-carrot incentive to stay at the table, the PF tried, sometimes desperately, to bypass the Front-Line States and to have the Conference disavowed by the OAU or UN. Both Western and Front-Line sources say that, almost to the day the Peace Treaty was signed, the PF sought, in the words of one observer, 'to wriggle out of the process'.

Muzorewa, too, came to Lancaster House against his will and with deep misgivings. Even to agree to discuss a new constitution was to acknowledge that there were deficiencies in the one that he and Smith had only recently agreed upon and, by implication, in the elections which had brought him to office. Moreover, Muzorewa must have been aware that the Conference agenda might, as indeed it did, go well beyond the constitutional issue and terminate his status as Head of State. Both he and his Government realized, however, that they had failed either to win international recognition or to end the war, which was going badly and bleeding the economy. Only by participating in the Lancaster House Conference could they hope to win international recognition and, probably of greater immediate importance, bring an end to sanctions which had at last begun seriously to affect the economy and the conduct of the war. Muzorewa had been assured of British recognition if the PF walked out of the discussions, a contingency which seemed not unlikely at the time. Moreover, he felt that he could count on greater South African military support, should things go really badly. Finally, both he and South African leaders were convinced that he would win re-election against the PF.

The Front-Line leaders, particularly Kaunda and Machel, also had a vital stake in the outcome of the Conference. A PF veto on the proceedings, and the ensuing lifting of sanctions, would lead to a rapid boost in outside aid to Rhodesia's war potential and might well bring South Africa into the war. Moreover, even the results of a Muzorewa walkout would not be all that different in terms of Front-Line interests; that is, intensified warfare with every likelihood of growing social and economic disruption in Zambia, Mozambique and Botswana – although in that contingency they might hope for greater international support of the PF and a greater willingness of others to help share the growing costs of the war to the Front-Line States. The Front-Line leaders thus had strong reasons for wanting the Conference to succeed, and were particularly determined that the PF should not be the cause of its collapse.

The Modus Operandi
The British decided in advance to avoid the open-ended wrangling that would result if all three delegations tabled draft proposals. Instead, Britain alone would present a draft; objections and suggestions would be heard, and then the British would revise the draft in private. Lord Carrington would present the revision on a take-it-or-leave-it basis, pressing the opposing delegations to accept it within a very short time.

Britain was well aware that the Front-Line States must play an important role in pressing the PF into accepting this 'gag-and-swallow routine', as one victim described it. Therefore she would try at each major step in the process to get the acquiescence of key Front-Line leaders in advance. Yet the British delegation also sought maximum flexibility in the negotiations; hence, it hoped to keep the Front-Line States from functioning as a *bloc* behind the scenes.

In this they were helped by the fact that the Front-Line leaders' preferred style was unstructured and *ad hoc*, with each state free to take whatever individual steps were felt would advance the general objectives of the group. Front-Line sources acknowledge, for example, that no attempt was made at formal co-ordination of Front-Line positions or agreed tactics in advance of Lancaster House. The Commonwealth Secretariat provided a useful venue for informal consultation during the Conference; indeed, such meetings took place more or less regularly every couple of days. Participants usually included the High Commissioners of Zambia, Tanzania, Botswana and Nigeria, plus Mark Chona, Kaunda's special envoy to the talks, and the Mozambican observer at the Conference, Fernando HonWana. They were normally joined by Anthony Duff and Derek Day – two key members of the British delegation.

The PF was not represented in these meetings, which the participants claim to have been an important forum for trying to reconcile divergent PF and British positions.

It is also clear that Machel, Nyerere and Kaunda, possibly in that order, were the key Front-Line figures in the peace process. Botswana, with a seriously ailing leader and far less influence with the PF, nevertheless played a useful and supportive role. Angola, also with a mortally-ill leader (President Neto), took virtually no part in the Lancaster House process. Machel was the most vocal of the Front-Line leaders and the closest to Mugabe. Machel's representatives in London for the talks are credited with being particularly astute and discerning: because Machel was kept accurately informed of current developments in the talks, he was able to bring constructive influence to bear at key moments in the fragile negotiations. While Western participants and observers generally feel that Machel played the most important Front-Line role, Front-Line participants stress the dominance of Nyerere. As the informally-acknowledged Chairman of the Front-Line Presidents, he spoke for them as a group. Unlike Kaunda and Machel, each of whom was the prime backer of one of the two guerrilla groups and hence suspect in the eyes of the other, Nyerere was seen as more or less neutral as well as being a strong supporter of the PF as such. This, together with his dominating personality, made him the court of last resort for the PF: only *his* word was considered final. Early on in the meetings, for example, he bluntly dismissed PF complaints about Carrington's autocratic running of the Conference, telling Nkomo and Mugabe: 'This is a *British* conference. Carrington is a *British* chairman. So don't waste your time telling him how to run it'. Yet, apparently because of poor communications between Dar es-Salaam and Tanzania's High Commission in London, Nyerere seems to have been sometimes out-of-date or ill-informed about what was going on. He would, for example, on occasion come out in strong support of a PF position on which the PF itself had already conceded a day or two before.[13] At times his intervention was seen, by both the PF and the British, to be counter-productive. Kaunda, like the other Front-Line Presidents, left the day-to-day liaison to his special representatives, and came to London only once during the fifteen-week Conference. The Zambian role was nevertheless an important one.

Thus, the Front-Line States approached the Conference with: a vital interest in its outcome; a general understanding as a group that they would take a low-profile but supportive position; a readiness on the part of individual leaders to intercede when each saw an opportunity to help the process along; and a realization that the PF would be a difficult *protégé*. As the negotiations moved tensely and uncertainly along, Front-Line intervention evolved along four lines:

– applying pressure on the PF not to break off the talks and to accept 'final' British proposals;
– mediating informally between the British and the PF;
– persuading the Communist States not to torpedo the talks;
– soliciting Commonwealth and UN support to put pressure on Britain.

The Front-Line States in Action
Britain's draft proposal for a new constitution was the first issue on the Lancaster House agenda. Initially, the PF balked at discussing a constitution before the modalities for a transitional government had been agreed. They dropped this objection after Front-Line officials had assured them that the constitution would be binding only if the entire peace package were agreed to and signed. The PF then rejected the Draft Constitution itself, claiming that it was directed more towards protecting white privilege than meeting the future needs of Zimbabwe. Although – unlike the Smith–Muzorewa Constitution – the new one contained no mechanism by which whites could block constitutional change, it did reserve twenty parliamentary seats for whites for a period of seven years, a provision to which the PF strongly objected, on the grounds that its effect would be to give Smith's Rhodesia Front Party 20 seats with which it would seek to obstruct the work of parliament. After holding out for two weeks

over this issue, the PF gave in under heavy Front-Line pressure, particularly from Nyerere, who had already expressed approval of the Draft which the British had shown him prior to tabling it at Lancaster House. To get the PF over this first hurdle, Front-Line officials told them: 'It's only for seven years; then you can change things to suit the conditions; but if you bolt the Conference now, the UK will recognize Muzorewa and will defend his Regime'.

The PF then balked at the provision that the future Zimbabwe Government would have to pay 'prompt and adequate compensation' to white landowners for any land acquired from them. Machel, noting that he was still paying compensation to the Portuguese, persuaded Mugabe to accept this idea. The PF then claimed that Britain and the US had earlier committed themselves (under the Kissinger proposals) to providing $2 bn for this purpose. At this point the Front-Line States toughened their stand. The PF was informed: 'Since you have already publicly accepted the really *major* provisions of the constitution, you cannot threaten to break up the Conference over a minor issue like compensation. The Front-Line will *not* back you up'. Recognizing, however, that the issue was a politically difficult one for Mugabe to concede, Front-Line representatives conferred with British and American officials and together they found a face-saving formula: in carefully-chosen and suitably non-committal language, Britain announced her agreement to promote the establishment of a multinational fund to which Britain, the US, the EEC, the World Bank and others would contribute. According to Front-Line sources, this agreement gave Mugabe something to sell to his rank and file followers as evidence that Britain had promised Zimbabwe massive aid to buy out white-owned land. With that the PF accepted the draft constitution.

The really critical moment at Lancaster House came on 19 October, when Britain tabled her proposal for a transition period to precede elections. The plan called for executive authority to be vested in a British Governor, who would control the armed forces and police. The existing (i.e., Rhodesian) police force would be responsible for maintaining law and order during the proposed two-month transition, and no provision was made for merging the guerrilla forces with those of the Rhodesian Government.

An earlier version of this plan had been modified under Front-Line pressure to meet major PF objections. The original British proposal had called for a two-week election campaign, proportional representation and no voter registration. The PF demanded a six-month election campaign, separate electoral constituencies and voter registration. In the end, the Front-Line States prevailed on Carrington to drop proportional representation, agree to voter registration, and to extend the election campaign to two months. The Front-Line States then persuaded the PF to accept the two-month campaign.

But the PF, still resentful of its failure to win a share of power during the transition, vetoed the 19 October proposal and threw the talks into deadlock. Their real sticking-point was the provision that law and order would be the responsibility of the Rhodesian police. To a degree, the Front-Line leaders backed them up: they insisted, as a matter of principle, that the PF forces be given equal status with the Rhodesian forces during the transition. After a three-week impasse which seemed likely to wreck the Conference, Kaunda flew to London where, at a working dinner with Mrs Thatcher and Lord Carrington, he urged major concessions in the British position. Out of this meeting came the compromise proposal which ended the deadlock: Britain would agree to pay, feed and house the guerrilla forces during the transition. This was, according to Front-Line officials, more than a face-saving device to allow the PF to climb down from its veto: it helped to establish the equality of treatment of the two opposing armed forces. Whether or not the idea was Kaunda's is of little relevance. The important point is that a Front-Line Head of State came away from an emergency session with Mrs Thatcher and Lord Carrington with important British concessions which he used to win PF acquiescence in the entire transition proposal on 15 November.[14]

The final item on the Lancaster House agenda was also the one most fraught with danger: the cease-fire arrangements. On 22 November, Carrington tabled the British proposal, which called for a brief (7–10 day) cease-fire, a monitoring force of several hundred troops from white Commonwealth countries, and 14 assembly points for the PF inside Rhodesia. Muzorewa accepted the proposals a few days later, but the PF – particularly Mugabe – flatly rejected them. Mugabe felt that a monitoring force of several thousand would be needed to insure against any attempt by the Rhodesian forces to annihilate his ZANLA troops in their assembly areas. He also wanted the monitoring force to include non-white troops, and he demanded a longer cease-fire period in which to get word to isolated guerrilla units and give them time to find their way to the assembly points.

Yet the chief obstacle – the one which stalled the Conference for almost a month and once again brought it near the point of collapse – was the question of troop disposition. The proposed 14 assembly points were all located along Rhodesia's periphery; in the North-west, East and South-east of the country. The Rhodesian troop locations were mainly in the centre of the country, but with some right on the borders. Thus the guerrillas in their assembly camps would be sandwiched between Rhodesian forces and cut off from escape to Mozambique or Zambia if attacked.[15] Moreover, Mugabe felt that it was essential that ZANLA forces be seen in Rhodesia's populous central areas during the transition, if his Party was to stand a chance in the elections.

At the urgent request of Mugabe, a Front-Line Summit Meeting was held in Dar es-Salaam on 24–25 November. Nkomo, who was planning to keep the bulk of his troops inside Zambia during the cease-fire, was ready to agree to the British terms. Mugabe, however, put a strong case. Apparently he won broad support for most of his objections, although, among the Front-Line Presidents, only Nyerere agreed with him that a six-month cease-fire was desirable. All the Presidents appear to have been irritated by Mugabe's insistence that his troops report wherever they happened to be, rather than at specified assembly points, but finally he dropped that proposal. In the end, however,

it was clear that he would not agree to arrangements which he saw as inciting a massacre of ZANLA forces. The Front-Line leaders agreed to put his case for removing Rhodesian troops from the border areas, and for increasing the size of the Commonwealth monitoring force to Lord Carrington.

This last was not to prove easy: the Front-Line States ruled themselves out, Muzorewa vetoed Nigeria, and Britain was unenthusiastic about Indian participation. On 28 November Carrington offered a compromise plan. Its major provisions were the withdrawal of Rhodesian troops from border positions to their bases and the enlargement of the monitoring force from Australia and New Zealand to 1,200 with the addition of contingents from Fiji and Kenya. The Front-Line States saw these concessions as essentially meeting the PF's major objections and they urged acceptance.

Though giving qualified approval on 6 December, the PF refused to sign the Agreement until their remaining demands for additional assembly points and an extended cease-fire deadline had been met, and consequently both Britain and the Front-Line States began to increase the pressure on the PF. Nyerere and Machel, through their London representatives, made it clear that they would not allow the Conference to be scuttled over such minor issues, claiming that no-one would accept it as a reason to break off negotiations. On 12 December Britain sent her Governor-designate, Lord Soames, to Salisbury and announced an end to sanctions.

But Mugabe and Nkomo, apparently acting independently of each other, decided around mid-December to make one last desperate bid to by-pass Lancaster House and the Front Line and try to win support for their position – or perhaps even to have the whole Lancaster House process condemned – at the UN. When word reached the Front-Line representatives that Mugabe and Nkomo had applied for visas to New York, Machel intervened personally to stop Mugabe from leaving London, and US, British, Zambian and Commonwealth Secretariat officials are all believed to have pressured Nkomo into staying.

Meanwhile Front-Line officials were successful in winning important last-minute concessions from Carrington: increasing the number of guerrilla assembly points to an initial 16, the last to be located in the centre of the country, at Que-Que; and agreement that additional assembly points would be established as needed.[16] Lord Carrington also announced that there would be some flexibility in the two-week deadline by which all guerrillas were to have reported to assembly areas. On 21 December 1979 the final peace accord was signed by all the parties involved.

Post-Lancaster House

The Front-Line States remained actively engaged in the Rhodesian affair between the signing of the Lancaster House Accord in December and the Zimbabwe elections in early March. Their chief function in this period was to build PF confidence in the pre-election process by demonstrating close support for the PF and vigilance against any possible British or Rhodesian attempts to use the cease-fire to gain military or electoral advantage for Muzorewa.

During early January and February all sides reported numerous violations of the cease-fire and incidents of political intimidation. By far the largest number of such incidents was attributed to those ZANLA guerrillas who remained outside the assembly areas. Lord Soames, fearing a complete collapse of the fragile cease-fire, and with scattered units of the 1,200–1,500-man Commonwealth monitoring force the only available neutral troops to call upon, announced a succession of measures directed at curbing abuses by the PF. In early January Soames announced that the Rhodesian army would be used to keep law and order, particularly to stop ZANLA guerrillas from infiltrating into the country at large.

Nyerere saw this move as a dangerous violation of the Peace Accord.[17] He also shared the PF's concern that there were 'thousands' of South African troops inside Rhodesia. On 14 January Nyerere threatened to sever diplomatic ties with Britain and persuaded the OAU Liberation Committee to denounce Lord Soames' actions. Nyerere also alerted the Chairman of the OAU, the UN Secretary General, and the Chairman of the non-aligned states. In the face of these growing pressures, Soames announced on 30 January the withdrawal of South African troops (said to have numbered only about two hundred) who had been guarding the Salisbury–Beitbridge rail line. Soames said that any other South African soldiers in Rhodesia were under Rhodesian military command and thus were authorized to be there. (Western intelligence sources estimated these latter to number 'several hundred', not the 6,000 claimed by the PF and the Front-Line States.) Nevertheless on 2 February the UN Security Council, pushed by the African group at the UN, demanded the removal of all South African forces, 'regular or mercenary', and called on Britain to ensure the speedy return of refugees to take part in the elections.

During the next two weeks, Soames threatened to cancel elections in areas of serious intimidation, and did in fact suspend Mugabe's ZANU(PF) Party from campaigning in two areas following ZANLA cease-fire violations there. On 21 February, following a meeting of 30 Commonwealth High Commissioners called by Tanzania, the Commonwealth Secretary General requested an 'urgent' meeting with Carrington to discuss the Commonwealth's 'crisis of confidence' in Soames. At the same time Nyerere himself called the British, EEC, and Nordic emissaries in Tanzania to warn their governments that Soames' actions were jeopardizing the Lancaster House Accord. He is said to have asked President Carter to guarantee the safety of the PF in the assembly areas.

On 25 February, again at Nyerere's request, the Front-Line Presidents met in Dar es-Salaam. Nyerere was incensed at the Governor's refusal to confine regular and auxiliary Rhodesian troops to their barracks and at what he saw as harassment of the PF's election campaign by Lord Soames. Nyerere's alarm was apparently not shared by the other Front-Line leaders: the joint communiqué following their summit expressed the mildest of reservations about Soames' handling of the election campaign, and notably failed to pledge Front-Line support for a resumption of the guerrilla war should the PF lose the election. On the same day (26 February) Soames and Mugabe resolved their differences: the Governor said he had decided not to cancel elections anywhere, and Mugabe pledged to accept the election results. A day later, Mugabe, who was by then confident that he would win the election, is reported to have met Nyerere to calm the latter's fear and to ask him to soften his criticism of Soames' running of the election campaign.

Meanwhile Machel had been quietly working to arrange a meeting between Mugabe and Rhodesia's Commander-in-Chief, General Walls. Walls, apparently at Machel's personal invitation had flown to Maputo on 23 February for secret talks with Mozambique's Foreign and Defence Ministers. The Mozambicans stressed their hope that a substantial white presence would remain in Zimbabwe after independence, and that the process of integrating the guerrillas with the Rhodesian forces would begin promptly. The Rhodesians were given assurances that Mozambique would accept the election results, and the Mozambicans in turn were assured that there would be no military coup if Mugabe should win the election. Three days later Walls and Mugabe met for the first time to discuss the integration of ZANLA troops and Rhodesian regulars.

Assessing the Front-Line Role

The Rhodesian Peace Settlement, from the Commonwealth Summit in August 1979 until the Zimbabwe elections the following March, brought the Front-Line States to a new level of diplomatic and political cooperation. Their leaders put aside or muted their individual preferences for a particular group or a particular political model in the interests of bringing the war to a close and seeing a freely-elected majority-rule government installed in Salisbury. By and large they played a responsible, honest-broker role, and it is almost certain that the Lancaster House Settlement would have failed without vigorous Front-Line involvement.

Officials operating *below* the Summit level played an important part in the joint Front-Line endeavour at Lancaster House. High Commissioners and special emissaries, like HonWana (Mozambique) and Chona (Zambia) conducted day-to-day informal mediation and liaison among the principals which went far towards finding common ground and easing the PF over difficult hurdles.

Front-Line behaviour in the Rhodesian Settlement revealed both the strengths and weaknesses of its usual (and preferred) mode of collaboration. The ad hoc style, with no formal plan of joint action or agreed individual initiatives, gave each national leader maximum freedom of action, and avoided the disagreements and frictions that might have surfaced had attempts been made to tie member states to more detailed commitments and actions. Yet this style also meant that coordination was weak where it should have been strong. Moreover, as in Nyerere's convening of the Front-Line Summit in late February 1980, better liaison and exchange of information could have avoided heightened tensions at a sensitive point in the pre-election period.

Moreover, in spite of the contributions made by the Front-Line officials below the leadership level, the tone and content of cooperation depended, as in earlier situations, on the personalities and inclinations of individual Front-Line Presidents and their personal ties with the PF. In the absence of permanent machinery (e.g., a secretariat) and formal procedures, success or failure rested on the unilateral actions of particular Front-Line leaders. Indeed, the personal intervention of individual Presidents was critical to the success of Lancaster House. Because of Nyerere's and Kaunda's stature as world leaders and champions of African liberation, and Machel's fresh revolutionary credentials, their counsel and assurances went far to overcome deep PF suspicions in the Lancaster House process and began gradually to build PF confidence in the outcome.

It is difficult to separate the roles of Nyerere, Kaunda and Khama as Front-Line leaders from their positions as Commonwealth Heads of State. Clearly their easy access to Mrs Thatcher and Lord Carrington and their interaction with the Commonwealth Secretariat and individual Commonwealth states (Nigeria, in particular) were made possible by their Commonwealth association. For example, Kaunda's key intercession with Lord Carrington over the transition impasse was undertaken in his role

as the current Chairman of the Commonwealth Heads of State. Thus both their Front-
Line and Commonwealth roles shaped their
performances during the Rhodesian peace
process.

What can be said with confidence is that
the Front-Line States co-operated with each
other and with Britain in a spectacularly successful process of bringing peace and independence to Zimbabwe. Their success
apparently gave them new confidence in their
ability to bring joint efforts to bear on other
regional problems, and in the usefulness of
working closely with Western powers on the
solution of such problems.

The following chapter offers an analysis of
joint Front-Line initiatives and responses in
several other regional security matters. None
of these other issues has yet called forth the
intensive, often day-by-day endeavour that
engaged the Front-Line States in Rhodesia.
Yet the confrontation with South Africa, the
long-standing Namibian conflict, and the
drive for economic security are all regional
security issues of importance in which the
Front-Line States play a substantial role.

III. POST-ZIMBABWE SECURITY CO-OPERATION

South Africa vs. the Front-Line States
Guerrilla threat to South Africa

The Front-Line leaders continue to see the
anti-apartheid struggle as a unique case. It is
viewed not as an anti-colonial struggle, but as
a campaign for majority rule, in which the
whites would have a political voice and a
permanent place in the future society. While
the Front-Line States acknowledge their
obligation to give political and material
assistance to South African national movements, they maintain that the struggle is
South Africa's and must not involve outside
aggression or direct foreign participation.
Moreover, for Botswana, Zambia, Zimbabwe
and Mozambique it is official policy not to
allow cross-border attacks on South Africa
from their territory. Zambia and Mozambique have permitted the most active South
African national movement, the African
National Congress (ANC) to open administra-
trative offices in their capitals while Zimbabwe has turned down an ANC application
to open another in Salisbury.

In spite of official Front-Line assurances,
however, the fact is that ANC attacks inside
South Africa have increased markedly since
1980, and most attacks appear to have originated in Mozambique. In February 1980
South African security forces reported dis-
covering the 'biggest cache of terrorist arms
and ammunition ever found in South Africa'
close to the Mozambique border in northern
Natal.[18] A few months later ANC saboteurs,
allegedly entering from Mozambique, used
limpet mines to blow up several large fuel
storage tanks in a dramatic attack on South
Africa's first oil-from-coal plant at Sasolburg.
Sabotage of two major power stations in the
Transvaal in July 1981 plunged one large
town briefly into darkness and took several
weeks to repair. A month later, several armed
attacks on police stations were followed by a
brief shower of 122mm rockets on South
Africa's largest army camp, near Pretoria.

Such attacks pose no serious threats to the
Government – 'political graffiti' is how one
correspondent characterized them[19] – but
they carry the message to black and white
South Africans that the resistance movement
is alive and active *inside* the country. Indeed
South African officials admit, both privately
and publicly, that the ANC now has at least
some personnel operating from within South
Africa herself. The Chief of the Security
Police claims that the ANC now offers 'crash
courses' in terrorism:

People leave the country legally, saying
they are travelling to neighbouring territories on a holiday or to visit relatives.
After a two-week course in the handling of
weapons and explosives, they return legally
to South Africa.[20]

He further stated that ANC people have
local 'bases', literally underground, three of
which were recently discovered in Soweto.

Neither the Prime Minister, Mr P. W.
Botha, nor any other South African leader

could afford to be seen as 'soft' in the face of this surge in ANC infiltration and sabotage. Toughness, particularly in the face of outside provocation, is a trait which the Afrikaaner people have always valued highly in their leaders. Because Mr Botha has been nurturing a reformist image in domestic race matters, he must take special care to demonstrate to the Afrikaaner rank-and-file that his Government is both sound on security and in control of events, and that the pace of reform will be dictated by the Government in response to perceived domestic imperatives, not forced on South Africa by guerrilla acts or outside pressures.

This domestic political factor, together with the Government's determination to give a sharp warning to those states believed to be supporting, or even thought likely to support, aggression against the Republic, indicated a bold and dramatic response to the ANC challenge. Such a response was no doubt made easier to decide upon in the more sympathetic environment of the Reagan and Thatcher Administrations, neither of which seemed likely to condemn any South African countermeasure, no matter how heavy, and both of which had taken a strong stand against international terrorism.[21]

The Botha Government's Response
Thus on 30 January 1981 a flying column of South African troops, driving eleven Soviet vehicles captured in Angola and subsequently painted in Mozambique's national colours, crossed into Mozambique and drove 50 miles by main road to Matola, a suburb of Mozambique's capital city. There they shelled and destroyed a building occupied by the ANC, killing 12 ANC members and capturing three, plus some weapons. While South Africa claimed that the building was a 'headquarters' or 'operational base', ANC and Mozambican officials said it was only a residence.

The Matola raid was the most blatant, but not the most destabilizing, act taken by South Africa against Mozambique. Far more unsettling has been her covert sponsorship of the Mozambican National Resistance Movement (variously abbreviated as MRM or NRM, and here called MRM). It is a group of dissident Mozambicans, numbering perhaps as many as 3,000, who were originally recruited by the Portuguese in the mid-1970s to combat Machel's FRELIMO guerrillas. After Mozambique gained her independence, the MRM forces fled to Rhodesia, where the Smith Government hired them to disrupt Mozambican transport and communication lines used to support guerrillas operating against the white minority regime in Salisbury. When Zimbabwe in turn came into being, the MRM moved once again, this time into the north-east Transvaal where Zimbabwe, Mozambique and South Africa meet.

From there, and also from smaller bases in Malawi, an invigorated and well-supplied MRM has succeeded in infiltrating at least four central and southern provinces of Mozambique. It has attacked isolated villages and government outposts, sabotaged power lines, destroyed bridges on the Beira–Umtali rail line, and launched sporadic rocket attacks on the main coastal road connecting the port of Beira with the capital, Maputo. Although such actions are consistent with operations by small patrols of 3–4 men, Mozambican authorities acknowledge that the MRM has on occasion fielded a guerrilla formation of up to 200. Perhaps of greatest concern to the Government is the MRM's success on some occasions in winning support of local villagers – a fact which Machel himself admitted in March 1981.

South Africa denies that she supports the MRM, but senior Front-Line military spokesmen say that they have tracked helicopters and transport planes from South Africa flying north along the sparsely-settled Zimbabwe–Mozambique border area to drop men and supplies. Western military observers and intelligence sources also believe that South Africa is directly involved. As one overt piece of evidence, they say that MRM forces have distributed among local villagers large supplies of food and clothing, goods which are virtually unobtainable in Mozambique. The MRM also appears to have been told to improve its image as a legitimate political movement, for, having operated since the early 1970s as a band of anti-FRELIMO mercenaries, in August 1981 it announced the rudiments of a political programme to include free elections and the de-nationalization of state enterprises.[22]

In addition to her direct and indirect military actions against Mozambique, South Africa has threatened to take similar steps against other neighbouring states if they provide bases for the ANC. On 9 May 1981 South Africa's Minister of Police warned Zimbabwe publicly that 'we are aware of the presence of ANC terrorists in Zimbabwe', and that South Africa would 'hit back hard' at countries harbouring guerrillas operating against the Republic.[23] In private conversation, South African officials acknowledge the difference between a guerrilla base and a guerrilla administrative office, which is all that Mozambique and Zimbabwe said they would allow, but South Africa asserts that in practice this distinction blurs, since the establishment of an ANC office inevitably leads to increased guerrilla activity from the host country – even though in some cases, they say, the host country may not be aware that such activity is going on.

This policy appears to be behind the South African raid into Lesotho on 9 December 1982 in which some 30 ANC members are believed to have been killed in Maseru, the capital of Lesotho. The raid was widely condemned by most Western and Third-world governments. The Head of the South African Defence Forces, General Viljoen, was quoted as saying , 'The South African Government has repeatedly warned governments of all neighbouring territories not to allow terrorists to use their territories as springboards against South Africa.' (*The Guardian*, 10 December 1982)

The Front-Line States suspect that South Africa is also supporting and training military forces of dissident Zambians and Zimbabweans for possible future use against the Kaunda and Mugabe Governments. In November 1980, Mugabe himself charged South Africa with recruiting and training large numbers of guerrillas from Zimbabwe.[24] Zimbabwe's Home Affairs Minister elaborated on this charge in May 1981, accusing Pretoria of training 5,000 disgruntled black Zimbabweans at Phalaborwa in the Transvaal. He further said that South Africa was also known to be funding the 'Mushala ban-

dits' (a group of long-time Zambian dissidents).[25] In private, senior Zimbabwe officials repeat the accusations, noting that the 5,000 Zimbabweans are the remnants of Bishop Muzorewa's auxiliary forces who left for South Africa following Muzorewa's electoral defeat in March 1980.

The validity of these charges is difficult to assess. It is known that, prior to Zimbabwe's closure of the South African diplomatic mission in Salisbury in July 1980, it had maintained a recruitment centre for members of the Rhodesian armed forces wishing to leave Zimbabwe and serve in the South African Defence Force (SADF). If this was the case, and if South Africa did indeed recruit 5,000 black Zimbabweans, the Botha Administration has not admitted it. Its silence may reflect domestic politics rather than a desire to conceal a plot against its neighbours. South African whites have always been uneasy about recruitment of blacks into the SADF and the Afrikaaner rank-and-file is inherently opposed to arming blacks. Moreover, the Government is concerned about the legal implications of recruitment, since military service implies citizenship status.

The Front Line's Response

While the Front-Line States publicly label South Africa's policy as a campaign to 'destabilize' the region, their responses to South African aggression have been based on a more subtle perception of the South African threat. From private discussion with senior Mozambican and Zimbabwean officials in the late Spring of 1981, it appears that neither government believes that Pretoria's leaders have been trying to overthrow them or were likely to invade their territories. Mozambique views the MRM as a troublesome problem which will be with her as long as South Africa finds it a convenient means of putting political pressure on the Machel Government. She speculates that South Africa will also try to keep the MRM alive as an in-country reserve that could be reinforced in a crisis, presumably if Mozambique's military ties to the USSR came to be seen in South Africa as a threat to South African security. Pretoria might then use the MRM as the nucleus of a force to occupy the southern half of Mozambique and declare it a 'Free Mozambique', but this is seen as an unlikely contingency.

Nonetheless, in spite of this relatively cool *post-facto* assessment of South Africa's intentions, the Front-Line States – particularly Mozambique and Zimbabwe, which feel themselves to be the most immediately threatened – could not allow such blatantly aggressive acts and threats against their security to go by without a response. On 31 January, the day after South Africa's raid on the ANC building in Mozambique, Mugabe said the attack:

is a signal, warning us not only to proceed with speed to strengthen our own defence forces, but also *to consolidate our military alliance with our Mozambican brothers.* (Italics added)[26]

Three weeks later, Mozambique's Deputy Minister of Defence went to Salisbury for a day of talks with the Chairman of Zimbabwe's Joint High Command, Emerson Mnangagwa. At a news conference later, Mnangagwa said that the discussion, which was the third in twelve months, would lead to continuing 'practical steps' to implement a 1980 agreement on 'the exchange of information on matters of security and defence'.[27] Although press reports continued to mention a 'defence pact', in private conversations senior officials in the two countries denied that any formal mutual defence agreement existed: according to them, there was no 'piece of paper', and the time was not yet ripe for such formal commitments. Yet Zimbabwe acknowledges her debt to Mozambique, and would (the author was informed) have to respond if Mozambique or another Front-Line State under attack asked Zimbabwe to come to her aid.

Meanwhile, informal military co-operation appears to have gone well beyond the 'exchange of information'. From both private discussion and press reports, it is apparent that Mozambique co-ordinates her counter-insurgency activities with Zimbabwe. She informs Zimbabwe, for example, of a forthcoming security sweep in time for Zimbabwe's forces to be moved to that particular border area; as MRM guerrillas flee across the border, they are intercepted by Zimbabwe

troops and turned over to Mozambique. Thus, in March 1981 Zimbabwe announced the capture of 40 MRM personnel along her Eastern border. Private Western sources also report that by the Summer of 1981 reconnaissance planes from Zimbabwe's air force had begun to patrol the sparsely-settled Mozambique border to seek out MRM concentrations and report their location to the Mozambican authorities.

South Africa's raid into Mozambique on 30 January 1981 also prompted a response from the Front-Line States acting as a group. A five-hour Front-Line Summit held in Lusaka on 17 February was attended by five national leaders, plus representatives from Angola (President dos Santos, successor to Neto, was unable to attend) and Nigeria, the *de facto* Front-Line State. Their communiqué condemned the attack, expressed deep concern over South Africa's 'destabilization policy in the region, particularly the continued training of dissidents from Angola, Mozambique, Zambia, and Zimbabwe' and 'reiterated the need to close ranks' in the face of the challenge posed by 'South African aggression'. The reactions and measured responses of the Front-Line States once again showed their proclivity to let the state or states most directly involved – in this case Mozambique and Zimbabwe – take the initiative, while the Front-Line States as a group offered only vocal and diplomatic support. (This pattern occurs again in the Front-Line States handling of Angola's clashes with South Africa, discussed below).

Hence, Mozambique, recognizing the limits to the support she could seek from the Front-Line States, turned to the USSR, which has been her supplier of advanced weapons. Machel quickly invoked his Treaty of Friendship with the Soviet Union and, on 9 February 1981, two Soviet warships dropped anchor in Maputo harbour. However, neither the USSR nor her Mozambican clients seemed intent on escalating the conflict: the Soviet Union perhaps feared that the appearance of any missile bases or similar weapons near the South African border might bring US military support to South Africa, while the Mozambicans – who so far have not permitted the establishment of any

Soviet bases in their country – appear anxious both to avoid increasing their dependence on the USSR and to avoid provoking South Africa.[28]

Mozambique's domestic response to the South African raid was to attempt to mobilize the people against further attacks by organizing Peoples' Militia Groups, training first-aid teams, and holding public meetings. The raid was thus seen as an opportunity to raise public awareness of the threat posed by South Africa, and presumably by the MRM, and to win support for the Government. Beyond that, such measures were taken to show that the leadership was taking vigorous action, rather than being passive and helpless, in the face of extreme provocation by an outside country.

Zimbabwe, too, responded unilaterally to South Africa's threats, and apparently did not think it appropriate or necessary to call upon the Front-Line States in what one official termed her 'war of words with Pretoria'. The day following South Africa's threat to attack Zimbabwe if she continued harbouring ANC terrorists, Mugabe's Minister of Home Affairs, Richard Hove, said Zimbabwe would defend herself with 'utmost vigour' if Pretoria carried out 'its long-conceived plan to invade'. He disclosed that Mugabe had sent a letter to President Reagan complaining of South Africa's 'bullying tactics'. Hove's tough language and accusations of South African terrorism against other states was balanced by a reiteration of Mugabe's policy of denying to any group permission to establish bases for launching cross-border attacks on neighbouring states, and a denial that the ANC had offices in Zimbabwe. The fact that Hove, rather than the Defence Minister or Mugabe himself, responded to South African accusations reflected the leadership's interests in keeping the war of words at a relatively low pitch.

South Africa, Angola and Namibia

During 1979–80 the long-simmering bush war in Namibia began to escalate rapidly. Small groups of SWAPO guerrillas infiltrated Namibia from their Angolan sanctuary to attack power lines, vehicles and isolated farms. Oil tankers and other lorry traffic were forced to move in armed convoys. In May 1980 a SWAPO mortar attack destroyed military aircraft at an advanced South African base.

In response, South Africa adopted a highly aggressive and pre-emptive strategy. South African forces in Namibia, numbering around 30,000 by the end of 1979[29], began to launch heavy cross-border attacks to seek and destroy SWAPO bases in Angola. In addition to such mobile ground and air assaults by her regular troops, South Africa was revealed to be engaged in covert operations as well. Following press disclosures by ex-mercenary officers, South Africa acknowledged the existence of a previously secret unit, the 32nd Battalion, made up of dissident Angolan troops (ex-members of Holden Roberto's now defunct FNLA movement) and led by West European and South African officers. Members of the 32nd have *operated almost continuously inside Angola* where, posing as guerrillas belonging to UNITA (Angola's dissident national movement), they have carried out missions both in support of UNITA and independently. According to former officers of the 32nd Battalion, one of their missions was to terrorize Angolan villages suspected of pro-government sympathies or of providing support to SWAPO. Although specific allegations could not be verified, accounts by newsmen later allowed to accompany the 32nd Battalion into Angola suggested that its activities did effectively terrorize the local populace and disrupt village life.[30]

By the Autumn of 1981 South African assaults, both overt and covert, had brought widespread chaos and desolation to southern Angola and had substantially raised the costs of the war to the Angolan Government. Between 1975 and early 1982, according to Angola's Foreign Minister, South African attacks had caused $7 billion worth of damage.[31]

Angola has not only been bearing the brunt of the Front-Line States' support to SWAPO but she seems to have received almost no military assistance and very little economic help from SWAPO's other Front-Line supporters. In May 1980 Angola's Foreign Minister called on the Front-Line States to take on more of the burden of supporting

SWAPO which 'is falling almost alone on Angola and costing many lives and hundreds of thousands (*sic*) of dollars'.[32] Other Front-Line States have expressed a readiness to extend diplomatic support to Angola and SWAPO but they have so far seen little opportunity to provide direct military support and little need to provide material aid. A senior Front-Line official said privately that SWAPO is already receiving more financial aid from the UN, Scandinavia and others and more military hardware than it can use. Hence the Front-Line States see it as their duty to follow the lead of Angola, as the Front-Line State most directly concerned, and to provide diplomatic support as needed.

Yet even the political and diplomatic role played by the Front-Line States in Namibia has been nothing like the prominent and forceful Front-Line initiative in the Rhodesian conflict. Western diplomatic sources assert privately that Nyerere himself initially put pressure on the late President Neto of Angola to get involved in Western-led peace initiatives. Zambia has favoured working closely with Angola on an informal and bilateral basis, rather than seeking a joint Front-Line *démarche*. Front-Line diplomatic sources privately confirm their difficulty in directing their Presidents' attention to the Namibian problem.[33]

The Namibian situation differs radically from that of Rhodesia. Unlike white-ruled Rhodesia, which at least three Front-Line States perceived as a political and economic threat to their long-run national survival, none of them, except Angola, are directly threatened by continued South African rule in Namibia. Moreover, Botswana, Mozambique and Zambia were suffering economically from the Rhodesian War, and the latter two were subjected to punishing Rhodesian attacks on their territory, whereas so far only Angola has suffered seriously from the fighting over Namibia.

The war itself is different. Front-Line leaders are unimpressed by SWAPO guerrilla actions to date and they are not at all enthusiastic about SWAPO's leadership. Following a report by the SWAPO leader, Sam Njoma, to a Front-Line Summit, Machel is said to have ridiculed SWAPO's war efforts:

'Don't tell me how many white farmers you ambushed. How many South African soldiers have you killed?'[34] As long as SWAPO is unable to mount anything like a credible threat to South African authority in Namibia, its weak bargaining position makes it difficult for Front-Line leaders to give strong support to its demands.

The Front-Line States' hypothetical option of committing troops to help Angola repulse South African incursions remains hypothetical. The risk of almost certain reprisal by South Africa's armed forces, which could easily occupy and devastate large areas of Zambia, Zimbabwe, Mozambique and Botswana (as they already have done in Angola) is too great. Depredations in Mozambique by the MRM, together with South Africa's alleged military training of Zambian and Zimbabwean dissidents, are additional reminders of South Africa's awesome covert capabilities.

A further constraint on Front-Line involvement is the array of domestic problems, both economic and political, occupying the attention of national leaders. In addition, the more activist of the Front-Line Presidents, particularly Machel and Kaunda, spent considerable political capital in the long struggle to bring majority rule to Rhodesia. As mentioned earlier, this endeavour led to severe strains internally, and to tensions among the Front-Line leaders. Shortly after the Lancaster House Conference ended in December 1979, Nyerere was reported to have said that the Front-Line States were 'exhausted' after the long conflict, and that it would be a long time before they could think about mounting another such effort.[35]

Generally the Front-Line States have had fewer cards to play in the Namibian conflict than in the Rhodesian. Unlike the latter, where Front-Line pressure on Britain (both direct and through the Commonwealth) was a key factor in bringing about a settlement, the Front-Line leaders have no significant leverage on South Africa. Furthermore, SWAPO is not as effective as the Patriotic Front – so far it has failed to make the costs of the war prohibitive for South Africa or to convince the South Africans that they cannot win in Namibia.

All this is not to suggest, however, that the Front-Line States have remained aloof from the Namibian conflict. Indeed, despite the constraints on the degree and quality of their direct intervention, the Front-Line States have nevertheless played a significant independent role – the more so as the Western Contact Group has engaged them in its continuing quest for a peaceful settlement.[36]

For one thing, Front-Line leaders have been instrumental in wringing occasional but substantial concessions from SWAPO's normally suspicious and unyielding leadership, and in reassuring it about the substance of specific Western proposals. In August 1979 the Front-Line Presidents persuaded SWAPO to drop its claim for bases inside Namibia at the time of a cease-fire. At the same time, the late President Neto of Angola joined the UN Secretary General in publicly proposing a demilitarized zone (DMZ) to straddle the Angola–Namibia border, and agreed in principle to a UN 'presence' inside Angola. Machel overcame strong SWAPO opposition to the idea of free elections, assuring SWAPO that it would win anyway, reportedly saying to Njoma:'What are you afraid of? Look at Mugabe.'[37] The entire Front-Line leadership took a strong stand in favour of elections, but informed SWAPO they were *not* committed to a SWAPO victory. At the same time, they assured SWAPO that they would help it campaign with posters, money, etc.[38] They also persuaded SWAPO to attend the abortive 'pre-implementation talks' in Geneva in January 1981, and to be prepared to make concessions. In the event, the SWAPO delegation was surprisingly conciliatory, and it was South Africa that refused concessions and caused the talks to break down.

The Front-Line States have also frequently taken the lead in pursuing the Namibia issue in other international fora. Thus, following the collapse of the Namibia Peace Conference in January 1981, they prompted an OAU call for renewed support of SWAPO's armed struggle, and the allocation of $700,000 in OAU funds for African diplomatic aid to SWAPO. They also revived the African demand for mandatory sanctions against South Africa, and took the lead in calling on the UN Security Council for the full-scale debate which took place on 21–30 April 1981.

The importance of the Front Line to the 'Western Five' negotiations is considerably enhanced by its influence over Soviet actions on Namibia, particularly at the UN. Western diplomats acknowledge privately that the USSR, even after bitterly denouncing the activities of the Western Contact Group, has invariably deferred to the views of the Front-Line States and has refrained from exercising her Security Council veto on Namibia. In early 1982, as Front-Line leaders were voicing misgivings about the Reagan Administration's emerging policy towards Namibia, Soviet UN representatives raised with their Front-Line colleagues the feasibility of taking the issue to the Security Council again. The Soviet officials then accepted Front-Line counsel against such a move.

But there are limitations on Front-Line effectiveness at the UN. Recently, for example, they were able to delay, but not prevent, the appointment of an Indian diplomat as the new Commissioner for Namibia, an appointment which they felt would give South Africa new grounds for charging the UN with bias on the Namibia question (since India was an original sponsor of a World Court challenge to South African rule in Namibia). Front-Line diplomats have said privately that an informal 'African contact group' at the UN has recently been taking the initiative on Namibian matters and that Front-Line representatives have found that the most effective way to influence this group is to lobby the Nigerian representative. If they convince Nigeria, the rest of the UN Africa group will normally concur.[39] This seems to suggest both some disarray or lack of cohesion among Front-Line UN representatives and a growing status for Nigeria among African states.

Front-Line Presidents and Foreign Ministers have also helped to shape the Western Five's settlement proposals for Namibia, and to ensure continuity in Western policy. The Front-Line States were unanimous in voicing strong reservations about the new American peace formula which was unveiled in April 1981 during a tour of the Front-Line States by Chester Crocker, the Reagan Administration's Assistant Secretary of State for Africa. Their misgivings centred on Crocker's proposal to change the order of events specified in UN Security Council Resolution 435, the centrepiece of UN peace efforts in Namibia and a formula to which *all* the parties to the conflict had earlier agreed in principle. They feared that the Crocker proposal to get agreement on a constitution *before* the holding of elections – a reversal of Resolution 435 – would lead to its unravelling and the collapse of four years of painstaking effort to narrow the gap between SWAPO and South Africa. They lobbied hard, and were eventually successful in winning the Contact Group's reaffirmation of Resolution 435 as the basis for a settlement, and probably in turning the US away from the notion of a full-fledged constitutional convention prior to elections.

They also had at least initial success in persuading the Reagan Administration to reverse its earlier intention of linking a Namibian settlement to the *prior* withdrawal of Cuban troops from Angola – a notion which the US and South Africa appear to have revived, though in diluted form, in mid-1982. In any event, by late 1981 it was clear that the Reagan Administration, like its predecessors, recognized that it must win Front-Line support if its settlement proposals were to be accepted by SWAPO and by the international community at large.

Whether the Front-Line States would assume a greater role in the Namibian situation if it appeared about to lead to super-power confrontation remains a moot question. The danger of a rapid escalation of the level of warfare was demonstrated in August 1981, following the introduction of a Soviet early-warning radar system and ground-to-air missiles in southern Angola. South Africa warned that this development threatened to rob her of the advantage of surprise in her cross-border attacks against SWAPO targets.[40] She further warned that a 'massive build-up' of heavy weapons had occurred in Angola, raising the spectre of a conventional attack being launched against Namibia. A few weeks later South Africa staged a heavy ground and air attack (the heaviest since 1975) deep into Angola. Unlike previous assaults, this one was not directed solely at SWAPO bases. Its main objectives were the destruction and seizure of heavy weapons and the demolition of radar and missile installations. Hence it was inevitable that South Africa would engage in combat with regular Angolan army units, the first such encounter since her invasion of Angola in 1975. At the end of her eight-day assault, South Africa claimed to have inflicted close to a thousand 'enemy' casualties, of which some 60% were regular Angolan troops. The South African troops also returned with an estimated 4,000 tons of captured equipment, mainly tanks, APCs, heavy lorries, anti-aircraft artillery and other heavy equipment which they had seized from the Angolan army.

On 14 September 1981 the Front-Line States plus Nigeria condemned the South African attack, and called on other African states (that is those distant enough from South Africa to avoid reprisals) to provide military aid to Angola. The Front-Line States were themselves believed to be quietly involved in channelling arms to the Angolans. A few days later, Mozambique reported that Libya and Algeria might send MiG-25 fighter-bombers to defend Angola from South African aggression, which was almost certainly an indirect threat that Angola was considering a request for such aid. Meanwhile, President dos Santos of Angola said only that Angola was 'entitled' to invoke Article 51 of the UN Charter (to call in allies to help a state repel aggression). But on 15 September he announced that Angola's Finance Minister (not, it should be noted, the Defence Minister) would go to Libya to discuss President Qadaffi's offer of military aid. Thus Angola, the Front-Line States and other African states orchestrated a response which purposely did not involve any directly provocative moves by Angola, but left the clear threat that this option was available and under serious consideration.

The Front-Line leaders recognize that, even acting in concert, they lack the power to bring about a Namibian settlement on their own. As much as they mistrusted the Crocker peace initiative in 1981, they were at the

113

same time concerned lest the US abandon the negotiations altogether, as Crocker had threatened to do if the talks reached a dead-end. Thus the Front-Line States have been playing a low-key multiple role in the Namibian conflict. They have acted as a partisan *amicus curiae*, supporting the Western peace initiative and advising the Contact Group on what would or would not contribute towards a settlement; they have supported SWAPO and built its confidence in the negotiating process; they have also applied pressure directly on SWAPO (and on South Africa and the West indirectly) to bring about an early transition to independence and majority rule *via* free elections; and they have provided diplomatic support to Angola in the face of South African armed attack.

Their interest in a settlement stems in part, of course, from an ideological commitment to black majority rule and the belief that this might be brought about sooner by negotiation than by war. The Front-Line States have also been concerned at the step-by-step escalation in the fighting since 1979, and at the growing risk of outside intervention. An East–West conflict fought on southern African soil comes close to being that which the Front-Line States dread most.

Some of the states – notably Botswana, Zambia and Zimbabwe – also fear that a prolonged war over Namibia might lead to an expanded and perhaps permanent Soviet or Cuban presence and influence in the region. Others – especially Angola and Mozambique – would like to see peace in the region because it would reduce or eliminate the threat from armed dissident groups supported by South Africa. Peace would also allow them to reduce their heavy military dependence on the Communist states and to make progress with the task of economic reconstruction.

With so much at stake, the Front-Line States will almost certainly continue to participate actively in the quest for a peaceful resolution of the conflict in Namibia. The constraints which have shaped and limited their role to date seem likely to remain dominant influences over their future actions in that conflict.

Economic Dimension of Regional Security
Genesis
Early in 1979 the Front-Line Foreign Ministers met in Botswana to discuss future economic co-operation in the region. The impetus for this meeting was twofold: first, the realization that the imminent independence of Zimbabwe would open the way, for the first time, to regional economic co-operation among the area's black majority-ruled states; and second, the Front-Line leaders' concern that South Africa might succeed in expanding her economic hegemony over the region through her offer (first announced in April 1979) to help create a 'constellation of states' in the region.[41] From the start, the Front-Line initiative had the twin objectives of raising the general economic level of regional states and reducing the degree of their economic dependence on South Africa. The latter aim incorporated a strong security element: it was 'to reduce as far as possible the vulnerability of the countries of the region to economic blackmail and reprisals'.[42]

How then have the Front-Line States gone about organizing regional economic security? How have they interacted with each other, with other regional states and with outside actors? And what are the long-term implications for regional security in its broad sense?

The Front-Line States formalized their intentions at a meeting held in Arusha in July 1979. The result was the Southern African Development Co-ordination Conference (SADCC) the name given both to the plan itself and to subsequent meetings of its member states (i.e., SADCC 1, SADCC 2). It was also decided at Arusha that, to be effective, SADCC should be open to all the majority-ruled states in the region. The Front-Line States therefore held off signing the 'Arusha Declaration' until the other states (Lesotho, Malawi and Swaziland) had been given an opportunity to discuss and accept the SADCC objectives.

When all nine states met in Lusaka the following April, however, it was clear that the Front-Line States were determined to keep intact the express objective of reducing the region's dependence on South Africa. Thus the other three states were offered a

114

chance to *subscribe* to the Arusha Declaration, but not amend it. The preamble was straightforward: the region's heavy dependence on South Africa 'is not a natural phenomenon', and 'it is necessary to liberate our economies from their dependence on the Republic of South Africa.'[43]

To sign a declaration so clearly directed at South Africa was a risky step for 'hostage states' like Lesotho and Swaziland. The former, in particular, is a small, poverty-ridden enclave surrounded by South Africa; and both states (like Botswana) are members of a customs union with South Africa which provides a large share of their total national revenues. Malawi is the first and only African state to maintain formal diplomatic ties with the Republic, and has profited economically from a cordial relationship. Therefore at Lusaka several of the SADCC states' leaders laid stress on SADCC's larger purpose of promoting the general economic development of member states. Thus Botswana's late President Seretse Khama said, 'It is not our objective to plot against anybody or any country but . . to lay a foundation for the development of a new economic order in southern Africa.'[44] There is little doubt, however, that Front-Line States' determination to reduce their vulnerability to South African economic pressure is the driving force behind SADCC.

This concern reflects both the region's heavy economic dependence on South Africa, and the latter's willingness to use her economic muscle for political ends. An analysis of regional economic dependence is clearly outside the focus of this study but a few illustrations should indicate the potential economic leverage that South Africa has at her disposal in the region.[45]

Economic Dependence

Botswana, Lesotho and Swaziland (the so-called BLS states) belong to a Customs Union with South Africa. Revenues are collected by South Africa and distributed according to a formula favouring the BLS members. In 1979 such revenue accounted for 34% of Botswana's revenues from all sources, 45% of Swaziland's, and 69% of Lesotho's. From the BLS standpoint, a serious drawback of the

Customs Union is its dampening effect on the development of local industry: all the member states have adopted South African tariff schedules, which are highly protective against *all* industrial products, including capital goods. Thus the BLS states are inhibited from starting up local manufacturing, and remain dependent on South African industry. South Africa also markets these countries' major export products (for example, Botswana's meat and cattle) and purchases a large share of their total exports. Moreover, as a US AID report noted:

Botswana, Lesotho, and Swaziland depend on South Africa for considerable investment capital and technical assistance. South Africans dominate the wholesale and retail trade . . .There is little private capital coming into the countries, other than from South Africa.[46]

The BLS states are not the only SADCC members heavily dependent on South Africa. In the mid-1970s South African-owned enterprises in Rhodesia amounted to an estimated £200 million – 35 to 40% of total foreign investments – and including at least five of the country's ten largest industrial establishments.[47] The Mugabe Government would like to reduce South Africa's preeminent position in the economy but Zimbabwe needs foreign capital and investment, and has been unwilling so far to risk the flight of capital and the drying-up of investment that might follow any measures directed at South African holdings. There are signs, however, that Zimbabwe will take steps to gain a measure of control over South African activities in Zimbabwe.[48] Zimbabwe has benefitted, however, from a preferential trade agreement with South Africa, which purchased over half of Zimbabwe's exports of manufactured goods in 1980. According to a Zimbabwean estimate, her South African trade preferences (which were renewed in the Spring of 1982) are worth $75 million and 6,500 jobs in her manufacturing sector.[49]

Mozambique is even more dependent on South Africa, and has less opportunity than Zimbabwe to do anything about it unilaterally. South African technical specialists manage and operate Mozambique's rail lines, airline and the port of Maputo. The 4 million tons of South African freight that pass through Maputo each year account for a third or more of Maputo's total, and are an important source of foreign exchange and employment. In 1978 Mozambique and South Africa agreed to double the rail line from Maputo to the Transvaal border.[50] South Africa repairs and maintains Mozambique's rolling stock, and South African orders for tank cars have kept a Mozambican factory in business.[51]

Six of the nine member SADCC states count on South Africa as a major source of employment, revenue and foreign exchange through migrant labour, chiefly in South Africa's mines. The number of migrant workers from each of the six states in June 1979, is shown in Table 1.

Table 1: Foreign Workers in South Africa

Botswana	32,463
Lesotho	152,032
Malawi	35,803
Mozambique	61,550
Swaziland	13,006
Zimbabwe	21,547

Source: Survey of Race Relations in South Africa 1980. (Johannesburg: South African Institute of Race Relations, 1981), p. 114. Data as of June 1979.

In 1977 migrant mineworkers' remittances from South Africa were as follows:

Table:2: Miners' Remittances (1977)

	(US$)
Botswana	10,659,508
Lesotho	24,842,287
Malawi	1,210,729
Mozambique	29,370,507
Swaziland	6,180,619
Zimbabwe	7,623,778

Source: Financial Mail (supplement), 28 July 1978.

Migrants working in South Africa account for roughly 40–50% of the total active work force of Botswana and Lesotho. Migrants' remittances contribute about half of Lesotho's GNP.

These are only some of the more obvious examples of dependence. The point is that South Africa, which boasts five of the region's ten seaports, a large and diversified industry, a sizeable grain surplus each year and (by regional standards) a large pool of technical and managerial skills, quite simply dominates the region's economy. Does South Africa use this power for political ends? Are the Front-Line States justified in undertaking a costly and long-range investment programme on the grounds that, to remain economically dependent on South Africa is to invite economic blackmail?

Economic Pressure

The South African Government has long shown an awareness of its economic leverage in the region, and a willingness to use it. As a former Prime Minister, Mr Vorster, candidly acknowledged, 'South Africa has never interfered in the internal affairs of other nations, except when her interests have been directly touched. But I must keep in mind that her interests can be touched.'[52]

South African use of the economic weapon has usually been carried out without fanfare. For example, when Mr Vorster was pressing Ian Smith early in 1975 to release a number of Rhodesian nationalist leaders from gaol to take part in settlement talks, South African deliveries of diesel fuel and other supplies critical to the counter-insurgency effort were deliberately slowed down without any statement or acknowledgement from Pretoria. South African annoyance at Lesotho two years later was reflected in a sudden withdrawal of grain subsidies, and delays in paying Lesotho her quarterly share of customs revenues.[53] Similarly, South Africa has quietly expressed her displeasure over Botswana's anti-apartheid rhetoric at the UN by cutting back the number of refrigerated railway wagons sent to pick up Botswana's beef for export.[54]

The most recent South African 'railway diplomacy' involved the withdrawal of 25 South African locomotives from Zimbabwe when their leases ran out in April 1981; that is, just as Zimbabwe farmers needed them to

116

move a bumper grain crop to market.[55] It was, moreover, at a time when more than a quarter of Zimbabwe's own locomotives were out of service for want of technicians to repair them. Zimbabwe, which severed diplomatic relations with South Africa soon after independence, indicated unofficially her need to lease 45 additional diesel locomotives from South Africa. Pretoria's Minister of Transport said that South Africa was ready to accommodate Zimbabwe, but that a request must be made at ministerial level. Apparently the issue has since been settled through secret talks at the sub-cabinet level, following US pressure on the Botha Government.

South Africa's original action against Zimbabwe in this instance was prompted by several unfriendly moves on the part of the Mugabe Government, including the unilateral severance of diplomatic and sports ties, critical public rhetoric and UN votes for sanctions against South Africa, and restrictions on repatriation of dividends by foreign-owned firms in Zimbabwe – the last an action affecting South Africa, by far the major investor, more than other countries. Thus South Africa was forcefully reminding Mr Mugabe that she had the power to throttle his economy should he step too far out of line in his actions towards South Africa.

The Front-Line States thus have reason to fear that any time their policies or actions offend South Africa, economic retaliation may follow. Indeed, Front-Line officials have expressed their conviction that South Africa is attempting to sabotage the SADCC initiative itself (through guerrilla attacks by the MRM on Mozambique's transport links to the interior, for example) in the hope of keeping the southern African countries in a state of permanent economic dependence on South Africa.

Front-Line Lead in SADCC Activities

In July 1979 when the Front-Line Foreign Ministers met in Arusha, Tanzania, for the first formal meeting of SADCC (SADCC 1), five regional economic studies, covering everything from transport to technical education, were presented; a declaration of intent (the Arusha Declaration) was drafted; the international community was informed and invited to help carry out the investment plans; and the decision was made to invite the region's three other majority-ruled states to join. The Arusha meeting also set some important guidelines for regional co-operation. First, the programme would be realistic: it was not a maximalist programme. There was to be no free trade area and no merger of airlines but rather the signatories would adopt a programme in which regional co-operation would take place only where it made economic sense and where the agreed objectives stood a reasonably good chance of being met. And second, the Front-Line initiators were determined to avoid creating a costly and overblown bureaucracy with a life of its own. Indeed, so important was this point that member states agreed only with great reluctance and after fifteen months' careful deliberation to establish a small permanent secretariat for co-ordinating SADCC activities.

It was apparent early on that Botswana and Mozambique were assuming leading roles in pushing SADCC forward. Together they are said to have 'held the thing together' in its early stages. At the Arusha meeting, Mozambique presented the clearest and best-defined sectoral study, an assessment of SADCC transport needs and priorities. Botswana took on the major organizational responsibility. Western financial officials who attended the important SADCC donors' conference in November 1980 (discussed below) later remarked on the efficiency with which Botswana had organized so large and diverse a gathering.

At the Lusaka Summit Meeting in April 1980, Lesotho, Malawi and Swaziland joined the Front-Line States in signing a declaration of their joint strategy for achieving closer economic integration of all nine states. They also approved a programme of action under which seven member states were assigned specific tasks as follows:

Mozambique: to establish a regional transport and communications commission;
Botswana: to lay the ground-work for a study on foot and mouth disease, and to organize a crop research institute;
Zimbabwe: to prepare a regional food security plan;

117

Swaziland: to survey the region's existing training facilities;

Tanzania: to devise a strategy for harmonizing national industrial development plans;

Zambia: to look into the establishment of a regional development bank;

Angola: to propose a plan to harmonize national energy policies.

Lesotho and Malawi, the two member states with the greatest reservations about the political implications of SADCC, took a back seat at Lusaka. The SADCC states' leaders scheduled an interim ministerial meeting in Salisbury in September 1980. They called for a multi-billion dollar southern African development fund, and put Botswana in charge of arrangements for an 'International Donors' Conference' in November of that year, referred to above. They further agreed that transport and communications were the key to regional co-operation and development, and gave the highest priority to establishing the Transport and Communications Commission.

At the September ministerial meeting, when the various national delegations were called upon to present action programmes in their assigned fields, it was clear that Mozambique had moved rapidly ahead on regional transport development. The Mozambicans, who had hired Danish technical specialists to assist them, put forward a clear statement of transport priorities and a provisional list of 97 projects for SADCC ministerial approval. Major projects, in order of priority, included:

- rehabilitation of existing transport and communications facilities;
- establishing telecommunications links and civil aviation infrastructures;[56]
- building new transport systems where feasibility studies had already been completed;
- undertaking feasibility studies for additional facilities.

By the Spring of 1981, Mozambican officials on the Transport and Communications Commission had good reason to be satisfied with their work. Of the 97 projects in the plan, 40 were already being implemented; that is, donors had made financial commitments, and the participating SADCC countries had given their final approval. Moreover, of the $2 billion in scheduled projects for transport and communications development, more than $800 million – over 40% – would be spent in Mozambique. If marginal projects are excluded, Mozambique's share rises to 70%. Even so, Mozambican officials expressed some impatience over delays in getting certain projects under way, since in some cases donors' aid commitments would expire if not taken up within a given time period.

Most of the foreign aid commitments were made at SADCC 2: the meeting of member states with prospective donors held in Maputo in November 1980. The sponsors succeeded in attracting to Maputo representatives from 35 industrial countries, including more than 20 cabinet ministers. International lending institutions were also well-represented, OPEC, the World Bank, and COMECON all sent representatives but pride of place went to Claude Cheysson, then EEC Commissioner for Development. COMECON representatives made no effort to dominate the proceedings or to seize the initiative from the West. According to observers, the Soviet bloc delegates remained silent, declining to take part in discussions, let alone make any commitments to provide SADCC with COMECON aid. This was in spite of repeated efforts by the host, President Machel, to draw them into discussions and give them an opportunity to show some evidence of support for SADCC.

In the end, SADCC 2 turned out to be more than just an occasion for donors to bid on the list of projects. Western aid officials criticized various elements of the programme, including its priorities. One Western representative made a forceful argument for giving a higher priority to agricultural development. Commitments, too, were substantial. At Maputo donors committed funds to cover more than a third of the total foreign investments needed to carry out the $2 billion transport and communications development programme.[57]

Prospects

Even under the most optimistic assumptions about SADCC's future, the reality of South African economic power over the region will remain. South Africa will continue to be the most important market, the major producer of food and manufactured products, the area's largest pool of technical, professional and managerial skills, and the dominant factor in regional transport. Angola and Tanzania will probably remain less involved economically with the sub-region but all the others will have to take South Africa into account in any major economic calculus. Heavy dependence on South Africa will be the dominant economic fact of life for land-locked Botswana, Lesotho and Swaziland. For the others, internal problems will continue to have prior claims on limited administrative and technical personnel and limited budgets, while for some their bilateral ties are likely to be more important than those of SADCC. The keys to SADCC success lie in Zimbabwe and Mozambique. Zimbabwe has the potential to offer an important partial alternative to South Africa as a supplier of grain, manufactured goods and skills to the region. Successful development of Mozambique's rail and port facilities would provide alternative access to sea ports for Zambia, Zimbabwe, Malawi, Botswana and Swaziland. Moreover, SADCC's plans to develop technical skills on a regional basis should enable their scarce resources to be used more effectively: for example, in the Summer of 1981, the SADCC Transport and Communications Commission was reported to have contracted with West Germany to establish a training programme for SADCC rail technicians.

It is too early, of course, to gauge the chances of SADCC success. Its concern is with long-range development, and its programmes are not planned to have any dramatic economic impact for perhaps a decade. In terms of future regional security, however, SADCC's most important contribution may well be its success, already manifested, in institutionalizing sets of intra-regional links that never existed before. SADCC programmes are bringing together in common endeavour cabinet- and middle-level officials of these states, officials who previously have had little or nothing to do with one another, and little or no knowledge of problems or developments outside their own countries. As such contacts inevitably multiply during the years immediately ahead, they will help to break down the tenacious and restricted colonial patterns of intercourse. Mutual ties established to carry out SADCC objectives should also lead to expanding political and cultural links among these states. Through SADCC, all the regional states will in future have increasingly more to lose through disruption of their regional ties. Moreover, since virtually all the major SADCC development projects will involve the West in supplying funds, capital equipment and technical expertise, the SADCC programme seems almost certain to bring the entire region, including Angola and Mozambique, which have been tied more closely to the Communist states, into closer association with the Western world economy.

In sum, if all goes reasonably well; that is, if member states are spared from serious political and ethnic conflict within their borders, and if Angola and Mozambique can contain the armed dissident groups which currently are disrupting economic activity, then the SADCC initiative will strengthen Front-Line relations and Front-Line influence in the sub-region. It will also help to move southern Africa towards greater regional interdependence, and away from being disparate states, each dealing bilaterally with South Africa, and it will strengthen the SADCC states' ties to the Western democracies. Significantly, the Front-Line sponsors of SADCC have made clear their limited expectations of it and have explicitly left a vacant place at the conference table for a future majority-ruled South Africa.

IV. CONCLUSIONS AND PROSPECTS

Achievements and Modus Operandi

How, then, should the Front-Line group be assessed? What are its strengths and weaknesses, its successes and failures? And in particular, what do these things tell us about its future role in regional security?

First, it must be noted that the Front-Line States were instrumental in bringing about the dramatic shifts in the regional balance of power which have occurred since 1975. Front-Line leaders were a moving force behind the collapse of Portuguese colonial rule in Angola and Mozambique, and of the white minority government in Rhodesia. They played a crucial part in the Rhodesian peace settlement, and have co-operated with the West in trying to find an internationally acceptable peace formula in Namibia. Moreover, since the Front-Line States have acted for the OAU in guiding and supporting the southern African guerrilla groups, they have served in the ambivalent position of a biased *amicus curiae* to Western peace initiatives, while helping guerrilla groups plan their political and military strategies.

The Front-Line States' influence with the national liberation movements is so widely recognized that diplomats of both Western and Communist states consult them rather than the OAU in matters affecting the various groups. Indeed, from the Anglo-US plan for Rhodesia to the Contact Group's Namibian initiative, the Western powers have enlisted Front-Line support in resolving regional conflicts, and have felt it essential to clear peace proposals with Front-Line leaders. In this role the Front-Line States have also acted as an effective buffer against direct Soviet intervention in support of the guerrillas. So far as is known, and with the glaring exception of aid to the MPLA in late 1975, Communist assistance has been arranged through, and with the prior approval of, the Front-Line sanctuary states. Perhaps of even greater importance, the USSR has followed the Front-Line lead on southern African matters at the UN, and on several occasions has agreed, with obvious and clearly-expressed misgivings, to withhold her veto of Western-led peace efforts which the Front-Line have supported. Moreover, by acting as champions to the national liberation movements, the Front-Line States have pre-empted the USSR, thereby denying her a role in peace negotiations.

These are astonishing achievements for a group of newly independent states (the newest member gained independence in 1980, the first only in 1964) which are militarily and economically weak, and which would seem to have little basis for exercising influence in international affairs. By sponsoring and supporting national liberation groups, the Front-Line States have waged war indirectly on the white minority regimes, most of the time managing not to become directly involved in the fighting.

Front-Line leaders have also been successful in drawing the Western powers into seeking a solution favourable to Front-Line objectives; objectives which could not have been attained without Western intercession. As Robert Keohane has noted, 'weak states have been able to exert leverage on great powers where the latter are intensely interested in regional events'.[58] In southern Africa, Britain's vulnerability to Front-Line pressure arose from her sense of responsibility for the outcome of the situation in her break-away colony of Southern Rhodesia, plus her concern with keeping the Commonwealth intact in the face of member states' criticism and threats over British policies in southern Africa. The US began to focus attention on southern Africa following the arrival of the Cuban combat brigade in Angola in 1975. From then on it was clear that she was directly engaged in the region and concerned over developments there. Successive American Administrations have been eager to seek peaceful and internationally-acceptable solutions to the Rhodesian and Namibian conflicts as a means of forestalling the spread of Soviet influence and power in southern Africa. This has given the regional actors – South Africa as well as the Front-Line States – significant leverage over Western policies and actions in the area.

Yet the Front-Line States recognize that their leverage is not all that strong or permanent and that it must be applied judiciously, or it might cease to be effective. If the Patriotic Front had rejected Britain's compromise proposals at Lancaster House, Britain would have recognized the Muzorewa Government and lifted sanctions, thereby tilting the balance against the guerrillas and confronting the Front-Line States with the prospect of supporting a prolonged and increasingly costly guerrilla war. Moreover, if the Western peace initiative in Namibia should reach a dead-end, the US, followed probably by the other Western states, might disengage, leaving the Namibian conflict without any authority with enough position and power to put pressure on South Africa and to mediate between South Africa and SWAPO. Thus the Front-Line States' success in engaging and influencing the great powers in regional conflicts has been a major factor in its achievements.

Of even greater importance has been the Front Line States' development of a *modus operandi* which has enabled the member states to function as a group. With the independence of Angola and Mozambique, collaboration between Presidents Nyerere, Khama and Kaunda was enlarged to five with the addition of Machel and Neto. The group of 'Five Presidents' was soon dubbed the 'Front-Line Presidents'. But these new additions made the Front-Line States a diverse group. Unlike Zambia, Botswana and Tanzania, the two new members were ex-Portuguese colonies and non-Commonwealth states with close and dependent political and military links to Communist states. Moreover, Kaunda and Nyerere had known each other and worked closely together for over a decade in the African independence movement. Neto was not close to either of them or to Machel; and both Neto and Machel were new and untried in the game of international diplomacy. If these leaders were to act together as a group in the growing Rhodesian conflict, clearly it would have to be in some loose and informal arrangement, something far less binding than a formal alliance.

Nor were the five leaders prepared to set up any permanent consultative bodies. Each President enjoyed a substantial, if not total, mandate to conduct his country's foreign affairs, and each wanted the freedom to act (or *not* to act) in accord with his perception of his own country's interests on any given issue or initiative. Hence the co-operating mode of the Front-Line States became one of *ad hoc* summitry. That is:

- any of the four leaders could call a summit meeting;
- Nyerere was Chairman by informal consensus;
- there was no fixed agenda at any meeting;
- no formal record was made of discussions;
- no votes were taken and issues were decided by informal consensus. Disagreements were simply allowed to stand.

Moreover, although normally a summit would reach agreement on a general conclusion or line of action, seldom were individual leaders tasked with any particular actions. Rather, each was left free to take whatever individual initiatives he felt would help attain the agreed objective, or to take no action at all.

The obvious weakness of this mode of action is that the Front-Line States have seldom presented a solid phalanx. This weakness was less serious a factor in relations with the PF, where an ultimatum from Nyerere or Machel was clearly being backed by other Front-Line leaders present. Even there, however, it seems likely that Nkomo would have played on the sympathy of his old friend Kaunda, while Mugabe would have felt that he could sometimes prevail on Machel to support his position. But in Front-Line dealings with the West, this lack of a solid, unified front was particularly manifest. At Lancaster House, for example, Britain found it possible (and much easier) to deal with one or another Front-Line leader, sometimes winning his support against the rest for a British position, instead of having to face a solid Front-Line bloc. The Front-Line States' awareness of their collective weakness is suggested by the actions of individual members, as, for example, when Kaunda sought to break a serious deadlock in the Rhodesian talks. Then he approached Britain not as a Front-Line Head of State, but in his role as current Chairman of the Commonwealth

Heads of State. The result, as noted earlier, was a private dinner with Prime Minister Thatcher and Lord Carrington from which a solution emerged to break the deadlock.

The strengths of the Front-Line States' loose and informal mode are less obvious than its weaknesses, but no less important. For one thing, it appears to have given the Front-Line States flexibility, a means by which to avoid getting locked into hard positions from which they could free themselves only at considerable political cost, either in terms of relations within the group or in the group's dealings with the outside world. Furthermore the same one-to-one relationships (Kaunda with Nkomo, Machel with Mugabe *et al*) that sometimes gave a guerrilla leader leverage over his Front-Line sponsor also created a bond of trust. For example, when Machel assured Mugabe that no more favourable terms could be extracted from Britain, Mugabe was inclined to accept it.

Most important, however, is the likelihood that any attempt to establish a more formal Front-Line organization, or a binding alliance, would quite simply have failed. The personalities of the leaders, particularly a strong and domineering individual like Nyerere, were crucial to Front-Line initiatives. Had the strong leaders been hobbled by voting procedures or a formal agenda, or had the weak states been forced to take specific actions approved or assigned by the more dominant members of the group, it is probable that the Front-Line coalition would not have come into being in the first place.

Prospects

Given the strengths and weaknesses of the Front-Line States as a group, and in light of the achievements of that group to date, will it be a driving force in future developments in the region? In particular, will the Front-Line coalition stay intact and weigh heavily in the settlement of future conflicts in southern Africa, or was Lancaster House the high-water mark of Front-Line collaboration?

The political and strategic situation in the region and the Front-Line States' perception of it are substantially different from the situation in the mid-1970s, when the Rhodesian conflict began to move towards a crisis. For one thing, as noted earlier, the major sources of current conflict differ in important ways from that of Rhodesia. The Rhodesian war spilled over directly into Zambia, Mozambique and Botswana, causing severe economic dislocation and threatening all three states with spreading warfare, civil disruption and political instability. Thus, for at least three of the (then) five member states it was imperative that the conflict be settled. The Namibian conflict, on the other hand, has so far directly affected only one Front-Line State, Angola. Thus, while other member states continue to back Angola and to support the Western-led UN peace initiative, only Angola has vital national interests at stake leading her urgently to seek a settlement. To the extent that other Front-Line States have become involved in the search for peace in Namibia, this seems to reflect the leaders' strong sense of need to support another member state, Angola, and a more generalized concept about the possible dangers of an escalating conflict over Namibia. Specifically they fear that a wider war might lead to conventional warfare between South Africa and Angola which could, in turn, bring outside powers into an East–West conflict in the region.

Nor is the South African domestic conflict, the long-developing challenge to white minority rule, perceived as analogous to that in Rhodesia. Black African leaders do not see South Africa as a colonial legacy. There is no colonial power to be prevailed upon to assume responsibility and South Africa's whites are acknowledged to be legitimate South Africans, not colonial settlers. The OAU has gone on record as encouraging a peaceful and gradualist solution to what it views as a complex internal problem, not lending itself to a simple transfer of power. As stated in the Dar es-Salaam Declaration on Southern Africa, adopted by the OAU in April 1975:

If current or future leaders of the apartheid regime should desire *to begin to move away* from the policy of racism in South Africa and to *seek the co-operation* of the Africans to that end, they could initiate *the necessary contacts and negotiations* from within. [Italics added]

Front-Line officials, though voicing support for the national liberation groups, have reiterated their view that this is an internal South African problem, and not one to be solved by external aggression. Indeed, they tacitly recognize that a civil war in South Africa would inevitably have the most serious consequences for the entire subregion.

Another new factor affecting Front-Line leaders' policies and actions is their heightened awareness of the dangers of outside intervention in local conflicts. This was not always the case. Robert Keohane has noted the ability of small powers to accept global patterns of politics as given, and 'to concentrate on a narrow range of vital interests and ignore almost everything else.' In particular, 'a small power can disregard or heavily discount the effects of its actions on the stability of international politics in general.'[59] This attitude seems to have prevailed among at least the dominant Front-Line leaders during the Rhodesian crisis. In the interests of bringing down the Smith Regime, they were prepared to see the British Commonwealth disrupted if not dismantled, and to allow large quantities of Soviet heavy weapons and large numbers of Soviet and Cuban military personnel to be introduced into the region. Several Front-Line leaders were even prepared to approve the rash (and abortive) Cuban plan of June 1979 (mentioned earlier) to declare a Free Zimbabwe under Nkomo and Mugabe in north-eastern Rhodesia and to intensify the war with expanded Soviet and Cuban arms aid. This scheme would not only have meant a greater Communist involvement in the war, but would almost certainly have brought South African troops into action, thus enlarging and prolonging the conflict and effectively negating Western peace efforts.

In the past couple of years, however, the Front-Line leaders have shown a growing concern over the possibility of East–West conflict in the area, and over the implicit threat posed by the continuing presence of Cuban combat troops. The blunt public warnings by Nigeria's Foreign Minister that the Cubans must not 'overstay their welcome' in Africa is a view shared by most Front-Line leaders. More recent statements by Portuguese and Angolan officials, and a joint Cuban–Angolan statement in early 1982 on withdrawal, indicate growing sensitivity on this issue. Such awareness stems in part from South Africa's increasingly aggressive posture towards Angola, Mozambique and Zimbabwe, and the threat it raises of Cuban and Soviet responses leading to a rapid escalation and spread of warfare in the region. It also reflects the concern of several Front-Line Governments that dissident national groups within their own borders might take advantage of growing disruption in the region to seek South African or Soviet help in launching an armed challenge to their governments.

How will all this affect future Front-Line joint action in regional affairs? How is it likely to balance out in terms of future Front-Line initiatives affecting regional security? The findings of this study support four broad propositions in regard to future prospects.

1) *The development of Front-Line collaboration over the next five to ten years is likely to be slow, cautious and piecemeal, with few, if any, dramatic new joint initiatives.*

Indeed, it appears likely that the notion of the Front-Line States as a cohesive group working closely together towards a common regional objective (as was the case in the Rhodesian conflict) will gradually fade. There are several reasons for this. First, no other crises in the region are likely to bear either the same high degree of urgency, with so much at stake for several member states, or to produce as high a degree of Front-Line unity. Second, other problems, mostly domestic, seem likely to take priority over regional issues. This is already happening in Zambia and Tanzania, whose leaders have been the driving force behind previous Front-Line initiatives, and in Zimbabwe. Inasmuch as the Front-Line States have no permanent mandate or organizational structure, but instead conduct their joint business through *ad hoc* summitry, the role of national leaders is crucial. To the extent that domestic conflicts and problems take their attention away from regional issues, the Front-Line States as such will be that much less active. Third, the increase in the number of Front-Line States from four (Zambia, Tanzania, Botswana and Mozambique) to six, with the addition of Angola and Zimbabwe, has tended to give the coalition greater psychological cohesion and strength but it also seems likely to reduce the chances for a quick Front-Line reaction to regional developments or for dramatic initiatives. Not only is there a larger number of national leaders to be consulted or convened on any given issue but the addition of Zimbabwe in particular has brought to the group a strong and influential member whose leader favours a pragmatic, low-key approach to foreign affairs. Only if Mugabe were to be replaced by a radical, outward-looking leader would Zimbabwe be likely to exert her influence towards a more activist role for the Front-Line States. And fourth, even in the realm of regional economic co-operation, the area where national self-interest is most likely to lead to increasing mutual co-operation (as discussed below), the regional group has been expanded from six to nine, thus reducing, formally at least, the role of the Front-Line States *per se.*

2) *There are likely to be few instances of joint defence operations or military collaboration*

This is the most sensitive area of Front-Line relationships. For one thing, this is the area where ideological differences which so far have not proved to be a serious obstacle to Front-Line co-operation, would give rise to deep misgivings and suspicions. The more conservative states – like Zambia, Botswana and Zimbabwe – in all probability would view with alarm any proposals for joint exercises, joint training or a combined command, let alone suggestions for a united Front-Line force. Such moves would involve their national armies (whose loyalty is not in every case all that certain) in joint activities with the Soviet- and Cuban-trained forces of Angola and Mozambique. The potential for radical political indoctrination, or for the smaller forces of Zambia and Botswana to be dominated by those of Angola or Mozam-

bique, would pose too great a risk. Mozambican officials are, in fact, aware that they project a radical image in the region which makes them suspect, and that they must avoid any initiative which other regional states could construe as a bid to export the Mozambican model.[60]

A practical obstacle to joint military activity is the lack of standardization of training, weapons or doctrine among the national armies. Moreover, since in most cases they are newly-established forces which have yet to be moulded into effective national armies, joint activities would risk the weakening of discipline and of efforts to instill a sense of nationalism.

At the foreign policy level, these states would be extremely reluctant to commit any of their forces to a joint command which could involve them in hostilities that they might otherwise have been able to avoid. This is particularly the case with regard to actions against the only perceived serious military threat to the region, the Republic of South Africa. These states know that they are militarily weak and vulnerable and that, even acting in concert, they are no match for the SADF. Any gesture, such as joint manoeuvres, which South Africa would almost certainly view as being directed against her, is quite simply out of the question for a long time to come.

So far one can note only three cases of known defence co-operation. First, in 1978 and 1979 Tanzanian troops helped defend Mozambique from Rhodesian attacks. Second, Zimbabwe has been co-operating with Mozambique in combatting the South African-supported MRM since early 1981, but here the co-operation has been both limited and informal: no written accord, no cross-border operations and no joining of forces has occurred. Both sides speak of 'exchanging information' but this appears to include parallel operations against the MRM guerrillas on each side of the border, as well as aerial reconnaissance by Zimbabwe along the frontier. The third case is that of Tanzanian training of Mozambican forces. Until the recently-concluded military training agreement with Portugal, Mozambique relied almost exclusively on Tanzania to train her soldiers.

(Advanced weapons training has been provided by Mozambique's Communist supplies of such arms.) None of this amounts to extensive collaboration, yet this is as far as Front-Line collaboration seems likely to go, at least during the present decade and probably beyond.

3) Co-operation in the political sphere is likely to remain ad hoc, occasional, reactive and conducted by summitry

None of the Front-Line States seems to want a more structured arrangement, let alone a permanent body, for Front-Line foreign policy co-ordination. Front-Line officials stress the effectiveness of the present system. Any of the leaders can call a summit when he sees the need for one. Moreover, the immediate and personal involvement of national leaders means that decisions can be taken on the spot, without going through any national or supra-national bureaucracies. National leaders, including the most recent addition (Mugabe) and the two successors to leaders who died in office (Masire of Botswana and dos Santos of Angola), are said to work well together, and appear to understand one another's sensitivities and domestic imperatives. Any permanent co-ordinating body would place intolerable strain on limited foreign affairs staffs, which already are stretched thin between UN, OAU, SADCC and bilateral demands on personnel. On a personal level, the existing *modus operandi* allows dominant Front-Line personalities, particularly Nyerere and Machel, to continue to run the meetings without hindrance from any bureaucratic staffs, formal procedures or agenda. Indeed, so dominant is the summit that Front-Line representatives at the UN do not regularly meet to plan joint initiatives.

All the Front-Line States have political and economic vulnerabilities which place serious constraints on the variety and intensity of joint political initiatives in which they can take part. Botswana, Zimbabwe, Mozambique and Zambia are all vulnerable to economic pressures, to say nothing of military actions, by South Africa. They must act with one eye on Pretoria, and try to avoid any action that might provoke South African retaliation. On any given regional or international issue, one or several Front-Line States will have more at stake, and a greater need or capacity for action, than the others. Hence it will be up to the most interested state or states to take the lead on a particular issue.

A further deterrent to joint political initiatives is the diversity of political outlook among Front-Line leaders. Zambian 'Humanism' is a far cry from Mozambique's or Angola's efforts to mobilize the populace along Marxist socialist lines. Zambia is believed to harbour fears about being 'squeezed' between two Marxist-leaning states which, from her point of view, have moved uncomfortably close to the Communist camp. Botswana and Zimbabwe have mixed economies and functioning parliamentary governments, and both countries depend on private initiative, domestic and foreign, to a far greater degree than the two ex-Portuguese territories. The leaders of Botswana and Zimbabwe follow a pragmatic, low-profile foreign policy, and seem to project a more narrowly national outlook than Nyerere and Kaunda, who are inclined to be internationalist in outlook and to let ideology have a somewhat greater influence on policy.

There are also political differences of a more personal kind. The Zambian leadership has been sympathetic to Jonas Savimbi and the UNITA national movement and took a long time to recognize Angola's MPLA government. Nyerere, too, was sympathetic to Savimbi at one time. During the Rhodesian crisis, Nkomo and his ZAPU guerrillas were the national movement favoured by Kaunda, while Machel and Nyerere were closest to Mugabe and ZANU. Hence relations between Zambia and the Mugabe Government have been distinctly cool. The lack of enthusiasm for the Namibian insurgency on the part of several Front-Line States probably reflects, in part at least, their doubts about the competence of the present SWAPO leadership.

In some cases pairs of Front-Line States will find their bilateral relations of greater importance than their association with the Front-Line States as a group. Mugabe and Machel have a particularly close *rapport*, which seems to go well beyond the fact that Mozambique was the major backer of

Mugabe's ZANU guerrillas. (Whether this closeness would survive the replacement of one or the other leader is of course questionable.) Mozambique also has close political, military and economic links with Tanzania, which was Machel's main source of support during his long fight against the Portuguese. Angola and an independent Namibia will almost certainly establish close bilateral ties for many of the same reasons.

Finally, some of the conflicts which may arise in the future would in all probability be politically more sensitive than the Rhodesian and Namibian conflicts where, after all, it was easy for all the Front-Line States to agree that white colonial rule should be removed. It would be more difficult for the Front-Line States to agree on joint action in the case of, say, a right-wing coup in Zambia or the coming to power of an aggressive military government in Tanzania.

4) *Front-Line collaboration will be most marked in the realm of economic co-operation which, in the southern African context, has an explicit regional security objective.*

The Front-Line States founded SADCC in July 1979 with the twin objectives of promoting the economic growth of member states and reducing their heavy economic dependence on South Africa. The latter goal was said to be necessary in order to minimize their vulnerability to South African economic pressure. Lesotho, Malawi and Swaziland also subscribed to these goals.

All nine member states stand to gain from SADCC plans, particularly in the area of transport development. Member states will staff the small permanent secretariat, as well as providing personnel for particular permanent commissions, like the Transport and Communications Commission, which is already functioning in Maputo. Thus, at the technical and planning levels, Front-Line personnel will increasingly work together on issues of common interest. They will also receive standardized training under joint regional programmes, such as the one which involves West Germany training railroad technical and administrative personnel for the entire region.

Some states will be far more involved than others in regional economic co-operation. Angola, for example, has few vital economic links to the other member states, and is far less dependent on South Africa. Therefore her involvement in SADCC activities will probably be limited and tangential. Tanzania will express her support of SADCC largely to demonstrate her political solidarity with its objectives but she will remain primarily concerned with internal economic problems and with East African regional economic affairs, which are of greater importance to her than future ties with the south. The BLS states have an important stake in SADCC but must move with caution to avoid antagonizing South Africa on whom they will remain heavily dependent.

Thus the core states in SADCC will be Zambia, Zimbabwe and Mozambique. This will be particularly the case during the remainder of this decade, as the ambitious programme to develop regional transport links begins to take effect. As that programme is implemented, these three states will be moving substantially closer together economically, with Zimbabwe as the hub.

Nevertheless, the constraints on the growth of SADCC co-operation are likely to be considerable. Most member states will continue to suffer a severe shortage of skills in this decade and beyond, thus limiting their ability to provide competent personnel for SADCC business. More important, this shortage could well slow the implementation of national development projects which are integral parts of regional development programmes. In addition, all the states except Zimbabwe are likely to find it difficult to raise agricultural output, particularly in the short term. This, in turn, will exacerbate the foreign exchange problems for several member states, and could inhibit their domestic investment plans. In short, these factors will make it difficult for some countries to meet their obligations to SADCC programmes, and will tend to lead some to look for their own national solutions to internal needs, perhaps at the expense of regional economic co-operation.

Much will depend, of course, on political conditions in the region. If all goes reasonably well (no civil wars or South African annexations and assuming that member states will be able to bring the several insurgencies under control), the SADCC programme should begin to forge some enduring economic and technical links among member states where such links have been non-existent in the past. The heavy involvement of Western industrial states in SADCC investment plans should gradually draw *all* the states closer to the Western world economy, as well as closer to each other. Although South Africa will undoubtedly remain by far the dominant economic power in the area, SADCC success will eventually give the other states in the region some alternatives, thereby reducing, to some degree, their vulnerability to South African economic pressures.

V. IMPLICATIONS FOR REGIONAL SECURITY

How, then, are the Front-Line States to be perceived? Is it, in the words of one Western diplomat 'more a slogan or a label than an operational phenomenon'?[61] Or should it be seen as something real and more lasting? Less than an alliance, certainly but more than a temporary, single-issue coalition?

More important than finding a suitable label are the implications of the Front-Line States for future regional security in southern Africa. Given the absence of a suitable regional power which could use its influence to prevent or dampen regional conflicts and to mediate disputes (since clearly South Africa will not be accepted in such a role for a long time to come) and given the usefulness of such an authority in promoting stability and peace in a region, can the group of Front-Line States acting in concert fulfil the role of a regional power? This question, of course, has important implications for Western policies in southern Africa. The short answer is: yes, within limits.

By far the major limiting factor is the regional imbalance of power between the Front-Line States and South Africa. South Africa enjoys roughly a 4:1 advantage over the Front-Line States in combat aircraft and a 10:1 margin in APCs, against the Front-Line States' approximately 2:1 advantage in troop strength, naval craft and tanks.[62] However, South Africa's armed forces are more experienced, better educated and trained, are generally better armed, and have had more combat training than the Front-Line national armies. Perhaps even more telling are the political factors. The political reliability of some Front-Line national forces is uncertain. Zimbabwe's 60,000-man army, for example, includes thousands of ex-ZIPRA guerrillas whose loyalty to the Mugabe Government has yet to be tested in combat. South Africa would appear to enjoy clear military superiority, and this, coupled with her tremendous economic power over the region, gives her so obvious an advantage that there seems virtually no chance of a Front-Line military challenge, much less a successful one, for a long time to come.

Only large numbers of outside combat troops supported by one or more great powers could make a difference. From a defensive point of view the Front-Line States can expect to do no more than increase the likely costs of any South African aggression, either by strengthening their own defence forces or by threatening to bring in forces from outside. So far, however, such threats have not deterred South Africa from undertaking armed incursions deep into Angola. In sum, the Front-Line States' lack of sufficient military power to prevent or retaliate effectively against South African attack severely limits their capability to establish and maintain security in the region.

Nevertheless, it has been argued in this Paper that the Front-Line States, as a loose coalition of national leaders, was a key factor in the success of the Lancaster House peace conference on Rhodesia, and is a moving force behind the current programme to expand regional economic co-operation among southern Africa's majority-ruled states. The Front-Line States are also deeply involved in the Western-led search for a peaceful resolution to the problem in Namibia. In all these endeavours, they have exerted influence outwards – towards the West, towards the

Communist camp and towards other African states, including South Africa.

How is this influence to be explained? Whence came the Front-Line's ability to pressure Britain into rejecting the Muzorewa Government, into agreeing to resume colonial authority, and into making substantial concessions to the guerrillas? And whence has come its status as an authority in regional disputes, an authority acknowledged by the Western powers, who have found it necessary to get the acquiescence of the Front-Line States to Western peace initiatives in Rhodesia and Namibia? The USSR, too, has had to take notice and has on several occasions withheld a UN Security Council veto because of Front-Line pressure. The OAU accepts Front-Line judgements and leadership in southern African conflicts and negotiations. Even, on occasion, South Africa, which has conducted discussions with individual Front-Line leaders on specific issues and which, under Front-Line pressure, forced Ian Smith to release Rhodesian nationalists from prison, has had to pay attention to the Front-Line States.

Part of the answer lies, of course, in the Front-Line States' control over the activities of the nationalist guerrilla groups operating against white-ruled territories. As the leading sponsors and supporters of such groups, Front-Line leaders have won their confidence and a generally-accepted right to represent their interests. Those who, like Machel and Mugabe, won independence through armed struggle, seem to have an especially close *rapport* with (and influence upon) SWAPO and the ANC. Moreover, the sanctuary, supply channels and arms conduits provided by one or more Front-Line States are essential to continued guerrilla operations. Indeed, the Front-Line States have the power effectively to close them down.

The authority of the Front-Line States over the Rhodesian and Namibian nationalists has made them invaluable to the West as a mediator and as a channel to the guerrilla groups, which otherwise would have been difficult for the West to reach and well-nigh impossible to influence directly. Moreover, since the Front-Line leaders were the chief advocates of national liberation and were the major sponsors and supporters of the guerrillas, they had the right credentials to receive the OAU's informal mandate to guide these struggles on its behalf. Similarly, since the USSR chose to defer to the OAU and go through the OAU in dealing with these movements, she too has followed the lead of the Front-Line States in its actions towards the guerrillas in southern Africa.

There are other factors as well. The original 'three Presidents' (Nyerere, Kaunda and Khama) were active Commonwealth Heads of State. This fact, together with their commitment to Nkrumah's maxim that no African state could be really independent until *all* were independent, earned them the respect of other Third-world Commonwealth States. The strong personalities of leaders like Nyerere and Kaunda, who had chosen to guide and mould their nations' political, economic and social development according to their own personal ideologies, were also an important factor. Indeed, it was largely their strong personal commitment (stemming only in part from reasons of ideology) to black majority rule that brought the Front-Line States into being

The effective roles played by the Front-Line States in the Rhodesian and Namibian settlement talks have given them status and momentum which seem likely to carry them forwards into other regional issues that may arise. Western, African and Communist governments now consult Front-Line States on any questions affecting the region, simply as a matter of course. In turn, all the Front-Line leaders, including the most recent to come to power, view their Front-Line role as an important element in their total international relationships, and are likely to continue to do so. They see the engagement of the Western powers as essential to solving regional problems, and their own co-operation as an effective means of keeping the West engaged. As a senior Front-Line official recently said in private:

The Front-Line States see themselves as working jointly with the Western powers, on Namibia, on SADCC, etc. And they know that after Namibia is settled, there will be the ultimate question: what to do about apartheid. And that, too, is a question on which the Front Line and the West will have to work together.[63]

There are clear advantages to the West in continuing to work with the Front-Line States on southern African issues, and in encouraging them to remain as a regional unit and to address these issues jointly. Seen in the purely regional context, the Front-Line States have access to, and influence with, important regional actors (with the exception of South Africa) to a degree not normally available to outside powers approaching such actors directly. Thus, to cite one example, during a Front-Line Summit meeting it was Mozambique's Marxist-oriented President Machel who persuaded SWAPO to agree to Namibian elections, a concession which no Western leader would be likely to have achieved by dealing directly with SWAPO's usually truculent and suspicious leadership. It is also likely to be in the West's long-term interests to see southern Africa continue to avoid regional rivalries, territorial conflicts and economic chaos that have, either singly or in combination, led to chronic political instability and warfare elsewhere on the African continent. In pursuing this objective, the West should find it useful to encourage the Front-Line leaders to work together as a group and with non-Front-Line States in the region. For example, the West could indirectly increase Front-Line States' incentives for acting jointly, and thereby raise the costs of their opting out of regional endeavours. In pursuing such a policy, however, the West would have to accept the fact that the Front-Line States value their official non-aligned status, and will continue to promote regional interests as they independently perceive them. Their perceptions will not always coincide with Western views, nor should the Front-Line States be seen as a potential 'agent' of the West in the region.

On the issue of apartheid, the Front-Line States are not likely to have much impact, particularly in the short term. It could be argued that on this issue alone it might be to Western advantage to have the Front-Line States divided, rather than pressing jointly for an initiative forced on the group by a dominant personality like Nyerere, who is normally the most militant of all the Front-Line leaders on this question. It could also be argued that the West, working through the Front-Line States' more pragmatic leaders, could encourage them to prevail on the group to take a moderate or more pragmatic stance.

In the East–West context, too, the Front-Line States are important for Western interests. To the degree that they continue to draw closer together as parts of a *regional entity*, they will inevitably draw closer to the West. It should be noted in particular that the leaders of the area's two self-declared Marxist states, Angola and Mozambique, have welcomed and indeed actively sought the involvement of the Western powers in the Namibian settlement process, while neither leader has sought to involve the USSR or other Communist states in that process. Indeed, the Front-Line States have on several occasions quietly rebuffed Soviet calls for rejecting Western initiatives. In the economic realm, too, any moves by the Front-Line States in the direction of regional development of transport, and regional cooperation generally, will further move all these states towards closer economic, technical and educational links with the West. This process of expanding and consolidating regional ties can work to reduce the dependence of Angola and Mozambique on the Communist countries, and diminish the chances of a regional split into pro-Soviet and pro-Western groups of states, a development which would increase the opportunities for an expansion of Soviet influence in the region.

In short, the West stands to gain by taking advantage of the Front-Line leaders' clear interest in enlisting Western participation in their joint efforts to find workable solutions to the region's problems. No convincing case can be made for ignoring the opportunities this offers to promote long-term Western interests.

It is a moot question whether the Front-Line experience offers a useful model for other regions of the Third World. This Paper has noted the peculiar circumstances which gave rise to the Front-Line States as a working group – the political and social background of the southern African states, the overwhelmingly Western and Christian orientation of their national leaders and cultures, the absence of strong traditionalist religious or political forces to oppose modernization and the struggle against white minority rule as a unifying ideology. Whether a roughly comparable set of circumstances in another region could give rise to something like the Front-Line States, at least in terms of its regional security potential, is impossible to say with any degree of confidence. The Front-Line experience at least demonstrates that it is possible for a group of weak and diverse states to work together towards a common political goal, and, by combining, to exert decisive influence over regional developments.

APPENDIX

The Nine-Point Peace Plan for Zimbabwe, endorsed by the Commonwealth Heads of State, 7 August 1979

The Heads of Government:

1 confirmed that they were wholly committed to genuine black majority rule for the people of Zimbabwe;

2 recognized, in this context, that the internal settlement constitution is defective in certain important respects;

3 fully accepted that it is the constitutional responsibility of the British Government to grant legal independence to Zimbabwe on the basis of majority rule;

4 recognized that the search for a lasting settlement must involve all parties to the conflict;

5 were deeply conscious of the urgent need to achieve such a settlement and bring peace to the people of Zimbabwe and their neighbours;

6 accepted that independence on the basis of majority rule requires the adoption of a democratic constitution including appropriate safeguards for minorities;

7 acknowledged that the government formed under such an independence constitution must be chosen through free and fair elections properly supervised under British Government authority, and with Commonwealth observers;

8 welcomed the British Government's indication that an appropriate procedure for advancing towards these objectives would be for them to call a constitutional conference to which all the parties would be invited; and

9 consequently, accepted that it must be a major objective to bring about the cessation of hostilities and an end to sanctions as part of the process of implementation of a lasting settlement.

Source: *Lusaka Highlights*, published by the Commonwealth Secretariat, London, August 1979.

NOTES

[1] For a fuller discussion, see Jan Pettman, *Zambia: Security and Conflict* (Lewes: Julian Friedman, 1974), and D. Anglin and T. Shaw, *Zambia's Foreign Policy: Studies in Diplomacy and Dependence* (Boulder, Colorado: Westview Press, 1979).

[2] For a detailed inside account of these discussions, see David Martin and Phyllis Johnson, *The Struggle for Zimbabwe* (London: Faber and Faber, 1981), Chapter 8.

[3] ZAPU was essentially a national organization of the minority Ndebele people. ZANU came to be identified as the political organization of the majority Shona people. ANC was a loose coalition of moderate black groups formed inside Rhodesia in 1971–72. FROLIZI, the Front for the Liberation of Zimbabwe, was a splinter group which soon fell into oblivion. For a detailed account of the complex nationalist politics of this period, see Martin and Johnson, *op. cit.*, in note 2. Only ZANU and ZAPU have survived.

[4] Martin and Johnson, *op. cit.*, in note 2, p. 251.

[5] *Africa Research Bulletin*, 1976.

[6] Martin and Johnson, *op. cit.*, in note 2, p. 286.

[7] Private discussions with Front-Line officials.

[8] *The Guardian*, 18 June 1979.

[9] Documents alleged to be Soviet instructions to Nkomo's guerrillas and seized by Rhodesian troops in 1979, however, warned Nkomo against resorting to conventional warfare which would, it was said, bring outside intervention by South Africa and the West in support of the Rhodesians.

[10] Although the final communiqué proclaimed only that the maintenance of peace in Africa was the responsibility of Africans alone, the discussion left no doubt that the key issue was the Cuban military involvement in the Angolan, Ethiopian and Rhodesian conflicts. Nigeria's Foreign Minister warned the Cubans 'not to overstay their welcome' in Africa, which would not 'exchange one colonial yoke for another'. Sekou Touré, while defending the need for Cuban technicians, noted that 'many' disapproved of the Cuban military presence.

[11] Data from *The Front-Line States: The Burden of the Liberation Struggle* (London: the Commonwealth Secretariat, 1979).

[12] Martin and Johnson, *op. cit.* in note 2, pp. 305–8.

[13] Communications presented a serious problem for all the Front-Line States during the Conference. Their London representatives could confirm Front-Line agreement on a particular question only after Nyerere, as Chairman of the group, had informed them that all five Presidents had agreed. In one instance the London press announced Front-Line agreement on the draft constitution. When a London Front-Line representative telephoned his Foreign Minister for confirmation, he was told, 'I must ring you back; the British High Commissioner is at my door, and he has the draft constitution in his hands.' (From a private conversation.)

[14] A Tanzanian official credits Machel with softening Mugabe's position on the law-and-order issue. Machel pointed out that the only alternative to the proposal was to assign the task to the two separate guerrilla armies (including Nkomo's heavily-armed forces) plus Muzorewa's army. Such an arrangement would have posed a greater threat to Mugabe than that of the Rhodesian police.

[15] According to a senior ZANU official, once the constitution issue had been settled, Mugabe (suspicious that Britain might try to strike a deal with Muzorewa) began deploying ZANLA's 'crack troops' deep inside the country. Taking no chances of falling into a trap, ZANLA commanders made sure that there were more ZANLA troops outside than inside the assembly points, a fact which General Walls, Rhodesia's Commander-in-Chief, is said to have known. Thus any treachery against ZANLA would have plunged the country immediately back into war.

[16] Britain had based her plans on an estimate of 16,000 guerrillas, while ZANU alone claimed to have 33,000. The guerrilla estimate was far closer, as bulging assembly points soon demonstrated.

[17] In fact, although the transition plan stated that 'the task of maintaining law and order in the pre-independence period will be the responsibility of the civil police', the ceasefire agreement provided that, 'in the event of more general or sustained breaches of the ceasefire, the Governor will decide what action to take to deal with them *with the forces which have accepted his authority*.' (Italics added.)*Southern Rhodesia: Report of the Constitutional Conference*, (London: Lancaster House, 21 December 1979).

[18] *South African Digest*, Pretoria, Department of Foreign Affairs, 22 February 1980.

[19] *New York Times*, 16 August 1981.

[20] Major General Coetzee, cited in *South African Digest*, 28 August 1981.

[21] See, for example, Patrick Laurence in *The Guardian*, 2 February 1981.

[22] *New York Times*, 28 September 1981.

[23] *Zimbabwe Herald*, 9 May 1981. The care with which South African leaders orchestrate their counter-measures is indicated by the statement of a South African official (in private) that the relatively junior Minister of Police was selected to issue the warning to Zimbabwe, since South Africa did not want to make a major issue of it at that particular time.

[24] *Sunday Times*, London, 30 November 1980.

[25] *Sunday Mail*, Salisbury, 10 May 1981.

[26] *Observer*, 1 February 1981.

[27] BBC, *Summary of World Broadcasts* (SWB) ME/6662/B/3, 2 March 1981.

[28] Mozambican officials stress, for example, that all their regular military training and ordinary weapons are supplied by Tanzania, and that they look to the Russians only for advanced weaponry and training. Recently Mozambique announced that agreement has been reached with Portugal to train Mozambican troops. (*Financial Times*, 29 April 1982).

[29] IISS, *Strategic Survey 1979*, (London: IISS, 1980), p. 91.

[30] See Stephen Glover in *The Daily Telegraph*, 10 March 1981.

[31] *The Guardian*, 19 January 1981.

[32] *Ibid.*, 21 May 1980.

[33] Conversations in February and April 1982.

[34] Front-Line official, April 1982, in private con-

versation.

[35] Private communication.

[36] Made up of Ambassadors from the five Western members of the UN Security Council: the US, Britain, Canada, Germany and France. Also known as 'the Western Five' or the 'Contact Group'.

[37] Private conversations in February and April 1982.

[38] *Ibid.*

[39] Interview in April 1982.

[40] *Citizen*, Johannesburg, 10 August 1981.

[41] A good analysis of the 'Constellation' idea is presented by Deon Geldenhuys, *The Constellation of Southern African States and SADCC: Toward a New Regional Stalemate?* (Bramfontein: South African Institute of International Affairs, January 1981).

[42] *SADCC 2: A Perspective* (Maputo: Conference Office, November 1980).

[43] *The Observer*, 30 March 1980.

[44] *The Guardian*, 1 April 1980.

[45] Since their trade with apartheid South Africa is politically embarrassing to the black states, neither South Africa nor most of her African trade partners publish data on this trade.

[46] *Development Needs and Opportunities for Co-operation in Southern Africa.* (Washington: US Agency for International Development, March 1979), p. 70.

[47] A. and N. Seidman, *Outposts of Monopoly Capitalism* (London: Zed Press, 1980). p. 271.

[48] *The Times*, January 1982.

[49] *Ibid.*

[50] *Development Needs, op. cit* in note 47. p. 71.

[51] *Wall Street Journal*, 9 December 1977.

[52] Prime Minister Vorster, cited in K. W. Grundy, *Confrontation and Accommodation in Southern Africa*, (Berkeley: University of California Press, 1973), p. 249.

[53] *Financial Mail*, 9 December 1977.

[54] *South*, January 1981.

[55] *South African Digest*, 11 September and 2 October 1981; *Die Burger*, 28 February 1981; *Washington Post*, 2 November 1981.

[56] As one example of the need for telecommunications, there are no telephone links between Maputo and Dar es-Salaam.

[57] In part this was a false total; the $380 million pledged by the African Development Bank was 'old money' (i.e., it would have been available anyway for viable projects in the region, though not for the particular projects on this list).

[58] Robert Keohane, 'The Big Influence of Small Allies', in *Foreign Policy*, No. 2, Spring 1971.

[59] *Ibid.*

[60] Based on private interviews in May 1982.

[61] Private interview, Spring 1981.

[62] Based on *The Military Balance 1979–1980*. (London: IISS, 1980).

[63] Interview in February 1982.

4 The Role and Impact of the OAU in the Management of African Conflicts

BUKAR BUKARAMBE

The Organization of African Unity (OAU), like other inter-governmental organizations, was formed under certain assumptions with certain objectives in mind. The OAU, established by independent African states in May 1963, was deemed to be a concerted structural response to the economic and political problems confronting the continent. Emerging out of recent decolonization, African states were new states with all the accompanying teething problems. Internally, the leadership that took over from the colonial rulers had to face the task of governing to meet the expectations of the people under political conditions where modern statehood barely existed before. Externally, African states had to find a mode of purposeful relations among themselves within the continent, and between themselves and others outside the continent.

There were two common assumptions in the background of the OAU – pan-Africanism (the concept of supra-nationalism and dedicated fraternity, predicated on the common socio-cultural bonds of the African peoples) and the need to protect the sovereignty of individual states. These assumptions were reflected in the objectives of the OAU, enumerated under Article II of the Charter. They are:

1 to promote the unity and solidarity of African states;
2 to co-ordinate and intensify their co-operation and efforts to achieve a better life for the peoples of Africa;
3 to defend their sovereignty, integrity and independence;
4 to eradicate all forms of colonialism from Africa; and

The author is a Research Fellow at the Nigerian Institute of International Affairs in Lagos.

5 to promote international co-operation having due regard to the Charter of the UN and the Universal Declaration of Human Rights.

Hence, the period since its formation marks the trial period for the OAU. The objective of this article is to determine, empirically, how the OAU has performed thus far in the management of conflicts in Africa. In the process, the article will dwell on the OAU's security environment, the causes of conflicts in Africa, the perceived role of the OAU, and its impact. Then on the basis of the trends discerned some suggestions for reform will be made.

The OAU's Security Environment

The OAU's security environment is influenced by five factors: the size and diversity of its membership, their new and developing status, super-power rivalry, modern ideologies, and elite perceptions.

In terms of size, the OAU membership currently stands at fifty. (But for the controversy, the admission of the Sahrawi Arab Democratic Republic could have brought the number to fifty one.) The diversity of its membership derives from the composition of the continent, which is Arab and Black, and the political, economic and administrative legacies of the different colonizing powers. The Black-Arab dimension shows within the OAU in what late President Nasser described as Egypt's concentric circles: the Islamic, Arab and African.[1] Thus, in addition to their membership of the OAU, Algeria, Egypt, Libya, Morocco, Mauritania, Sudan, Somalia and Tunisia are also members of the Arab League and the Organization of Islamic Conference (OIC).[2] The dual membership forcefully extends the frontiers of the OAU to the world of Arab and Islamic

133

politics. Issues that are extra-continental and essentially Arab affairs reverberate on to the continent. Occasionally the Organization experiences the effect of policies that are based not on African, but on Arab and Islamic foundations – e.g. Arab (particularly Middle Eastern) support for Somalia and Eritrea against Ethiopia.[3] Apart from the long-standing boundary problems, the colonial legacies are factors now mainly due to the ties (strong in some cases) maintained with the former metropolitan powers.[4]

The new and developing status of the membership relates to the fragility of their political and economic systems. Independence brought the joy of self rule, but it also brought the brutal reality of development administration. The nationalist leaders had to face the problems of building a nation out of the multiplicity of ancient kingdoms and establishing a modern infrastructure with scarce and undeveloped resources. Low levels of economic, industrial and structural development[5] make inter-African economic co-operation less easy, as the mainly monocultural and undiversified economies remain externally oriented except, say, through collective bargaining in the ACP–EEC fashion or through low-level regional arrangements such as the Economic Community of West African States (ECOWAS). Further, their fragility also paves the way for the quick internationalization of African conflicts, since such states often have the capacity to initiate a war but seldom the strength to go through with it.

Internationalization of conflict also gives vent to super-power geostrategic rivalry on the continent. Because of their divergent and competitive views, roles and goals, the super-powers almost invariably end up supporting opposing sides, thereby indirectly transferring their rivalry into local conflicts; and through the 'assistance' they render, they make their interests a factor in the trend as well as the outcome of such conflicts. For example, even though Somalia's decision to attack and escalate the Ogaden war in 1977 was influenced by Ethiopia's domestic turmoil at the time, it was also encouraged by the American announcement in June that the United States would supply arms to Somalia and the message in September that Washington, 'was not averse to further guerrilla pressure in the Ogaden . . .'[6] The Soviet Union, for her part, initially tried to make the best of the situation in the region by proposing a confederation of 'progressive' states grouping Ethiopia, Somalia, Djibouti and South Yemen. When that failed to reconcile the animosity between Ethiopia and Somalia, she opted to support the former. In retaliation, Somalia abrogated the July 1974 Friendship Treaty and expelled all Soviet and Cuban citizens in November 1977.[7] Moscow did not take kindly to that, probably incensed by the parallel between the Somali action and earlier experiences in Sudan and Egypt. Thus, before leaving Mogadishu, the Soviet Ambassador said: 'we will teach the Somalis a lesson they will never forget. We will bring them to their knees.'[8] That was translated into massive Soviet–Cuban support for Ethiopia.

Clearly, given the earlier encouragement, Somalia expected the US to fill the gap left by the departure of the Soviet Union. But the help never materialized. Thus, in the end Somalia got nothing out of the war, while the super-powers were able to restore their positions in the region by swapping 'friends'.

Finally, elite perceptions have been especially important in the circumstance of African states, where the concentration of power in the hands of the leadership has meant that their personal attitudes, fears and whims can be easily translated into national policy. The injection of a personality factor into OAU politics has tended to produce elastic politics which seek to accommodate all interests.

Environmental attributes are also the source of conflicts in Africa. First, there is the colonial legacy of arbitrary borders[9] which, apart from major conflicts like those in the Western Sahara and the Ogaden have also pitched Algeria and Morocco, Nigeria and Cameroon and Chad and Libya among others, against each other. And most of these are still active, often sustained by the mineral wealth of the disputed areas. With regard to Morocco and Somalia, the governments in both countries have made the territorial question so central to their policies that even their legitimacy seems to hinge on it. Trapped as they are in years of pent-up national sentiment, the costs of retreating from this course, in spite of successive failure and collective opposition, seem as monumental as pursuing it.

Second, African conflicts are also caused by perceived inequalities in the distribution of domestic power, usually along ethnic or regional lines. Such situations have often been largely the result of administrative policies pursued by the colonial powers. In Chad, for instance, French policy favoured the more receptive South over the North.[10] At independence, political, economic, military and administrative power came to rest with the Southerners. Resentment of that situation and other sideline factors led to the insurgency. The situation was reversed in Sudan where Britain's colonial policy divided the country into two regions, uniting them only in 1947. At independence, the North emerged relatively more educated and developed with an Islamic and Arab culture, while the South – isolated during colonial rule – emerged as more Christianized but less developed. Northern Sudanese independence leaders reneged on an agreement to work out a federal structure[11] to provide some elbow room for local differences and failed to work out a satisfactory *modus operandi*.[12] Cumulative discontent forced the South into a rebellion that spanned a decade.

Third, conflicts can arise from differences in ideological perception between states, particularly where they feel threatened by activities across the border, or where one of the states has felt it a duty to carry its ideological commitment further. While a reaction to the latter posture could be taken as an opposition to imposed values, the former denotes a response by a leadership that is apprehensive of any demonstrative effect on its own domain, especially where governmental and organizational processes are not well entrenched and are consequently susceptible to erosion through overtures.[13] Related to this is the fourth factor of personality clash where leaders, as individuals, might fall out with one another and drag their countries to war with that as a major determinant. Ideological differences and elite disaffection were largely responsible for the demise of the East African Community.

Thus, for example, relatively moderate Kenya was wary of Tanzania's Ujamma radicalism and of President Obote's brand of common man's charter in Uganda. Nevertheless, when Dr Obote was overthrown in 1971, President Nyerere refused to recognize the military government led by President Amin, whom Nyerere loathed.[14] This disaffection also played a role later in the Uganda–Tanzania war, which resulted in Obote regaining power. A similar pattern unfolded in

the Maghreb where Libya under Gaddafi combined a brand of radical fundamentalism with relative affluence sustained by oil wealth. The failure of Gaddafi's attempts. to unite Libya with her neighbours on a pan-Arabist basis produced apprehension and recrimination leading eventually to the July 1977 border war between Libya and Egypt.[15] At the personal level, relations between Libyan and Sudanese leaders deteriorated to such an extent that President Numeiri of Sudan openly wished that Colonel Gaddafi 'should be taken out, killed'.[16] Finally, there is the conflict brought about by the presence of colonial and minority regimes against whom African states have sanctioned a nationalist war.[17]

This admixture underlines the nature of African conflicts. They tend to be, in the main, either short and limited conventional wars, border clashes (even skirmishes), civil wars or wars of attrition – i.e., guerrilla warfare. On another plane, the conflicts show up as subversion or as export of rebellion, where the belligerents resort to aiding and abetting insurgency against each other.

African conflicts have demonstrated a certain degree of intractability. Thus, after some two decades of independence, territorial and border disputes are still frequent, problems of domestic power-sharing remain a potentially disruptive factor and, in spite of pan-African sentiments – particularly since the formation of the OAU – elite incompatibility is still a formidable phenomenon in intra-African relations. Apart from keeping the African conflict situation bubbling, these factors have led African states to continue to divert their meagre resources to armament.[18] Of course, military spending in Africa remains low in comparison to other regions of the world. But it is pertinent to note that the African states with comparatively large military establishments, such as Libya, Ethiopia, Morocco, Nigeria, Somalia, Algeria, Sudan and Zaire,[19] have either fought a civil war or are threatened with one, and face problems of domestic insurgency or have strained relations with their neighbours.

Expectations of the OAU
Africa was supposed to have been saved from this dilemma by the OAU, which was expected to foster a continental consensus that would avert or solve such problems.

135

Such expectations were the result of the pan-African assumptions that led to its formation. Historically, pan-Africanism, as a movement, started among the Blacks of the diaspora in response to the deprivations of their new abode. From its inception, the spirit of pan-Africanism entailed a consciousness of origins and the quest to 'encourage a feeling of unity and to facilitate friendly intercourse among Africans in general.'[20] At the early stage, the movement was essentially a commitment to the Black race, but from the mid-1940s onwards it became an 'allegiance'[21] to the African continent as well. Its ideals came to be articulated within the context of independence movements. Further, by encompassing both the Arab and Black nature of the continent, pan-Africanism in its new form extended across the Sahara, and was dominated by sovereign states rather than by individuals and associations as before.[22]

Therefore, as they emerged from colonial rule, African st..tes nestled on a sense of community feeling forged by a perceived legacy of common history and geography. A year after Ghana's independence in 1957, President Nkrumah convened a conference of independent African states to discuss issues of 'mutual interest'. On the eve of this he said in a national broadcast:

... for too long in our history, Africa has spoken through the voices of others. Now what I have called the African personality in international affairs will have a chance of making its impact and will let the world know it through the voices of Africa's own sons.[23]

Attended by representatives from both Arab and Black African states (Ethiopia, Egypt, Liberia, Morocco, Sudan, Tunisia and Ghana), the conference became a milestone in African independence. It was followed by a succession of others. Political parties, trade unions and other associations soon followed suit.[24] The climax of the diplomatic activities that ensued was the May 1963 Addis Ababa conference and the formation of the OAU. Thus, the OAU became for African states an achievement as well as an instrument. This conferred on the Organization a symbolic force which turned it into a rudimentary power centre within which African states sought to create a wider political community. These expectations determined its roles; with regard to conflict they include:

1 Serving as a body under whose aegis African problems could have African solutions. In fact, conflicts (though predominating) are not the only problems that could be referred.
2 Legitimizing certain positions in a conflict on the basis of provisions of the OAU charter or resolutions. These represent the areas of consensus among the member states; going against them will invariably mean loss of general support.
3 Mediating conflicts. This stems mainly from the roles enumerated above. The OAU Charter provides for a Commission of Mediation Conciliation and Arbitration (CMCA), but it has never been used. Typically mediations are either by *ad hoc* committees, personal diplomacy, or through the good offices of another member state.

OAU as Conflict Manager

As the embodiment of African sensitivities and an institution for their collective pursuit, the impact of the OAU has been felt primarily in forging a broad consensus over issues of major interest to the member states. This denotes that there will be dissent and, indeed, there has been. Given the OAU's security environment, it cannot be otherwise. But at the end, what is generally seen as the 'African position' invariably emerges. That in reality is the dominant view – the view of the majority of the members as carried in the resolutions. For the members who disagree, it is a sort of *fait accompli*. Their dissent does not usually alter the general position.

From this stems the OAU style in conflict management. Acknowledging pervading sensitivities, pan-Africanism has been invoked to settle disputes.[25] Through a common stance, some incipient disputes have been discouraged, while attempted secessions like those in Nigeria and Sudan have failed to win African support and got blunted in the process. Furthermore, the collective approach has succeeded in legitimizing nationalist wars against colonial and minority regimes – providing the national liberation movements with a diplomatic umbrella and material aid – and has induced the OAU to withhold action on issues perceived as contrary to the African spirit. Thus, for example, African states rejected the idea of dialogue with apartheid South Africa as suggested by Ivory Coast in 1971,[26] refused to recognize any of the so-called homelands in

South Africa and, during the 1977-8 Ogaden war, declined to condemn the Soviet–Cuban intervention against Somalia because the Somali goal would have amounted to a forceful rather than a peaceful alteration of borders.

Against this background, it can be said that the OAU has, over time, succeeded to some extent in institutionalizing a pattern of behaviour for African states in conflicts, especially where borders, secession, minority regimes and foreign intervention are concerned. The importance of this factor is that member states or parties who have sought to change the established norms, inevitably have found themselves faced with the displeasure of the overwhelming majority of African states.

But while the positive side remains, it is also a fact that, at times when it has suited their purpose, member states have ignored or violated the resolutions of the OAU and the provisions of its Charter, and have abandoned OAU principles. Mediations have run out of steam, peaceful structures established by the OAU have been quashed, and the Organization has been presented with a *fait accompli*. In almost all such cases, the hoped-for results failed to materialize due to lack of support (moral and resources) and commitment by member states.

The OAU and Chad

The OAU involvements in, say, Chad or the Western Sahara are illustrative. Though the conflict in Chad had started by 1968, active participation by the OAU did not begin until one decade later. By then adversary positions had hardened, institutional structures in the country had been virtually destroyed, and the insurgent groups had splintered through a combination of personal acrimony and competitive sponsorship.[27] Peace conferences never seemed to build confidence among the adversaries; the results were invariably little more than shortlived ceasefires and tottering coalitions.[28] Peaceful structures set up as African endeavours collapsed soon after[29] or even failed to take off[30] because of failure by member states to meet their commitments, disagreement between the adversaries and some sponsoring African states, and unceasing recriminations among the adversaries themselves.

The failure of the OAU Peace-keeping Force (OAUF) in Chad, deployed in March 1982, showed even more. The OAUF was meant to replace the Libyan troops who had intervened in November 1980. Sudan, Egypt, Saudi Arabia, France and the US were very opposed to this intervention and quickly came to the aid of the defeated Defence Minister, Mr Hissene Habre, who resumed fighting. After American and French promises of support, the leader of the transitional government (GUNT), President Gaukhouni Weddeye, finally asked Libya to withdraw; obviously angered, she refused to synchronize her withdrawal with the deployment of the OAUF and departed abruptly. However, the OAUF did not arrive until mid-December, after a month's delay spent in fresh negotiations among the countries volunteering to send contingents, the transitional government of Chad, and the OAU over the terms of the force. And of the seven countries mentioned as providing troops only three (Nigeria, Senegal and Zaire) sent contingents while the inadequacy of promised Western assistance soon became apparent as the OAU appealed for UN assistance. At the same time, Habre's advance continued, aided not only by Sudanese and other external assistance but also by the lack of co-operation in battle among the factional fighting units under GUNT. The OAUF meanwhile, deployed without securing ceasefire, pledged neutrality and stood by (it was not meant to be a fighting force anyway) until Habre captured the capital, N'djamena on 4 June 1982. No sooner had the capital fallen, than the contributing states started to withdraw their troops.[31]

In retrospect, the whole process raises some important questions: Why did the countries, particularly the African states that supported Hissene Habre continue to do so even after the withdrawal of Libyan troops and the deployment of the OAUF? Why did Libya, a member of the OAU, refuse to synchronize the withdrawal of her troops with the deployment of the OAUF? How was it feasible for the various groups that made up GUNT to persist in recrimination and fail to co-operate even in the face of Habre's success?

There could be more questions. But the answers to these would suggest that:

(a) The various groups in Chad were in the alliance under GUNT only for tactical reasons and that was not sufficient to sustain a strong central authority;

137

(b) The conflict in Chad, once internationalized became an appendage to African as well as extra-African interests and feuds – hence the network of American, French, Sudanese, Egyptian and Saudi Arabian participation in re-establishing Habre who was known to oppose Libya; and

(c) Libya, once she perceived that she could not have her way in Chad, lost interest momentarily in the affairs of that country and even worked against that.

Thus the OAU endeavour in Chad was quashed by the same forces that called for it. In addition, the reliance on Western support (inadequate as it was) and the call for UN assistance suggest a distinct lack of resources available to the OAU to mount and sustain peace-keeping operations.

Conflict in the Western Sahara
The Western Sahara conflict presented a different angle. The OAU ultimately set up at the July 1978 Khartoum summit a six-nation *ad hoc* committee, to address the issue, but by then *Polisario* (Popular Front for the Liberation of Saguia el Hamra and Rio de Oro) had already formed a government-in-exile (in February 1976) the Sahrawi Arab Democratic Republic (SADR), which had been recognized by at least seven African states. As a result, a pattern of diplomatic encampment had started to form within the OAU. Therefore, once the OAU waded into the conflict the issue became two-pronged – it was necessary both to find a solution to the conflict and to contain the latent disruptive bloc politics within the Organization. That required the active co-operation of the parties to the dispute – Algeria, Morocco, Mauritania and the *Polisario*. But it was not forthcoming, particularly from Morocco, which rejected a series of OAU recommendations and offered instead a 'controlled referendum' who would effectively confirm her sovereignty over the territory.[32]

Utterly powerless to determine anything of substance in the face of Morocco's rejection, the OAU drifted. Meanwhile, the SADR was winning in the diplomatic front such that by July 1980, twenty-six African states had recognized it and were pushing for its admission into the OAU. The move was stalled for about two years through compromise and threats of walk-out by Morocco and her supporters until February 1982 when the

Secretary-General invoked his powers under Article 28 of the Charter and admitted the SADR during a council of ministers meeting in Addis Ababa.[33] Morocco and eighteen other states walked out on the grounds that the act was illegal. Thereafter, the OAU could not hold any successful meeting, including the 1982 annual summit, due to lack of a quorum. The split has immobilized it. And so, by an ugly irony, the OAU, instead of helping to solve the Western Sahara conflict, has been incapacitated by it. Since then the issue has become the OAU itself – that is, how to get it back on its feet again. The solution to the conflict has become secondary.

Operational Problems
The experiences of Chad and the Western Sahara are examples of the OAU's operational problems. In the first place, its resolutions are only advisory, not binding on the member states. It has no coercive power and cannot mount sanctions of any sort except to register disapproval. Hence, once a member state decides to ignore OAU resolutions or the principles of the OAU Charter (which all have pledged to observe) there is nothing else the Organization can do other than to re-affirm its general position. Against this background, it is hardly surprising that foreign powers are not inhibited from intervening in African conflicts.

Second, African states have failed to mollify micro-nationalism in order to strengthen the continental organization. Perhaps inadvertently, by making national prerogatives sacrosanct without giving equivalent status to the ideals of pan-Africanism, the member states succeeded only in cutting pan-Africanism into fifty odd pieces. This is not to suggest that national obligations can be abandoned. But African states, by concentrating mainly on the prerogatives of the nation state, have failed to give their collective goals the optimum legal and political attention. The net effect of this is that pan-Africanism decisively ends at the borders of states. And the implications are obvious: without the required commitment resolutions became rhetoric.

Third, the Organization is thus internally weakened by the attitudes of, and relations among, the member states. The Charter exists and every independent African state is a signatory, but at the same time, apart from the southern African

Front-Line States virtually every member state sees their continental neighbours as a threat. Accusations range from support of dissent, export of rebellion and military incursions, to facilitating foreign invasion or intervention. For example, Uganda accused Kenya of aiding and abetting the July 1976 Israeli raid on Entebbe;[34] Benin accused Morocco and Gabon of involvement in the Cotonou raid of January 1977 and boycotted the OAU summit in Libreville that year in protest.[35] Before that, in 1965 the Francophone West African states boycotted the OAU Accra summit after accusing President Nkrumah of fomenting dissent in their countries.[36] The list is extensive.

Fourth, member states make demands on the Organization without ensuring that it has the resources to meet them. When measured against the security, economic and administrative needs envisaged by member states, the OAU budget is modest indeed. Worse still, the Organization has been plagued by excessive default in payment. President Stevens, the out-going chairman at the June 1981 Nairobi summit, elaborated on the resource problem of the Organization:

> ... The arrears in contribution ... have made it difficult for the General Secretariat to operate effectively or to carry out the tasks we have assigned to it. It also appears to me that the present premises are inadequate to house staff. With more recruitment and an increase in the Secretariat's activities, it was evident to me that we will be faced with more serious problems in the not too distant future.[37]

The trend has not altered. At the Council of Ministers budget session at Addis Ababa in March 1982 the Secretary-General reported that only $4 million had been received for the 1981/82 financial year, that only ten members had paid their dues all or in part, and that lack of funds forced the Organization to borrow money in 1981 to pay staff. Undaunted, the Council adopted a budget of nearly $22 million.[38]

Finally, the OAU is inevitably affected by the lack of unanimity under certain conflict situations. Dissenting groups are sometimes powerful enough to produce OAU positions which are unrepresentative of the views of most of its members or else to prevent it from taking any action at all. Meanwhile, either external solutions would be applied to the conflict while African

states stand by harassing each other or else initiatives would be taken by some African states but outside the OAU framework. During the April 1977 Shaba crisis, for example, the OAU watched while France (with US, West German, Chinese and Belgian support) ferried 1,500 Moroccan troops to help quell the uprising.[39] For the second Shaba crisis in May 1978, Western action was even bolder: the US, Britain, France and Belgium went ahead to emplace a 'Pan-African Force' made up of troops from Morocco, Senegal, Central African Republic, Gabon, Ivory Coast and Egypt to police the province and allow Franco–Belgian troops to withdraw.[40] The OAU in those instances stood by, rendered redundant and immobilized.

Suggestions for Reform

A basic dilemma thus confronts the African states. Even if the impact of Africa's security environment is acknowledged, the dilemma is still largely of their own making. It is difficult to avoid the conclusion that African states are still not decided on what type of OAU they want. Perhaps that is to be expected. Since African states were looking for a collective forum in the OAU they could only decide on one with an elastic charter. Nevertheless the OAU often fails not only because of what African states cannot do, but also actually because of what they do. One such area is finance. If the OAU is to function at all, it must have optimum subvention. This has never been met. Another area is the relationship between member states and the OAU – that is, how member states fashion their national behaviour within the African framework. In designing the charter, African states wished to preserve their own discretionary power, constraining the powers of the OAU such that there is no independent elbow room for the Organization. This suggests that if the member states wish the Organization to function with good effect, then the reins on OAU discretionary powers should be loosened. But how far, if at all? African states are not decided on that. African states cannot logically expect the OAU to succeed, if after taking a collective decision some of them will still feel free to adopt and implement policies that they know will ultimately erase the effects of the general one.

Could this dilemma be attributed to the decline of pan-Africanism, or the waning of felt needs? Neither seems to be the case. The roots of the dilemma are as old as the Organization itself; and in spite of the deficiencies of the OAU, members states are still charmed by it. They still have sufficient loyalty towards it to continue to refer to it, invoke its provisions, and endeavour to be seen to be on its side. The dilemma, therefore, is the result of a question that arose with the formation of the OAU but has not been answered for the past two decades.

Hence, there are no better suggestions for reform than those which seek to eliminate this dilemma and the ambivalence that stems from it. The premise of the suggestion is that what the OAU needs is a proper definition of what it should be and do. It has been under-utilized since its birth.

To start with, the Organization can be strengthened by giving its resolutions a more binding character. This can be done by altering Article VI of the Charter to remove, or at least reduce, the discretionary power of the member states. The aim would be to contain the tendency of member states to vote for resolutions that they have neither the intention nor the capacity to implement. Such a step would also, indirectly, give the Organization some reserved coercive power.

Then, the OAU's resource base can be enhanced by making the payment of dues compulsory; the Charter can be amended to the effect that defaulting member states would lose their voting rights (as under Article 19 of the UN Charter). Clearly, the aim is to deny countries the means to vote for provisions that they cannot help sustain. Quite often a false image of support is created by votes of states that do not even pay for the basic maintenance of institutional structures. To spread the burden more evenly, some concessions can be given to the countries that are in economic difficulties, while those that are relatively richer can contribute a little more to fill any gap. These suggestions are essentially a call for African states to stem their own power in favour of the OAU and to commit themselves more. Therein lies the greatest obstacle. Still, a sudden re-awakening to necessity might do it.

This article is, therefore, not supportive of reforms that recommend extra bodies. Given that the OAU is under-utilized and under-financed, then extra bodies do not stand a chance of making any impact. Instead, they will only add to unfulfilled promises and require extra financial outlay which the OAU is in no position to meet. Besides, the OAU's chequered record is replete with institutions that have been allowed to decay even though they were established at the request of African governments.[41]

But an area worth looking into for the future is the role which regional organizations like ECOWAS would play in conflict management. Such organizations could help ease the problems of diversity and territorial expanse by providing a federal framework for the continent. Furthermore, they have the advantages of manageable size, regional contiguity, relatively higher socio-cultural affinity, non-reliance on the OAU for subvention, and a more enduring need for economic co-operation. Regional organizations could also build on established traditions of intra-group mediation and military co-operation agreements among neighbouring states.[42] This would in effect introduce a tier system, where the regional bodies can serve as a level of first hearing while the OAU becomes a sort of clearing house in addition to what it is currently, and would complement the decision by African states to set up 'by the year 2000 . . . an African Economic Community' based on the foundation of regional groupings.[43]

In the final analysis, international organizations can be dependable only to the extent that its members are capable of and willing to endow them with credible commitments. It is the lack of such commitments that explains the OAU most.

NOTES

[1] Gamel Abdul Nasser, *The Philosophy of the Revolution* (English edition, Buffalo, 1959) pp. 74.

[2] Not all of these countries are Arab. Mauritania is Berber-Black, Sudan is Black-Arab, while Somalia is Black. Apart from these Guinea, Gabon, Guinea-Bissau, Uganda, Sierra Leone, Djibouti, Chad, Gambia, Mali, Upper Volta, Niger and Senegal are also members of the OIC. See *The Middle East and North Africa 1980–81*, (London, Europa Publications Ltd., 1980).

[3] Colin Legum (ed.), *Africa Contemporary Record*, 1978–9 (London: Africana Publishing Co., 1979) pp. A38–9. See also Patrick Gilkes, 'The Arabs and the Eritreans', *Middle East International*, (London), No. 156, 14 August 1981, pp. 10–11.

4 Ali A. Mazrui, *Africa's International Relations. The Diplomacy of Dependence and Change.* (London: Heinemann Books, 1979), p. 63.

5 *What Kind of Africa by the Year 2000. Final Report of the Monrovia Symposium on the Future Development Prospects of Africa Towa ds the Year 2000.* (OAU: February 12–16, 1979), pp. 13–14. See also, *OAU: Lagos Plan of Action for the Economic Development of Africa 1980–2000.* (Geneva: International Institute for Labour Studies, 1981).

6 Said S. Samator, 'The New Rivalry in Africa: America and Russia in the Recent Crisis of the Horn'. *The Pan-Africanist* (Evanstor, Illinois), No. 8, July 1979, p. 37. See also W. S. Thompson, 'The American–African Nexus in Soviet Strategy'. *Horn of Africa* (New Jersey), January–March 1978, Vol. 1, No. 1, p. 43.

7 Jiri Valenta, 'Soviet–Cuban Intervention in the Horn of Africa: Impact and Lessons'. *Journal of International Affairs*, Vol. 34, No. 2, Fall-Winter 1980/81, pp. 361.

8 Said S. Samator, *op. cit.* in note 6, pp. 44.

9 On African boundaries, see: Saadia Touval, *The Boundary Politics of Independent Africa* (Cambridge, Mass: Harvard University Press 1972) and Carl Costa Widstrand (ed.) *African Boundary Problems* (Uppsala: Scandinavian Institute of African Studies, 1968).

10 See Virginia Thompson and Richard Adloff, *Conflict in Chad* (London: C. Hurst & Co., 1981).

11 Abel Alier, 'The Southern Sudan Question', in Dunstan M. Wai (ed.) *The Southern Sudan. The Problem of National Integration.* (London: Frank Cass & Co., 1973), pp. 18–21.

12 Mansour Khalid, 'The Southern Sudan Settlement and its African Implications', in Yassin El-Ayouty (ed.). *The OAU After Ten Years. Comparative Perspective* (New York: Praeger, 1975), p. 178.

13 Raymond W. Copson, 'African International Politics: Underdevelopment and Conflict in the Seventies', *Orbis* Vol. 22, No. 1, Spring 1981, p. 229.

14 Ibrahim S. Wani, 'Humanitarian Intervention and the Tanzania–Uganda War'. *Horn of Africa* (New Jersey), Vol. III, No. 2, 1981, p. 24.

15 John Wright, *Libya: A Modern History* (London & Canberra: Croom Helm, 1982), pp. 204–7.

16 International Herald Tribune, 8 July 1981, pp. 4.

17 The application of the phrase 'colonial and minority regimes' may be feasible no longer since what remains of that is apartheid South Africa and her occupation of Namibia. But the phrase will be maintained throughout the discussion because it dates from 1963 when, in addition to South Africa, there were also the Portuguese colonies and Zimbabwe (Rhodesia).

18 Jacques Revol, 'African Countries: Defence and its Problems'. *Africa Defence Journal*, No. 9, May 1981, p. 40. See also, *Africa Now*, (London) July 1982, pp. 15–29.

19 See Ruth Leger Sivard, *World Military and Social Expenditures, 1981*, (Virginia: World Priorities 1981), pp. 22–7.

Also, *The Military Balance 1981–82*, (London: IISS, 1981).

20 Imanuel Giess, *The Pan-African Movement. A History of Pan-Africanism in America, Europe and Africa.* Translated by Ann Keep (New York: Africa Publishing Co., 1974), p. 190.

21 Ali A. Mazrui, *Towards a Pan Africana. A Study of Ideology and Ambition* (University of Chicago Press, 1967), p. 3.

22 Ali A. Mazrui, *op cit.* in note 4, p. 68.

23 Kwame Nkrumah, *I Speak of Freedom. A Statement of African Ideology.* (New York: Praeger Inc., 1961), p. 125.

24 See Colin Legum, *Pan-Africanism; A Short Political Guide* (New York: Praeger Inc., 1962), pp. 38–80.

25 B. David Meyers, 'Intra-Regional Conflict Management by the OAU'. *International Organization*, Vol. 28, No. 3, Summer 1974. R. A. Akindele, 'The Organization of African Unity and the United Nations', *Canadian Year Book of International Law* Vol. IX, 1972, pp. 30–58.

26 A. Bolaji Akinyemi, 'Africa – Challenges and Response: A Foreign Policy Perspective', *Daedalus* Vol. III, No. 2, Spring, 1982, p. 247.

27 Thompson and Adloff, *op. cit.* in note 10.

28 Note, for example, the outcome of the Conferences in Libya and Sudan in 1978. See, *Keesing's Contemporary Archives*, 12 May 1978, p. 28977. *Africa Research Bulletin*, March 1978, p. 4781 and August 1978, p. 4958.

29 Such as the Kano Agreement that provided for a transitional government and deployment of Nigerian Peace-keeping Force. See *Keesing's Contemporary Archives* (London), Vol. XXVI, 1980, pp. 30065–7.

30 The August 1979 Lagos Conference provided for a OAU force. That did not materialize due to lack of funds. Member states balked. Only Congo Brazzaville sent a contingent that had to withdraw after a short while. See, Thompson and Adloff, *op. cit.*, in note 10, pp. 96–7, *Keesing's Contemporary Archives*, 1981, pp. 30559 and 30694.

31 Details of the unfolding conflict in Chad can be found, *inter alia*, in the contemporary issues of *West Africa* (London), *Africa Research Bulletin, Africa Now* (London), and *New Nigerian* (Lagos).

32 For more details see, *Africa Research Bulletin*, February 1976; pp. 3942–5; Susan Morgan, 'The OAU and the Sahara', *Middle East International*, 18 July 1980; *Africa Research Bulletin*, July 1978, p. 5330 and September 1980, p. 5794.

33 Secretary-General, Edem Kodjo in an interview. See *Africa Now* (London), August 1982, pp. 18–19.

34 Kenya, however, denied the allegation and accused Ethiopia instead. See *Africa Research Bulletin*, July 1976, p. 4080.

35 *Africa Research Bulletin*, February 1977, p. 4311 and July 1977, p. 4489.

36 Zdenek Cervenka, *The Unfinished Quest for Unity: Africa and the OAU* (London: Julian Friedmann, 1977), p. 81.

37 *West Africa* (London), 29 June 1981, p. 1459.

38 *West Africa* (London), 8 March 1982, p. 640.

39 *Africa Research Bulletin*, May 1978, p. 4858.

40 *Ibid.* pp. 4704–5 and 4861.

41 OAU, *Lagos Plan of Action, op. cit.*, in note 5, p. 91.

42 See *ECOWAS Policies and Programme Series*, Lagos No. 1. 1981, p. 2; *Executive Office of the President*, Lagos, Press Release No. 866, 31 May 1981; *African Research Bulletin*, June 1981, pp. 6071–2. The Southern Africa Front-Line States also have similar security co-operation agreements. See also O. Aluko, 'African Response to External Intervention since Angola', *African Affairs*, Vol. 80, No. 319, April 1981, p. 169.

43 *Lagos Plan of Action, op. cit.* in note 5, p. 128.

5 South Africa: A New Military Role in Southern Africa 1969–82

CHRISTOPHER COKER

Events in the 1970s transformed the South African Defence Force (SADF) from a limited military force into a powerful arm of the state. In part the change was prompted by the belief that the West no longer considered the Republic a useful ally; America's failure to come to South Africa's assistance in Angola convinced her that it was no longer in her interests to act as a member in all but name of the Western Alliance. In recent years this has given rise to a conflict between the army's basic philosophy, with its emphasis on close relations with the West, (peppered, to be sure, by frequent conflicts and crises) and the ever sharpening recognition that its objectives may no longer meet with Western acquiescence. In particular, the SADF has played a major role in South Africa's attempts to undermine the settlements pursued by the Western powers in Namibia and Zimbabwe.

Judged in the light of the events of the past five years the role of the SADF is infinitely more significant than its own conception of it could possibly have suggested to itself or anyone else in 1968. No-one then could possibly have foreseen that the US failure to prevent the Soviet Union from intervening in southern Africa would have left South Africa an independent military power.

South Africa and Rhodesian security 1968–80

South Africa first deployed her forces beyond her frontiers in September 1967, against the African National Congress (ANC), the nationalist movement which was involved at the time in minor, and largely unsuccessful, operations along the Zambezi with the Zimbabwe African People's Union (ZAPU) led by Joshua Nkomo.[1]

The presence of South African troops in Rhodesia should have given rise to serious doubts about her future intentions. This was the first time that South Africa had made clear that

The author is a Lecturer in International Relations at the London School of Economics.

the defence of the *laager* recognized no frontiers – that if necessary she would be prepared to extend the fight beyond her borders whether invited to do so or not. Secondly, the scale of operations was more extensive than generally recognized. By 1969 the number of South African troops at the front reportedly reached 2,700, only a thousand short of the Rhodesian regular army.[2]

By the time of the Lancaster House agreement in 1979 South Africa's presence in Rhodesia comprised at least two airborne units with *Puma* helicopters and armoured cars,[3] or the equivalent of an infantry battalion and two fire-force groups,[4] deployed not along the Zambezi but in the south-east of the country against the operations of the Zimbabwe African National Union (ZANU). Without South African arms and assistance Rhodesia would never have survived until 1979. Given her own extended lines of communication South Africa did not have the resources to defend Rhodesia herself; to have done so would have meant doubling the borders for which her own security forces were responsible, as well as inviting an attack on the Transvaal through Mozambique. She did have forces, however, to *frustrate* British and American plans and might well have continued to do so but for her belief that Bishop Abel Muzorewa would be returned by the majority of black voters in the election of March 1980. It was a serious miscalculation but a useful illustration of how South Africa was quite prepared to live with a destabilized Rhodesia rather than act as midwife for a Zimbabwean government not of her own making.

South Africa and Angola 1975–6

South Africa's intervention in Rhodesia was, at least, at the behest of a *de facto* administration in Salisbury. Her intervention in Angola was taken against the wishes of first the colonial power (Portugal) and then the government which succeeded it. The most interesting feature of the initial operation was that it was remarkably small, involving no more than 500 men, two-thirds of them African. When fighting began in earnest, after the capture of Benguela and Lobito, the strength of the force still stood at only 1,500. The South African High Command did not commit substantial mechanized or air forces. The army fought well under its true strength.

This was not surprising. With Cuban troops arriving in increasingly large numbers, South Africa would have needed to call upon extensive air strikes to have pressed ahead and she was not prepared to hazard her *Mirage* IIIs without some assurance from the West that her losses would be made good. If Pretoria believed that the United States would intervene rather than allow the Frente Nacional de Libertação de Angola (FNLA) and União Nacional para a Independencia Total de Angola (UNITA) to collapse, it was soon disabused. As one US government official told Congress, no American government could agree to resupply South African forces *during a conflict in which its own forces were not engaged.* He underlined the point by reminding it that throughout the conflict the US had scrupulously adhered to the arms embargo.[5]

The main lesson of the Angolan operation was a simple one. Given that the West had opted for a view of stability in southern Africa which had begun to differ in nearly all respects from South Africa's, and that it would no longer be prepared to resupply arms in a conflict in which it was not itself engaged, the SADF could only really be employed in limited engagements. Nevertheless, this has far from limited its operations.

South Africa and Angola since 1976

It is striking that the conflict which saw the triumph of the Movimento Popular para a Libertação de Angola (MPLA) and prompted some Western observers to dismiss South Africa as a military power has been followed by a significant increase in SADF operations. Since 1976 it has repeatedly crossed the frontier into Angola to attack road and rail communications and the bases of the South West Africa People's Organization (SWAPO), against which it has been fighting for the past fifteen years. Although these operations have been described as raids the term is somewhat misleading. Most recently they have amounted to full-scale invasions, involving armoured cars, fighter bombers and large detachments of troops – much larger, in fact, than those involved in 1975. Clearly, Pretoria's increasingly obvious failure to contain the forces of change at home has prompted it to compensate by putting even more emphasis on the use of force beyond the *laager*.

Until recently these raids tended to be seen almost exclusively against the backdrop of negotiations for a settlement in Namibia. After 1976 South Africa obviously felt that she had to show that armed struggle need not necessarily triumph as it already had in Angola and Mozambique. She seemed to have made a profound connection between the chances of peaceful change at home – on her own terms and at her own pace – and military victory or defeat, actual or perceived, in Namibia.

But for raids like the Cassinga (1978) and Savate (1980) incursions the United States would never have been able to link South Africa's withdrawal from Namibia with the withdrawal of the Cubans from Angola. For the presence of the Cubans was in large measure contingent on UNITA's continuing challenge to the MPLA and the support UNITA received from South Africa.

From the beginning, the Front-Line States have been critical of linkage because Namibia's independence is an *unqualified* obligation mandated by the International Court of Justice and the Security Council. Nevertheless, under President Reagan the US has accepted it as a *sine qua non* of further progress in the negotiations. As Chester Crocker, the Assistant Secretary for African Affairs, told an audience in Honolulu in August 1981, America wondered:

> how a young government in the fragile new state of Namibia can be expected to survive and prosper with a seemingly endless civil war on its northern border, with a substantial Soviet–Cuban presence nearby, and with the *consequent prospect of a new sequence of intervention involving both South African and Communist forces.*[6]

These remarks were revealing because they were the first recognition that linkage worked both ways. Obviously, it was in America's interest to get the Cubans out of Angola but once they have departed the problem of South African intervention will still remain. Angola

143

and Namibia have both become battlefields in which the Soviet Union and South Africa have developed surprisingly similar objectives. Both countries expect political gains from a continuation and increase in hostilities; both have been lukewarm, if not openly hostile, to the West's attempts to find a permanent solution to regional problems which, in one form or another, have preoccupied the US and the Front-Line States for the better part of five years. The remarks made by the South African Foreign Minister during Crocker's most recent visit to Pretoria suggest that South Africa would prefer a low-level conflict on the Angolan–Namibian border to a Namibia in which the ANC would be able to operate without hindrance.[7]

Nevertheless, the raids that have continued since 1980 cannot be interpreted entirely as attacks against SWAPO. Certainly, South Africa has tried for fifteen years not to be blackmailed, coerced or persuaded by the Western powers that a SWAPO government would be for the best when, at times, the West itself has been far from certain about the outcome. A critical and as yet unanswered question, however, is what South Africa really hopes to gain; whether other motives explain the frequency and scale of her operations; indeed, whether SWAPO is any longer the principal target.

It is interesting, in fact, to compare *Operation Protea* in August 1981, with the invasion of Angola five years earlier. The second operation demonstrated that South Africa had learned much from the past:

- The number of men involved in *Operation Protea*, 11,000 in all, was considerably greater than in 1975. The deployment of three infantry brigades in *Operation Smokeshell* (1980) had represented the largest mobilization of South African military strength since 1945.
- *Operation Protea* not only called upon a greater number of aircraft but also the use of high-speed bombing strikes against the civilian population. No attempt was made to win civilians over to UNITA. In fact, South Africa deliberately injected new uncertainty into the Angolan scene, which is now as tense and potentially dangerous as any in southern Africa. *Operation Smokeshell* also involved three squadrons of *Mirage* III and *Buccaneer* bombers which might well have turned the tide

of battle had they been used four years before.
- In addition to relying on air support, the SADF was also equipped with tanks. Ninety *Centurion* tanks, as well as 250 armoured cars, entered Cunene at the end of August 1981. At the same time 120mm and 155mm guns were used in combination with the air force to bombard Angolan towns before ground troops moved into the area.[8]

The reason for the increase in force and equipment numbers is that South Africa was no longer fighting a guerrilla force but a highly trained, well-equipped modern army, with sustained experience of modern combat. And it was the Angolan army, not the Cubans whom they engaged. The Cubans were so unreliable and their morale so suspect, that they were used almost exclusively for garrison duty in the main towns.[9]

Operation Protea yielded 3,000 tons of equipment, including 300 vehicles, more than a hundred SAM-7 missile launchers, many still in their crates, and ammunition cases stacked ten feet high. The capture of such spoils confirmed that the Angolan army, to whom most of the vehicles and heavier weapons belonged, lost even more in the assault than SWAPO. At a press conference in Luanda President Eduardo dos Santos reported that, contrary to South African claims, the operation had been directed against regular army units who had suffered 60 per cent of the total casualties.[10]

A subsequent raid on two Angolan missile sites under construction at Cahana and Chibemba, two towns north-west of Xangogo, was the first time that the Angolan army put up any real resistance, bringing to an end a tacit understanding that the two countries would not engage each other's forces along a narrow corridor running 200 miles north of the border. The South African Commander, General Viljoen, later claimed that despite alerting the Angolans of the assault, they had 'awaited' the advancing column and attacked it 'with premeditation', an episode which, if true, marked the first time that the army of a neighbouring state had tried to stand its ground against South African forces.

Since the beginning of 1981 South African incursions into Angola (the majority of which have gone unreported),[11] have taken one of four forms: reconnaissance flights over the provinces

144

of Mocamedes, Huila and Cuando-Cubango; reconnaissance flights and bomber raids into the eastern province of Moxico; operations intended to extend UNITA's operational area northwards; and long-range sabotage missions by special units of which by far the most dramatic was the attack on the Petrangol state oil refinery in Luanda in November 1981.

It remains to ask why these raids have been carried out; why, for that matter, Angola has become the principal target. Although South Africa has an interest in destabilizing the MPLA regime, she would probably not wish to overthrow the government by force. She prefers to keep it on the defensive. Like the Soviet Union, her freedom of manoeuvre is only as great as the instability which exists (and which, to some extent, she promotes). Indeed, her actions are intelligible only in relation to the MPLA's continuing presence in government.

By supporting the UNITA guerrillas South Africa has been able to harry the government at the point where its control of the country is weakest. Although the conflict in the south has produced many conflicting, exaggerated and unverifiable claims, the movement has undoubtedly disrupted the life of the community. From a demoralized band of 3,000 men who fled into the bush six years ago, UNITA's leader, Jonas Savimbi, claims to have built a force of 30,000 who are active in every province up to the tenth parallel. The true extent of South African support to UNITA is unknown but it is clear that the South Africans work closely with Savimbi. Most of the trucks and petrol used by the guerrillas are supplied by Pretoria, as are some, though not all, of their weapons. Savimbi's reason for fighting on is to force the MPLA to re-open negotiations with him on equal terms. It is doubtful whether his allies are really interested in such an outcome. With UNITA in the government, rather than out of it, they would have no excuse for destabilizing Angola or for focusing attention on what is happening elsewhere in southern Africa rather than on what is happening in South Africa herself.

If that is the South African objective the raids have so embarrassed the United States that she has been forced against her better judgment to re-open negotiations on diplomatic recognition of the present regime. Even after Savimbi's visit to Washington in December 1981 the State Department went out of its way to insist that it did not consider UNITA an alternative to the government in power, only a legitimate political force that it would be foolish to ignore in any discussion of the country's future.[12] The US was forced into these negotiations largely by her European partners in the Contact Group (Britain, Canada, Germany and France) who were embarrassed by their demonstrable failure to prevent the border incursions and raids of the past three years.

It is much more likely that South Africa's main interest is not the support of Savimbi, but the economic dislocation of Angola. Although the country is one of the world's least developed states, she has been forced to spend more than 50 per cent of her budget on defence.[13] The report prepared by the Angolan Government for the second session of the International Commission of Enquiry estimated that in the eighteen months between 11 June 1979 and 31 December 1980 the total value of the damage produced by the raids was $230m, nearly as much as during the preceding three years.[14]

Undoubtedly, the worst economic dislocation has been the refugee problem which, after Somalia's, is the second worst in Africa. Since 1975 half a million Angolans have been made homeless by the fighting. *Operation Protea* alone added 80,000 refugees in three weeks. One of the worst hit targets, Lubango, is the operational centre for the storage and distribution of relief supplied as part of the UN Emergency Programme. Having abandoned their fields and lost their herds of cattle, many thousands of peasants have been reduced to what may well become a permanent state of dependency. Many have become refugees in their own country. Intermittent warfare has turned southern Angola into Africa's southern Lebanon and, like the Lebanon, the government's pleas for international assistance have gone largely unheeded.[15]

Destabilization of southern Africa
Many Western analyses have tended to focus almost entirely on the threat to Angola and to interpret the operations of the SADF as essentially an extension of its campaign in Namibia. Nothing could be more misleading. The destabilization of her neighbours has become one of the most important and persistent South African concerns since 1978, as she has tried to turn Western

145

attention to the instability of the countries beyond her borders in the hope of dissuading it from putting pressure on the one country that appears to be immune from disorder.

Since 1980 she has extended the scope of her raids in an attempt to prevent the ANC from attacking power plants, rail links and government installations in the Transvaal. She has also tried to prevent the nine members of the Southern African Development Co-ordination Conference (SADCC) from escaping her economic orbit. While this activity continues Pretoria can be reasonably assured that it will be able to dominate the region.

The SADF regularly describes Zambia as a centre for subversion. One reason sometimes advanced in private conversations for the retention of Namibia is that it offers the SADF the ability to station itself on Zambia's border.[16] In April 1982 a defence White Paper described Zambia as 'a Marxist satellite state' engaged in Soviet-inspired conspiracy against the Republic – a euphemism that nearly always can be taken to mean that the country concerned has become a target for destabilization.

What evidence there is of attempts to undermine President Kaunda's authority has tended to emerge from the trial of dissidents. At the Commonwealth Conference in Melbourne Kaunda announced that up to 600 Zambians were being trained by South Africa. South African involvement in at least two conspiracies has been uncovered by the police since 1980, though the claim that Pretoria has been behind the recent upsurge of labour unrest in the copper belt should not necessarily be taken at face value.

Far more serious in the short term is the incontrovertible evidence of economic destabilization which was brought to light by a joint commission of the EEC and the 57 African, Caribbean and Pacific signatories of the Lomé Convention. The commission found that since 1980 direct attacks on Zambian villages had been launched from the Caprivi strip. The most sustained form of aggression had been the laying of land mines which, in addition to causing loss of life and a decline in agricultural production, had also deterred mining companies from prospecting in the area.[17] Zimbabwe's independence prompted an immediate escalation of attacks from Caprivi: in April 1982 two bat-talions of South African troops attacked villages and burned their crops.[18] The strategy of destroying the economic infrastructure of the Western Province became apparent in July when the Zambian government declared the region a disaster zone.

If Zambia is the most notable example of destabilization, Botswana is one of the most recent. A series of protest notes by the Botswanan government following several border incidents in 1981 elicited little or no response from the South African government beyond, in some cases, flat denials that the incidents ever occurred. In an interview at the end of 1981 Botswana's President disclosed that his government was increasingly concerned at indications that Pretoria was fabricating evidence of border incursions as a way of justifying counterattacks by the SADF.[19] The incidents so far recorded in the Western press have involved border violations or exchanges of fire between Botswanan and South African forces, particularly near the Caprivi strip; as well as attacks on the South African refugee population living in the country; and the illicit importation of arms to facilitate armed robberies and other crimes.[20]

South Africa's concept of security is not confined to the protection of communication centres and other installations within her own borders. She has also sought to pre-empt attacks by launching pre-emptive strikes against neighbouring countries harbouring ANC guerrillas. (By a 1976 amendment to the Defence Act the definition of 'service in defence of the republic' has been redefined to include the suppression of any armed conflict outside its borders.) Since the Soweto summer of 1976 the ANC has been deluged with young recruits crossing the frontier into Botswana, Lesotho and Swaziland from where they have gone to training camps in Zambia and Angola. One of the most important developments of recent years has been the re-emergence of the ANC as the most popular nationalist movement.

Pretoria has not, however, launched pre-emptive raids indiscriminately. For example, in January 1980 the SADF carried out a daring assault on the ANC headquarters in Maputo, destroying three planning and control centres in the course of the attack. During the raid a great deal of evidence was also seized which later helped to convict three ANC members then operating in the Transvaal. Any assessment of the scope of South African operations must take note of the opportunity that similar raids may provide in the future, not only to 'take out' guerrilla positions but to disrupt communication links between the ANC control centres and its operatives in the field.

South Africa's operations have not only been confined to Mozambique. In Lesotho the government of Chief Jonathan faces opposition from an offshoot of the Basotho Congress Party which is now in exile. Ever since the head of the South African security police warned that Lesotho was becoming an ANC staging post the rebels opposing Jonathan have been allowed free passage through the Orange Free State.[21] It is doubtful whether Pretoria would want to oust the present administration but clearly it wishes to demonstrate that it is quite prepared to reciprocate if the ANC is allowed to operate without restriction. In one way or another this is a message which South Africa appears intent on sending to her neighbours.

In recent months African diplomats have become increasingly alarmed by the growing depredations of the *Resistencia Nacional Mocambicana* (MNR) which has successfully launched attacks against 1,000 km of Mozambique's main north–south road and virtually halted traffic between Zimbabwe and Malawi. The MNR was originally set up by Rhodesian intelligence in 1977 before passing under South African control after the Lancaster House Conference. It now has a training camp at Zoabostad in the Transvaal and its forces in Mozambique are regularly supplied by air and by sea north and south of Beira.

It is notable that since South Africa took over the movement little interest has been shown in its earlier objective of creating 'liberated' zones and winning popular support. Instead, the MNR has set about producing the maximum disruption to local life in the seven provinces in which it is active. Because of Mozambique's size and geography it is almost impossible for government forces to patrol every line of communication. Yet the country's road and rail links are absolutely crucial to the SADCC – particularly the rail line from Zimbabwe to Maputo and Beira, the road and rail bridges near Beira and the oil pipeline from Beira to Mutare (Umtali), which opened six months behind schedule because of

guerrilla attacks.[22] As long as the MNR's attacks continue the West is most unlikely to invest the $800m needed to improve Mozambique's communications infrastructure and without this the nine members of the SADCC will not be able to escape South Africa's stranglehold on their economies.[23]

Conclusion

In suggesting the future pattern of South African operations we must deal with two matters: the objectives Pretoria will set itself and the response its actions will elicit. In Namibia the raids will almost certainly continue for as long as South Africa remains in occupation. Although South Africa recently agreed to the Contact Group proposals for independence sometime in 1983 she will still be reluctant to allow SWAPO to contest free elections in an organized manner. That is why the raids will probably continue until the elections have been held. South African success in the past will make it difficult to withdraw into the *laager* for the duration.

The raids against the ANC will also continue. Black spokesmen in South Africa appear to have drawn the same conclusions as the whites: that the West will not intervene. As Buthelezi, the leader of the largest black movement allowed in the Republic, remarked after the raid on the ANC offices in Maputo: '. . . apart from the protests from the international community not a single country has taken a bold practical stand against what amounted to an infringement of territorial integrity of Mozambique'.[24] The raids have obviously reinforced the government's position. Indeed, it has sold them to the white electorate as the best means of pre-empting the onset of a guerrilla campaign that, in all probability, would be sustained for many years to come.

Even more important still will be the West's response to the crisis. Given South Africa's willingness to launch raids into Angola in the face of diplomatic *démarches* from the Western powers, the US has already found herself in an impossible dilemma. Since the MPLA attaches such importance to the Cuban presence for its own security (2,000 more Cuban troops were airlifted after *Operation Protea*) Washington will have to find some way to alleviate Angolan fears after the Cubans have departed. The same holds true for an independent Namibia. Certainly, both countries will expect a better guarantee than her word that South Africa will not attack again. The US has no leverage over Pretoria to prevent such an occurrence. There are no arms sales which can be cut off, no military sanctions which can be taken. The only real American option would be to sell arms to Luanda and Windhoek but Congress would probably embargo their despatch. It can always be argued that it is precisely the powers who *can* act as intermediaries which have influence, the best intermediaries being not those with the least bias, but with the most leverage.[25] But precisely because this is true the US is likely to find herself in difficulty. It is not the Reagan Administration's bias which is likely to tell against it, but the fact that the arms embargo has robbed America of any control over the use of force by the South African government.

If the raids continue much longer and the Namibian question remains unresolved the US and Europe are likely to find themselves increasingly at odds. America clearly believes that the best way of deterring South Africa from attacking her neighbours would be to deter raids into South Africa by the ANC. This is a curious reading of South Africa's motives. She has already put forward a plan to create a *cordon sanitaire* between the Republic and her neighbours.[26] The Europeans, by contrast, have much less faith in South Africa's intentions and are doubtful that the US approach to South Africa can succeed. Angola's application to join the Lomé Convention in the company of Mozambique has been paralleled by the EEC's decision to boost the SADCC, to become, as the European Commission remarked, 'directly involved in the development process right up to the frontiers of *apartheid.*'[27] What this may mean in security terms in the future is suggested by an initial French suggestion that French forces replace the Cuban troops, a proposal originally made in Cuba during a visit by Jean Assueil, the head of the Africa department of the Quai D'Orsay. Luanda feels, perhaps with justification, that the presence of European troops would afford the most plausible deterrent to South Africa. It is precisely because of its implications that the US is unlikely to favour the suggestion. The Reagan Administration's doubts represent a failure of 'nerve', an introspective withdrawal of faith in the scope of its own influence, a tendency met and reinforced by a converging pessimism that without South African support the West's interests cannot be defended.

Europe has every reason to be concerned. No country in the region is likely to acquiesce voluntarily in what amounts to South African hegemony. If South Africa continues to threaten her neighbours she will have to face the consequences. It is doubtful whether she has thought the consequences through. Quite apart from the Western powers whom she appears to hold in no particular esteem she may have to contend with the Soviet Union. As long as South Africa insists on intervening, even to pre-empt attacks by the ANC, the Front-Line States will see no recourse but to ask for help from outside. There appears to be every likelihood that, the more implacable and unyielding South Africa remains the more they will feel impelled to look to Moscow, and the greater is the danger of Soviet influence.

Indeed, in a telegram to the UN Secretary-General in August 1981 Angola warned that she might be forced to invoke Article 51 of the UN Charter and invite outside assistance to avert what was threatening to become 'a war with unforeseeable consequences'.[28] Such commitments of assistance can be found in the Treaties of Friendship which both Angola and Mozambique have signed with the USSR and GDR. The treaty with Mozambique was activated for the first time in January 1980 after the raid against the ANC offices in Maputo. Within days of the attack, the 16,000-ton carrier *Alexander Suvorov* and another warship arrived in Beira.

South Africa's complete failure to take note of the new situation raises the question whether she has any real interest in defending Western interests, as opposed to her own, which are somewhat more narrowly defined. Her operations have provided the USSR with an opportunity to sell 135 fighter aircraft, 527 tanks, 704 armoured cars, 778 troop carriers and 738 medium artillery pieces to Angola, Mozambique, Zimbabwe and Zambia and 30 armoured cars to Botswana.

Pretoria often claims that these sales present a threat to the region, irrespective of whether they are in response to its own actions. In the short term, there is no evidence to support this contention. Indeed, the SADF's own Chief of Staff, Lt-Gen. Jannie Geldenhuys, admitted recently that the evidence that Soviet officers had trained SWAPO to engage in combat operations was mostly circumstantial. Their main concern appeared to be the defence of Angola.[29] A hard look at Soviet arms transfers tends to bear out this analysis. It discloses that much of the equipment is defensive in nature and dated in technology, and that it poses a threat, if at all, to forces crossing the border. Although Mozambique has MiG-17 fighters, they are first generation aircraft, a poor match for South Africa's *Mirage* IIIs which were supplied by France in the 1970s. Similarly, the missile defences at Mapai and Maputo are so old that they offer very little protection despite the fact that they have been recently improved by the installation of anti-aircraft radar tracking and guidance systems.[30]

To South Africa the supply of weapons seems a more significant phenomenon than the brief intervention of Cuban forces in 1975. Yet, in the light of the defensive equipment supplied since 1978 the Soviet Union's first priority appears to be to deter a full-scale South African invasion, not to discourage South African raids. It is obviously impossible to study the manifold pressures that mould Soviet policy without reflecting upon the common interest that both Moscow and Pretoria share: the destabilization of the region. Yet one ought to beware of pressing the analysis too far. For the Soviet Union

has no wish to encourage her clients to involve themselves in a conventional confrontation with South Africa which they would almost certainly lose without substantial Soviet assistance. There is little prospect of it being forthcoming. In spite of considerable Soviet aid and the presence of 15,000 Cuban soldiers, Ethiopia, her other client in Africa, has been unable to defeat or contain the many nationalist movements within her territory. The USSR for the moment cannot afford to extend her commitments in southern Africa above and beyond their present level.

Nevertheless, the West's position in the region has been seriously undermined by South Africa's increasingly confident use of her forces. Having embarked on the peace process the United States may find that, as it evolves, she will not be able to ignore the threat faced by many of the states with whom she has worked so assiduously to reach a settlement in Zimbabwe and Namibia. To some extent, even America has become the prisoner of her own commitments. Having entered into the negotiations she cannot easily jettison the process even though it has become more complex and problematic. Indeed, she may well have to ask herself whether a diplomatic clash with Pretoria can be postponed, much less avoided, for much longer.

NOTES

[1] In 1968 South Africa's Minister of Defence publicly warned Zambia that acting as a base for guerrillas could provoke airstrikes against military targets analogous to Israeli reprisal raids against PLO bases in the Middle East.

[2] *The Economist*, 10 May 1969.

[3] *The Financial Times*, 11 March 1980.

[4] *The Times*, 11 March 1980.

[5] Statement of John Reed, Director of Africa Regional Office of the Assistant Secretary of Defense, *Disaster Assistance to Angola*, Hearings before the Committee on International Relations, subcommittee on Resources, Food and Energy, House of Representatives, 94th Congress, 2nd Session 1976, p. 56.

[6] Chester A. Crocker, Assistant Secretary for African Affairs, Address to the American Legion, Honolulu, 29 August 1981, reprinted in *Africa Report* 26:6, November–December 1981, p. 10.

[7] *The Washington Post*, 12 September 1981.

[8] Notes taken by the International Defence Aid Fund Research and Information Department at a public meeting in London, 27 October 1981, *Focus*, January–February 1982.

[9] In fact the number of Cuban troops in Angola fell from 30,000 in 1976 to 10,000 by the Autumn of 1981. (*The New York Times*, 8 January 1982).

[10] *The Times*, 9 September 1981.

[11] For a complete list see the two Angolan submissions to the International Mission of Jurists June 1979–July 1980 and 1–9 October 1981 published by the Centre against Apartheid, UN Department of Political and Security Council Affairs 2/81 and 12/82.

[12] *The New York Times*, 13 December 1981.

[13] *The Guardian*, 29 July 1981.

[14] *Report of the People's Republic of Angola to the Second Session of the International Commission of Enquiry into the crimes of the racist and apartheid regime in Southern Africa* (Centre against Apartheid: Department of Political and Security Council Affairs 12/82 1982). The damage was caused largely by aerial bombing, sporadic attacks by South African troops in *Puma* and *Alouette* helicopters; and armoured car attacks supported by airstrikes.

[15] Ramsay Clark, the former US Attorney-General and one of the members of the International Commission of Enquiry, has compared the situation in the south to that

in southern Lebanon. 'We found generally there what could be called a state of war. There was a constant military presence and alertness of a defensive nature, networks of trenches and bunkers and reports of daily depredations by South African military personnel.'

[16] *The New York Times*, 30 April 1982.
[17] Interim Report of the ACP–EEC Consultative Assembly Fact finding mission to the Front-Line States 23 January 1982 to 1 February 1982.
[18] *New African*, April 1981.
[19] *The Star*, (Johannesburg), 5 December 1981.
[20] *The Financial Mail*, 6 March 1982.
[21] *The New York Times*, 17 September 1981.
[22] See two articles on the MNR in *Africa Confidential*, Vol. 23, Nos. 15; and 16, 1982. The information of South African involvement is based largely on documents captured at a guerrilla base at Garagua on 7 December 1981.
[23] The SADCC comprises Angola, Botswana, Swaziland, Lesotho, Mozambique, Malawi, Tanzania, Zambia and Zimbabwe.
[24] *The Financial Times*, 24 February 1981.
[25] Pierre Hassner, 'Super-power Rivalries, Conflict and Co-operation' in *Diffusion of Power, Part II: Control and Conflict*, Adelphi, 134 (London: IISS, 1977).
[26] *The Sunday Times*, 10 October 1982.
[27] *The Guardian*, 11 October 1982.
[28] Communiqué issued by the Angolan Ministry of Defence, 17 August 1981.
[29] *The Times*, 7 April 1982.
[30] *The Washington Post*, 16 September 1981.

6 Southern Africa: Shifting Security Concerns

An increase in armed conflict and a catastrophic drought between them caused severe strains in almost every state in Southern Africa during 1983. In Angola, Jonas Savimbi's UNITA (*União Nacional para a Independência Total de Angola*) insurgents began a sustained hit-and-run offensive in late summer that struck at towns within 125 miles of the capital, Luanda. The African National Congress (ANC), South Africa's oldest and most influential national liberation movement, raised the intensity of its war against the apartheid system to a new level in 1983, and its attacks prompted South African reprisal raids against suspected ANC-occupied buildings in the capitals of Lesotho and Mozambique as well as threats of similar attacks on other South African neighbours. Early in 1984, however, South Africa and Mozambique seem to have found a peaceful *modus vivendi.*

Attempts to resolve the continuing conflict in Namibia engaged the Western powers (particularly the US), South Africa and Angola in high-level talks during 1983. While Angola tacitly accepted the US and South African proposition that the withdrawal of Cuban troops must be an element in an overall settlement, a wide gulf separated Pretoria and Luanda on the sequence of and conditions for such a withdrawal. Two additional factors, though not officially acknowledged, complicated the negotiations and inhibited movement towards a settlement: the disarray in Namibian internal politics, and the recent expansion of UNITA's guerrilla activities in several Angolan provinces. US officials believe that South Africa and Angola are genuinely interested in a resolution of the conflict, and that they will implement UN Security Council Resolution 435 once agreement has been reached on the terms of a Cuban withdrawal. Other observers suspect South Africa of deliberately creating conditions which make

such a withdrawal impossible, thereby postponing the day when she must release her hold on Namibia.

Internal developments in several southern African states in 1983 also had important implications for future regional stability. Mozambique increased her military and economic ties with the West and moved significantly away from the Soviet economic model and towards a mixed economy. Zimbabwe completed her third year of independent Black rule without either the massive exodus of Whites or the degeneration into civil war that opponents had predicted. Early in the year, however, disgruntled ex-members of Joshua Nkomo's now disbanded guerrilla forces instigated a rash of banditry and murders in the western province of Matabeleland around the city of Bulawayo. Prime Minister Mugabe dispatched the so-called 'fifth brigade', trained by North Koreans, to pacify the region, but its five-month campaign, marked by indiscriminate destruction and killing, exacerbated longstanding political and ethnic tensions between the largely Shona ruling party and Nkomo's Matabele tribe.

By far the most damaging development in 1983 was the severe drought which affected virtually the entire region for the second year in a row. Rainfall less than half the normal caused shortfalls of 60–70% in major crop yields and heavy losses of livestock (Botswana, alone, lost a half million head of cattle), and some 10 million people in five states required emergency food aid from abroad in order to survive the summer. Even South Africa, normally one of two net food exporters in the region (Zimbabwe is the other), had to import 1.5 million tons of grain as she suffered her worst drought in 200 years.

While the precise political impact of the drought cannot be assessed, some general consequences seem clear enough. First, the drought highlighted the region's economic dependence on the West and reinforced its growing ties with the Western world economy. Second, southern African leaders were far more concerned with domestic crises in 1983 than with larger ideological or global political issues. Moreover, the parlous economic condition of countries like Mozambique, Lesotho and Zimbabwe made them less able to withstand South African economic pressures on issues such as the control of ANC personnel within their borders. Of longer-run concern are the effects of hunger and the disruption of traditional farming communities brought on by the long drought. Even more alarming is the concern of meteorologists that the drought may be part of a long-term cycle and may not yet be over.

Deadlock in Namibia
The Namibian conflict also continued unabated in 1983. The opening move occurred in February, when the South West Africa People's Organization (SWAPO) infiltrated guerrillas (some 1,600, according to South African sources) into the territory in their annual rainy season campaign of sabotage, mine-laying and abductions. Three months later South African forces were pursuing a small remnant of that group still at large inside Namibia. In May South Africa's Defence Minister, Magnus Malan, claimed that pre-emptive action by his forces had prevented a new 'massive incursion' by SWAPO. The absence of any large-scale South African attacks on Angola at that time, however, suggests that SWAPO's 'offensive' had so little punch that Pretoria could afford to show the restraint that Washington had been urging on it.

In January South Africa had begun pursuing a new peace initiative with Angola. At unprecedented direct talks in the Cape Verde islands, South African Foreign Minister Roelof Botha proposed a two-stage cease-fire: first, the opposing armed forces (South African, Angolan, Cuban and SWAPO) would remain in place but cease fighting; then, after two months of successful cease-fire, all South African units in Angola (around 1,500 troops) would withdraw to Namibia, and Cuban forces would move back to 185 miles (and SWAPO forces to some 250 miles) north of the

Namibian border. This second stage would remain in force until agreement had been reached on a political settlement in Namibia and the complete withdrawal of Cuba's 25,000 troops from Angola. South African forces in Namibia, approximately 20,000, would remain in the territory through the second stage.

A further round of talks in February, to which South Africa sent a lower-ranking official, made no progress. The gap between the two official positions was revealed in August, when Angolan President dos Santos listed four pre-conditions for a Cuban withdrawal. The Cubans would leave 'progressively', he said, if South Africa unconditionally withdrew from Angola, implemented the UN settlement plan, halted all aggression against Angola, and terminated military aid to 'puppet groups'. (This last point was a reference to UNITA, whose forces had gone unmentioned in South Africa's January cease-fire proposal.)

The growing importance of UNITA as a complicating factor in the negotiations was highlighted by its late summer offensive. With an infusion of vehicles and heavy arms from South Africa in 1982–83, UNITA broke out of its central plateau bases and attacked Angolan towns in Moxico and Bié provinces. After an eleven-day battle in September, in which it was supported by South African air strikes, it captured Cangamba in the far south-east corner of Angola, and may have still held it at the end of the year. Other towns were taken and held only for a day or two. Although the territory under effective UNITA control may not have greatly increased, UNITA's expanding operations put the Angolan army on the defensive in the country's more populous and economically important areas and aggravated an already serious food shortage.

There is little doubt that Savimbi and UNITA have their own objectives in Angola, independent of those of South Africa. Indeed, Savimbi has been vocal in asserting UNITA's claims to a place in any settlement talks. South Africa may have already found Savimbi a difficult and unmanageable protégé, and an obstacle to negotiations, and South African Prime Minister P. W. Botha has occasionally hinted at differences between them. But in 1983 the resurgent and aggressive UNITA clearly served South African interests. By maintaining heavy military pressure on Angola, it has been an effective *de facto* proxy for South African forces. This was particularly welcome since the South African Defence Forces, apparently under US pressure to show restraint, refrained from heavy attacks on Angola until the very end of 1983.

Dissension in Windhoek

Another, though somewhat less serious, obstacle to a peace settlement is the continuing political discord inside Namibia. Since 1977 South Africa has been striving to build a strong, cohesive political structure in the territory, excluding SWAPO participation from the process. A 1978 internal election held 'to choose political leaders', which was boycotted by SWAPO, was won by a moderate, multi-ethnic coalition, the Democratic Turnhalle Alliance (DTA), backed by South Africa. Executive responsibility remained in the hands of an Administrator-General appointed in Pretoria.

In order to survive, the new DTA-led National Assembly had to be seen by Namibia's 90% Black majority to be doing something to dismantle apartheid in the territory. However, when it passed a spate of desegregation measures it caused a political revolt by Namibia's conservative and highly vocal White community. The Botha government, anxious to avoid further splits in Afrikanerdom, made enough concessions to the Whites effectively to block the Assembly's anti-apartheid moves. This led the Black parties to drop out of the DTA coalition, which collapsed in January 1983 with the resignation of its White chairman, Dirk Mudge, as head of the Council of Ministers.

A new Administrator-General, Willie van Niekerk, appointed in February 1983, established 'councils of local citizens' to help him administer the territory, and in July announced plans for an interim constitution, to be drafted by a State Council. Members of the 50-member council were selected from Namibia's 40-odd political parties, but only a few of these agreed to take part. Thus the group assembled in Windhoek in November to draft recommendations for a new constitution was even less representative than the defunct National Assembly.

Some Western diplomats discount internal Namibian politics as a possible obstacle to such a settlement, but there is little doubt that the issue is important to South Africa. Three Administrators-General, including a former head of the prestigious Afrikaner *Broederbond*, have been assigned to the territory since 1977, and in 1982 the head of Military Intelligence was sent to Namibia to try to bring squabbling political groups together. In September 1983 the Theron Commission, appointed to review the territory's governmental structure, delivered a stinging indictment of its multi-layered system of government, finding widespread mismanagement, inefficiency and corruption. There is thus good reason to believe that South Africa will seek to postpone an electoral contest against SWAPO until some cohesion has been brought to Namibia's faltering political structure. However, the problem reflects a deep Black–White fissure which is not amenable to a quick solution. Despite the search for an effective ruling coalition, SWAPO will continue to command near-total support in Namibia.

Diplomacy and Combat

Diplomatic initiatives resumed late in the year. After his visit to southern Africa in late August, the UN Secretary General reported to the Security Council that South Africa's insistence on a Cuban troop withdrawal from Angola was the chief barrier to an accord. In November a Soviet UN official warned South African representatives that Pretoria's military activities in Angola, including its support for UNITA were 'unacceptable'. France signalled her lack of hope for early progress towards a settlement by announcing that she would not attend further meetings of the Western Contact Group. In mid-December South Africa, apparently after US prodding to make some move to break the Namibian impasse, offered to pull her troops back to the Namibian border on 31 January 1984 for a 30-day cease-fire, on condition that Angolan, SWAPO and Cuban troops observed the cease-fire and stayed north of the border.

A few days after this cease-fire offer, South African forces began their largest military operation inside Angola for almost 18 months. Defence Minister Malan described the attack as a 'limited campaign' against SWAPO, which, he said, was preparing to launch its annual rainy season offensive, but it may also have been designed to weaken SWAPO and Angolan army offensive capabilities before the 31 January cease-fire. However, South Africa soon reverted to diplomatic moves. On 16 February she and Angola signed an agreement which called for the withdrawal of South African troops from southern Angola in return for an Angolan promise that SWAPO guerillas would not be allowed to move southwards. Nine days later a joint Angolan/South African commission met in Cuvelai to establish a monitoring system for the disengagement of troops. By mid-March, however, over 800 SWAPO guerrillas had managed to slip through the cease-fire zone, thus delaying the withdrawal of South African forces. Tensions were still high at the end of March, when Angola was angered by a South African call for round-table peace talks between all the parties directly involved in the conflict in Angola and Namibia (she argued that the UN should not be bypassed), while South Africa was annoyed by a Cuban/Angolan statement, issued from Havana, which laid down very stringent pre-conditions for a withdrawal of Cuban troops. Nonetheless, the agreement seemed to be holding. South Africa had begun to withdraw her troops from Angola, and Angolan forces had clashed with SWAPO guerillas to keep them from infiltrating across the border.

Internal Political Developments
Despite the unrest that his plans for a new constitution had brought to South African politics during 1983, Prime Minister P. W. Botha succeeded in winning approval for them in November 1983. The newly-adopted constitution provides for separate parliamentary chambers for Whites, Coloureds and Indians; each chamber has responsibility for its own 'community concerns', while all legislation affecting the apartheid system, national and foreign policy will be handled jointly. This tricameral arrangement will bring the Coloured and Indian minorities (2.5 and 0.8 million respectively) into the parliamentary system. But the system will still be one in which the Whites (4.5 million) will continue to maintain effective control. Not only will they retain

overall numerical advantage (their House of Assembly will have 178 seats, the Coloureds' House of Representatives 85, and the Indians' House of Delegates 45), but certain other stipulations will ensure that their entrenched power is not lost.

The new constitution specifies that the three chambers will select an Executive President who will have greater scope than the present Prime Minister (the first incumbent is widely expected to be the present Prime Minister), who will make cabinet appointments and will be able to decide what legislation is put before each chamber. Any disputes that the chambers might have will be settled through the newly constituted President's Council. The precise composition and activities of this body have not yet been disclosed, but it is known that the senior members of the President's cabinet will automatically be among its members.

While the new dispensation would bring Asians and Coloureds into the central legislature for the first time in a quarter of a century, it makes no provision at all for South Africa's 22 million Blacks, who continue to be assigned citizenship in 'independent' tribal homelands. In February, as if to emphasize that they will have no place in the proposed constitutional arrangements, Botha appointed a seven-man all-White cabinet committee to evolve a policy for Blacks living in urban areas away from their tribal 'homelands'.

Reactions to the constitutional plan have reinforced the deep divisions in South African society, both between and within racial groups. In January the leading Coloured party, the South African Labour Party, held a stormy eight-hour debate on the new proposals. After scuffling and disorder had threatened to break up the meeting, its members finally voted to take part in the new arrangements, though criticizing them for excluding Blacks and entrenching ethnicity.

During the summer various Black groups joined together in two separate and broad coalitions to oppose the constitutional change. Representatives of some 400 civic groups, unions and other organizations met in August and established the multiracial United Democratic Front. Its first success was a widespread boycott of elections to Black municipal councils under a government-sponsored plan to give Blacks somewhat greater local autonomy (the turnout was only some 5% of eligible voters). In addition, the leaders of six tribal homelands met with leaders of Black urban councils and formed the South African Federal Union to promote the idea of a Black federal parliament. However, like all Black opposition groups in South Africa, both these bodies face an uncertain future.

In the Afrikaner community the split deepened between Botha's reformers and the conservative advocates of the *status quo*. Early in the year the former were cheered by an opinion poll among Whites showing only 13% support for the right-wing Conservative Party's idea of a separate 'homeland' for South Africa's 2.6 million Coloureds. The long-heralded White referendum on the constitutional reform took place in November and gave the Prime Minister an impressive 2:1 vote in favour of his proposal.

But the painful dissension within the Afrikaner fraternity continues. In July it emerged in a struggle for control of the still-powerful *Broederbond*, the 65-year-old secret society whose rolls include most of the leaders of the Afrikaner community. Theology professor Carel Boshoff – son-in-law of the late Prime Minister Verwoerd (the 'architect of apartheid') – was forced to resign as its chairman when he became an active opponent of the Botha policy. In spite of the reformers' recent victories over conservative opponents, the struggle within Afrikanerdom will not soon be resolved; even the *Broederbond* is said to be divided 60:40 on the constitutional issue, the majority favouring Botha's proposals.

The Prime Minister took action against internal violence by both Left and Right in 1983. In May he announced the start of an inquiry into the activities of a right-wing extremist group, the Afrikaner Resistance Movement, and its 'private armies' committed to an Afrikaner state maintained through violence. Later on, in a clear but futile effort to dampen growing Black sympathy for the African National Congress, the courts began giving stiff sentences for any signs of support: eighteen months' jail to a factory worker who drank from a mug decorated with ANC slogans, and four years to two pop musicians for singing ANC songs. Such repression may slow, but is unlikely to stop, the growth of support for the ANC.

ANC Attacks and Pretoria's Response
The struggle between the Botha government and the ANC led to a rapidly-rising spiral of violence in 1983. South Africa's draconian security laws and pervasive intelligence network failed to blunt ANC sabotage attacks, which totalled 26 in the first nine months of the year – equal to the record level of such attacks in 1982. But more ominous than the number of incidents was their changed nature.

In May the ANC car-bombed the South African Air Force headquarters building on a busy Pretoria street during the rush hour. That attack, which killed 18 people and injured over 200, was the first in which the ANC chose a method, place and time which were certain to cause multiple civilian casualties. Oliver Tambo, the ANC's exiled leader, acknowledged it as a 'tactical change' and said that the organization would extend its future operations to 'attacking enemy forces', of which this was an 'example'. He claimed the attack was in retaliation for South Africa's raid into Lesotho in December 1982, in which 29 ANC members and 13 Lesotho civilians were killed. Other leaders also pointed out that the ANC only went after military or strategic targets; that it refrained from engaging in a race war; and that it did not assassinate South African diplomatic or other personnel abroad. For all that, the Pretoria attack moved the organization dangerously close to the sort of indiscriminate terrorism practised by others elsewhere in the world.

The Botha government, claiming that ANC attacks originated in neighbouring states which either abetted or turned a blind eye to them, struck back quickly at suspected ANC sanctuaries. After the Pretoria bombing South Africa cut off all traffic to and from the tiny enclave state of Lesotho – forcing her to agree to expel some 3,000 South African refugees, including known and suspected ANC members – and also launched an air attack against suspected ANC quarters in a suburb of Mozambique's capital, Maputo.

Lesotho, in turn, charged South Africa with supporting the Lesotho Liberation Army, a group of dissidents which carries out sporadic sabotage and raids on Lesotho police and border posts. In November her foreign minister claimed that pressure from Pretoria was directed not so much at the ANC presence (which Lesotho had already agreed to curtail) as at forcing her to support South Africa's alleged demand that her nominally independent Bantustans be allowed to join the Southern African Customs Union (which embraces South Africa, Botswana, Lesotho and Swaziland). In December 1982, to demonstrate Lesotho's defiance, Prime Minister Leabua Jonathan had announced his government's intention to establish diplomatic relations with the USSR. In retaliation, South Africa launched a series of sabotage attacks against Lesotho, which led Chief Jonathan to proclaim that a state of war existed between South Africa and Lesotho. While it is unlikely that he will carry out this threat, Jonathan has at least managed to win substantial Atlantic Community economic support to help his country withstand South African economic pressures. He has also discredited the Lesotho Liberation Army by making clear that it is a tool of Pretoria.

Mozambique, too, suffered from growing South African pressure. In January 1983 the Mozambican National Resistance Movement (MRM) blew up part of the Beira–Mutare pipeline (which carries almost all Zimbabwe's vital petroleum imports), – part of its wide-ranging campaign of sabotage and attacks on isolated villages and farms during the previous couple of years. The MRM has no real political programme, nor an identifiable constituency inside Mozambique, and this, together with its sophisticated arrangements for communications and air drops, suggests that it is little more than a proxy force for South Africa (a connection widely believed by Western diplomats, and one which South Africa no longer

bothers to deny). A Mozambican army counter-insurgency drive in the summer of 1983 apparently succeeded in destroying several MRM bases and capturing 200 of its guerrillas. In October, an alleged ANC planning office was bombed in another South African air raid, this time in retaliation for an ANC attack on a Transvaal fuel depot. Defence Minister Malan accused Mozambique of helping the ANC organize its attacks; a charge the Machel government denied.

South Africa's aggressive response to ANC attacks allegedly originating across its borders ('Limpet mines . . . do not just fall from the sky,' said Defence Minister Malan) appear to have had some success. Swaziland had already concluded a secret mutual security accord with South Africa in 1982, and Lesotho was pressured into taking action against her South African refugees during 1983. On 16 March 1984 Mozambique and South Africa signed the 'Nkomati Accord', each undertaking to eliminate from her territory bases, training centres, places of shelter, accommodation and transit for elements which intend aggression against the other. The ANC reacted to this by announcing its intention to intensify its offensive against the South African regime.

South African officials acknowledge both privately and publicly that the ANC probably has established some sort of a support network inside South Africa. If so, Pretoria's policy of clubbing its neighbours into more vigorous action against ANC personnel within their borders will undoubtedly make ANC attacks more difficult, but is unlikely to bring them to an end. In the longer run, South Africa's so-called 'destabilization policy' will have reinforced local mistrust of the region's armed Colossus, and will have wiped out for a long time to come any illusion that she could be a benign regional power, willing to show restraint towards weaker neighbours.

Index

157

S. African economic intervention in 55

reaction to S. African threats 110
role as front-line state 88
S. African economic pressure on 116–17
value of S. African economic connection
  115
See also Rhodesia
Zimbabwe African National Union (ZANU)
  10, 59, 91–4 *passim*, 104, 142
  feuding within 10

Zimbabwe African People's Union (ZAPU)
  10, 91–5 *passim*, 142
  guerrilla campaigns in Rhodesia 53
Zimbabwe National Liberation Army
  (ZANLA) 95, 97, 103, 105
  cease-fire violations 104
Zimbabwe People's Army (ZIPA) 93
Zimbabwe People's Revolutionary Army
  (ZIPRA) 95, 127

SOCIAL SCIENCE LIBRARY

Oxford University Library Services
Manor Road
Oxford OX1 3UQ
Tel: (2)74093 (enquiries and renewals)
http://www.ssl.ox.ac.uk

This is a NORMAL LOAN item.

We will email you a reminder before this item is due.

Please see http://www.ssl.ox.ac.uk/lending.html
for details on:

- loan policies; these are also displayed on the notice boards and in our library guide.

- how to check when your books are due back.

- how to renew your books, including information on the maximum number of renewals.
  Items may be renewed if not reserved by another reader. Items must be renewed before the library closes on the due date.

- level of fines; fines are charged on overdue books.

Please note that this item may be recalled during Term.